Enterprise Security: A Data-Centric Approach to Securing the Enterprise

A guide to applying data-centric security concepts for securing enterprise data to enable an agile enterprise

Aaron Woody

BIRMINGHAM - MUMBAI

Enterprise Security: A Data-Centric Approach to Securing the Enterprise

First published: February 2013

Production Reference: 1120213

Published by Packt Publishing Ltd.
Livery Place
35 Livery Street
Birmingham B3 2PB, UK.

ISBN 978-1-84968-596-2

www.packtpub.com

Cover Image by Artie Ng (artherng@yahoo.com.au)

Credits

Author

Aaron Woody

Reviewers

Lee Allen

Shon Robinson

Acquisition Editor

Mary Jasmine Nadar

Lead Technical Editor

Susmita Panda

Technical Editors

Worrell Lewis

Charmaine Pereira

Pooja Prakashan

Lubna Shaikh

Manmeet Singh Vasir

Project Coordinators

Priya Sharma

Esha Thakker

Proofreader

Bernadette Watkins

Indexer

Hemangini Bari

Graphics

Sheetal Aute

Valentina D'silva

Aditi Gajjar

Production Coordinator

Shantanu Zagade

Cover Work

Shantanu Zagade

About the Author

Aaron Woody is an expert in information security with over 15 years of experience across several industry verticals. His experience includes securing some of the largest enterprises in the world. Currently, he is a Security Consultant in the public sector. He is also a speaker and active instructor teaching hacking and forensics, and maintains a blog n00bpentesting.com.

Aaron can also be followed on twitter at @shai_saint. He will be launching a companion website (http://www.datacentricsec.com) for this book. To contact him for consulting please e-mail him at aaron.m.woody@gmail.com.

I sincerely thank my wife Melissa and my children, Alexis and Elisa, for sharing me with this project.

About the Reviewers

Lee Allen is currently the Vulnerability Management Program Lead for one of the Fortune 500 companies. He is also the owner of MiDGames.com that is dedicated to bridging the gap between learning and fun, by providing 3D video games that reinforce and teach complex subjects such as Linux command line and penetration testing skills.

Lee is the author of *Advanced Penetration Testing for Highly-Secured Environments: The Ultimate Security Guide*, Packt Publishing.

> I would like to thank my wife Kellie and our children for allowing me the time needed to review this book. I would also like to thank Aaron Woody for allowing me to be a part of this work. This is an excellent book that contains information that every security professional should know. Aaron does an excellent job of making the knowledge available in an easy to understand and comprehensive manner. I would also like to thank George and Helen Slocum; without your encouragement and support throughout the years, I would never have chased my dreams.

Shon Robinson has been working in IT for 17 years, with 15 of these spent dealing with various aspects of the security field. Over the years, he has worked for a large financial services company in a number of roles including securing the online banking platform and performing application vulnerability assessments across all lines of business applications. Currently, he is a Principal Consultant for a business security company. He has also been a reviewer for *Hakin9* since its first issues.

In addition to an MBA and Master of Theological Studies, Shon currently holds a number of active certifications including CISSP, ISSAP, ISSMP, CISA, CISM, CRISC, CEH, and a number of others on security, application, and operating systems.

In his copious free time, Shon tries to help teach the Central Ohio ISSA CISSP prep class.

I would like to thank Aaron for recommending me as a reviewer. I have, even after all these years, been able to learn more about security architecture from the experience. I would especially like to thank my wife, Tammy, who has been a supportive partner and inspiration in life even when I make her life difficult; and my son, Jesse, who is my joy and reminds me daily to be thankful for and enjoy every second.

www.packtpub.com

Support files, e-books, discount offers, and more

You might want to visit www.packtpub.com for support files and downloads related to your book.

Did you know that Packt offers e-book versions of every book published, with PDF and ePub files available? You can upgrade to the e-book version at www.packtpub.com and as a print book customer, you are entitled to a discount on the e-book copy. Get in touch with us at service@packtpub.com for more details.

At www.packtpub.com, you can also read a collection of free technical articles, sign up for a range of free newsletters and receive exclusive discounts and offers on Packt books and e-books.

http://packtlib.packtpub.com

Do you need instant solutions to your IT questions? PacktLib is Packt's online digital book library. Here, you can access, read, and search across Packt's entire library of books.

Why Subscribe?

- Fully searchable across every book published by Packt
- Copy and paste, print and bookmark content
- On demand and accessible via web browser

Free Access for Packt account holders

If you have an account with Packt at www.packtpub.com, you can use this to access PacktLib today and view nine entirely free books. Simply use your login credentials for immediate access.

Instant Updates on New Packt Books

Get notified! Find out when new books are published by following @PacktEnterprise on Twitter, or the *Packt Enterprise* Facebook page.

This book is dedicated to my grandmother Helen L. Woody (1932 – 2001).

Table of Contents

Preface

Information security in the enterprise is challenging and has been considered a roadblock to enterprise innovation and use of new services such as cloud and bring your own device (BYOD). One of the primary reasons for this is the paradigm from which information security is being approached in today's ever evolving and agile businesses. Strict security requirements as an overlay to a perimeter-focused network architecture does not adequately secure enterprise data, failing the agile enterprise.

This book covers the current state of enterprise security and a new model for implementing security in the enterprise. Data-centric security architecture is introduced in the context of a layered security approach for end-to-end security. By looking at each component of the data-centric architecture, the realization of applying these concepts to information security creates a new paradigm to operate from where information security is agile and becomes a business enablement process supporting the latest trends in business such as cloud and BYOD.

The book is a guide to leveraging existing investment in traditional network- and host-based security tools. It introduces the data aspect of security and how to provide complete coverage of enterprise security. With several diagrams to illustrate concepts, and resources for further development in the areas of enterprise information security, this book serves as a go-to reference for IT professionals responsible for securing enterprise networks and data.

What this book covers

Chapter 1, Enterprise Security Overview, introduces readers to the concepts of information security by providing an overview of information security, where we went wrong, and the road map to securing the enterprise.

Chapter 2, Security Architectures, covers the drivers of redefining security architecture from a network-based concept to a data-centric focus as today's ever-changing business landscape has invalidated the traditional security architecture. The chapter introduces trust models and how they can be applied to existing data and infrastructure.

Chapter 3, Security As a Process, covers the importance of security as a process through policies, standards, risk analysis, and security review of changes. For security to be effective in the enterprise, it must be an integral component of everyday business processes.

Chapter 4, Securing the Network, is the first of several chapters diving into the layers of the data-centric security architecture. Methods to secure the enterprise at the network layer leveraging the latest technologies to mitigate threats at the network edge and segmented portions of the network are presented. The reader will also be given guidance on how to secure common network services.

Chapter 5, Securing Systems, presents methods to secure the systems that store, transmit, and process enterprise data. A look at effective approaches to securing systems when traditional methods fail is covered in detail. A list of tools is provided in *Appendix C, Security Tools List.*

Chapter 6, Securing Enterprise Data, presents readers with methods to secure data in the various states within the enterprise. Encryption, hashing, data loss prevention, and data classification are covered in detail to provide readers with several approaches to secure enterprise data.

Chapter 7, Wireless Network Security, provides coverage of securely implementing wireless networking in the enterprise. Methods to mitigate the most common and dangerous attacks against wireless are discussed. Lastly, the chapter covers proper segmentation of wireless infrastructure from critical segments and assets within the enterprise network.

Chapter 8, The Human Element of Security, takes a look at the weakest link in the enterprise security program: *humans*. The chapter examines social engineering and security awareness program development. Once a program is developed, consistent testing of the effectiveness of training is presented with several resources to get this portion of the program up and running.

Chapter 9, Security Monitoring, covers the many times overlooked, yet very important aspect of security monitoring. First, the chapter covers monitoring at the various layers of the new security architecture, then dives into leveraging SIEM solutions and providing monitoring for privileged users, systems, and the network.

Chapter 10, Managing Security Incidents, covers security incidents and management. Making the determination on what a security incident is and how to develop the response is the focus of this chapter. Guidelines for developing an incident response capability, along with supporting processes, are also provided to the reader.

Appendix A, Applying Trust Models to Develop a Security Architectuture, walks the reader through applying the presented security architecture and trust models to a real-world scenario. This exercise will strengthen the new concepts presented in *Chapter 2, Security Architectures.*

Appendix B, Risk Analysis, Policy and Standard, and System Hardening Resources, provides a list of available resources to help the reader develop the necessary enterprise security processes: risk analysis, vulnerability and patch management, and policies and standards.

Appendix C, Security Tools List, covers a list of security tools that can be used to provide security at the network, system, and data layers of the data-centric architecture. In addition to tools for securing the enterprise, the reader is provided tools for testing security, vulnerability identification, and security monitoring. It also provides a list of available resources to help the reader develop the necessary enterprise security processes: risk analysis, vulnerability and patch management, and policies and standards.

Appendix D, Security Awareness Resources, provides the reader a jumping board for building a security awareness program in the enterprise. Resources to learn presentation and teaching skills are provided along with tools to facilitate social engineering testing. Lastly, the reader is provided links to security awareness training materials and safe computing resources.

Appendix E, Security Incident Response Resources, provides a sample incident response process flow along with sample incident response forms and resources for incident response.

Who this book is for

This book is for the IT professional in security or responsible for any component of the enterprise that is affected by information security policies, standards, and processes. This book can also be a valuable resource for a reader wanting to learn about and implement information security in the enterprise leveraging sound architectural principles. IT staff tasked with securing enterprise data while supporting new business initiatives such as cloud and BYOD will find this book a valuable reference on how to make information security a *business enabler* by implementing security in an agile manner built on data-centric trust models.

Conventions

In this book, you will find a number of styles of text that distinguish between different kinds of information. Here are some examples of these styles, and an explanation of their meaning.

Code words in text are shown as follows: "...a MD5 hash is calculated for secretfile using the md5 command..."

Any command-line input or output is written as follows:

```
Macbook-pro$ md5 secretfile
MD5 (secretfile) = 273cf6c54c2bdba56416942fbb5ec224
```

New terms and **important words** are shown in bold. Words that you see on the screen, in menus or dialog boxes for example, appear in the text like this: "...a secret file (secretfile) has been created with the text **This is a secret file.** inserted..."

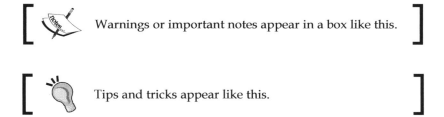

Warnings or important notes appear in a box like this.

Tips and tricks appear like this.

Reader feedback

Feedback from our readers is always welcome. Let us know what you think about this book—what you liked or may have disliked. Reader feedback is important for us to develop titles that you really get the most out of.

To send us general feedback, simply send an e-mail to feedback@packtpub.com, and mention the book title via the subject of your message.

If there is a topic that you have expertise in and you are interested in either writing or contributing to a book, see our author guide on www.packtpub.com/authors.

Customer support

Now that you are the proud owner of a Packt book, we have a number of things to help you to get the most from your purchase.

Errata

Although we have taken every care to ensure the accuracy of our content, mistakes do happen. If you find a mistake in one of our books—maybe a mistake in the text or the code—we would be grateful if you would report this to us. By doing so, you can save other readers from frustration and help us improve subsequent versions of this book. If you find any errata, please report them by visiting http://www.packtpub.com/submit-errata, selecting your book, clicking on the **errata submission form** link, and entering the details of your errata. Once your errata are verified, your submission will be accepted and the errata will be uploaded on our website, or added to any list of existing errata, under the Errata section of that title. Any existing errata can be viewed by selecting your title from http://www.packtpub.com/support.

Piracy

Piracy of copyright material on the Internet is an ongoing problem across all media. At Packt, we take the protection of our copyright and licenses very seriously. If you come across any illegal copies of our works, in any form, on the Internet, please provide us with the location address or website name immediately so that we can pursue a remedy.

Please contact us at copyright@packtpub.com with a link to the suspected pirated material.

We appreciate your help in protecting our authors, and our ability to bring you valuable content.

Questions

You can contact us at questions@packtpub.com if you are having a problem with any aspect of the book, and we will do our best to address it.

Enterprise Security Overview

1

Today's enterprise security approach is the product of an elaborate façade created by for-profit security vendors and outdated perimeter-focused security architecture. The focus has been shifted from protecting assets to guarding the network edge, while data continues to be exfiltrated, and data breaches are at an all-time high. This shift in focus has created a cat-and-mouse game of securing the enterprise from the latest threats at the expense of our budgets, network infrastructure, creditability, and maybe sanity. In response, we have self-imposed several challenges in the security industry and created a roadblock perception for the enterprise security team and enterprise security program. Let's reset our focus on securing what is most critical to the enterprise, its *data*.

This chapter will cover:

- The complex façade of enterprise security
- The failure of perimeter-focused security
- An introduction to security architecture
- Challenges of implementing security in the enterprise
- A road map to securing the enterprise

The façade of enterprise security

In concept, securing the enterprise may seem like a binary statement or universally understood idea, but a common solution continues to elude us. We have been trained to think that if we take certain steps such as developing secure processes, providing security training, and implementing security technologies, then we have secured the enterprise. This is in fact the "façade" of today's enterprise security approach. Security is not binary in an enterprise and implementation should be approached with a flexible and agile security architecture based on risk to enterprise data, therefore making the implementation of security more gray than black and white.

The static and inflexible approach meets compromise when a solution does not fit into the defined security architecture introducing undesirable risk, followed by the fall of idealistic enterprise security. In order for us to get to where we need to be, we need to understand the façade of enterprise security and take a look at how we got to the idea of enterprise security that is driving security purchases and the security industry today.

The history and making of the façade

In the earliest enterprise networks, there was not much call for a DMZ due to there being no real Internet presence like today. One example of early networking that drew the attention of malicious users was enterprise dial-up networking connections. Modems were used to make outbound calls and accept inbound calls to primarily process batch jobs for large backend systems. Security of this implementation was not much of a concern because the phone numbers had to be known and the systems connected to the modems were expecting very specific data from the calling modem. Eventually, modems became the method used by network and system administrators to connect to the enterprise network remotely for support functions. This was an excellent out-of-band method to access critical network infrastructure. If security was enabled, there may have been DIP switch settings that enabled password security on the receiving modem. This was until war dialing became a method to identify modems in large banks of phone numbers for attackers to gain unauthorized access to the connected equipment or network.

 War dialing is a method of dialing large pools of phone numbers looking for a modem attached to gain unauthorized access to a network. Non-local calling was expensive so this led to hackers exploiting **Private Branch Exchanges (PBXs)** using a method called phreaking. **Phreaking** is a method of sending tones through the phone to the PBX that tricks the PBX to allow the calls for free.

Specialized equipment was designed and sold to enterprises to provide security for the modem infrastructure. As more advanced networking technologies were developed and enterprise assets became accessible on the Internet, weaknesses in the systems and network security were quickly identified. Attackers were eager to exploit any vulnerability that was discovered. This behavior influenced network equipment manufacturers to begin developing security products to defeat specific security threats as they were identified. Point solutions were chosen not accepting that this was a "band-aid" approach that would fuel a narrowly-focused security industry.

As more threats were observed, more point solutions were developed to mitigate the threats. It was this natural progression of networking capabilities and threats that launched the security software and hardware manufacturing industry of today. We have continued this pattern of reaction-based development of security tools driven by mitigating specific threats as they are identified. In lockstep, we implemented the new technology to protect against the new "threat". Anti-virus, firewalls, intrusion detection/prevention, and other security technologies are the direct result of an existing threat, and are *reactive*.

Our efforts had been focused on securing the infrastructure and we forgot about the data, applications, processes, and users. It is easier to just buy the new technology of the day and support the illusion that we are secure from the "threat". This is the trend today. Advanced persistent threat mitigation became a hot topic because it became a real threat and instead of rethinking our security architecture, we purchased and implemented another technology, and probably implemented the solution at the network perimeter. This should seem familiar. We bought the story the security vendors had to sell. If there is a threat, buy our product and it will make you secure.

The next diagram shows the progression of point solutions being developed over time as new threats are detected. It also shows that detection and mitigation of threats becomes more complex over time as the threats themselves become more complex. As Threat 1 is identified, then Product 1 is developed to specifically mitigate Threat 1, and so on. We are seeing some traction in hardware and software that is capable of mitigating several threats. However, integration, management, solution scalability, and ability to provide deep coverage in all areas is yet to be seen. This continues the trend observed to date.

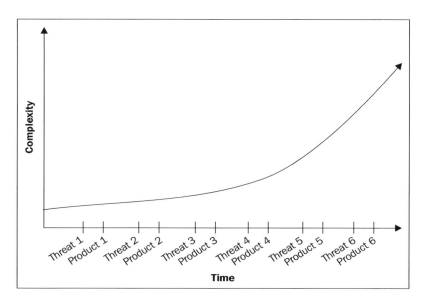

Having observed the history of enterprise security and the status quo reaction, we didn't realize we were buying into a false thought. So we implemented poorly-integrated security controls to address the enterprise's need to secure its assets while allowing business to continue. Unfortunately, what we designed was a relatively secure network perimeter instead of functioning, extensible, enterprise-wide security architecture. In fact, most developed security architecture is sound network design with an overlay of security that dictates what communication is allowed to and from the unique network zones.

Whether it is called a DMZ, a business partner zone, or a remote office zone, it is perimeter security by design and function. Until recently this made sense; though not true, it was thought that the known threat has always been external. Networks may have been large, but not overly complex, with multiple business partner connections or multiple DMZs. Typically, if there were services to be made available to an outside entity, we would place the assets providing the service in a perimeter zone, give it a name, and implement according to a defined security architecture. Such was the extent of implementing a secure solution.

This mentality has led to bloated security budgets, crowded perimeter zones, and very little increase in security. Because we have purchased and implemented the latest next-generation firewall technology, intrusion prevention systems, advanced persistent threat mitigation, data loss prevention, and file integrity monitoring, we think we have secured the enterprise. However, we have only increased the complexity in mitigating low-hanging fruit threats at the network perimeter and decreased our effectiveness in mitigating threats holistically. This is the security façade we've jointly created with our security software and hardware manufacturers.

Our current approach to security

We as a security industry have found ourselves in a unique position with significant changes in the way enterprises are conducting business. The late 1990s solidified the Internet as the premier method to market, provide services, and sell products in a global economy. This also meant that to be competitive, outsourcing of internal work would occur, remote access to critical systems was required, and more complex applications would be implemented with access to the most critical systems and data. This changed the threat landscape. Our focus became more on protecting all external threats, while losing focus on the most risky access we so quickly gave away, so that the business could grow.

Security architecture 101

In order to have a consistent approach to security, security architecture must be defined. Enterprise security architecture is the blueprint for securely implementing enterprise solutions to meet business requirements. Much like a house has blueprints for properly constructing it, security architecture serves the same purpose for the enterprise security design and implementation.

Up to this point, we have been discussing the implementation of security technologies as point solutions not necessarily as part of a defined security architecture. The progression of network technologies and business drivers created the first security architecture, but it was network focused and failed to address the enterprise as a whole taking into account data, processes, applications, roles, and users. Implementing to the network-based architecture with a security overlay limits the ability to sufficiently secure these components of the enterprise with agility and flexibility.

The current "security" architecture addresses user access to data in a very generic manner, focusing primarily on what protocols can be used at what tier of the network regardless of who the user is, the application used, type of data, and data interaction. An example of this approach is shown in the following diagram:

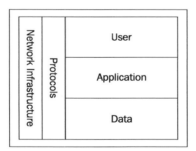

If the approach for securing the enterprise is to constrain all solutions the enterprise implements into this defined "security" architecture, then there will be three possible outcomes:

- Implementation in accordance with defined security architecture; there is no deviation from design or defined security architecture
- Implementation in accordance with security architecture cripples the solution and implementation of the solution is aborted
- Implementation not in accordance with security architecture weakens the effectiveness of the security architecture to make the implementation successful and introduces risk to the organization

This inflexible security architecture often requires the enterprise to quickly decide if the "risk" of not following security architecture is acceptable or if another method is available to secure the implementation without jeopardizing the project (investment on the table). By risk, I am presenting the fact that this is usually a determination of whether properly securing the implementation is too costly and difficult versus accepting the perceived risk and proceeding with the implementation. To reduce the risk associated with not following the architecture, compensating security mechanisms may be implemented. A continued cycle of this resolution leads to an overall less secure enterprise.

Let's look at an example of our current method of implementing security in line with our common and generic security architecture. Today, we have done a good job at creating segmented networks at least at the network layer using **virtual LANs (VLANs)**, internal firewall segmentation slowly being introduced, and assigning our users to groups according to job functions. I am careful to imply we have commonly defined roles within our architecture, so I will use functions, usually no more than a team designation. An example would be a VLAN called DBA_VLAN that is for the database administrator job function. Each VLAN will have its own unique IP subnet, so the database administrator "team" can easily be identified by the IP address of their system on the network. We can then implement firewall rules (if implemented) to allow this unique IP subnet access to the systems with databases. This is a very simple implementation and very ineffective security. In this previous example, the only unique identifier is the IP address in an assigned IP subnet belonging to the database administrators. This method does not constitute a secure authentication method, which should be more granular and performed at the user level.

The teams responsible for the security of the databases would present that the database security itself is the most important, so it doesn't matter who is sitting on the DBA_VLAN because ultimately only authenticated individuals can access the database systems. Unfortunately, this architecture allows for many misuse scenarios that increase the risk of a data breach through unauthorized access over trusted communications. We may have implemented security mechanisms, but I am willing to bet they are threat specific and lack the broader threat perspective required to secure the implementation. This is not security architecture, it is security patchwork often focused only on the product side of security because we have never figured out how to properly secure our people through roles, processes, policies, and standards. The example presented is the unacceptable yet accepted norm; recent data breaches have proven this is not a sufficient method to secure data.

A new approach to security

Our approach to securing the enterprise should go beyond simple threat mitigation. After all, this is exactly why we are in the not-so-effective security state that causes the breaches we see regularly in the news. As with all good design and architecture there are many factors that must be taken into consideration to properly influence the correct implementation. There is network infrastructure, system architecture, applications, and data that need to be designed, implemented, and secured. There are also people and systems that will access these components provided by the enterprise to use a service, and so on.

I recently traveled to Savannah, Georgia (GA) and was able to appreciate this very principle in home and building architecture and design. Did you know that any home built in historic Savannah has to be externally period correct? The requirement is to maintain the well-thought-out and aesthetically pleasing architecture. The original architects had many influences and deep reasons for the materials, layout, functionality, and design of the buildings at different points in history. Each home and building was not approached with a single thought or idea for its only purpose; instead, there is a standard that must be followed. The architectural standard allows the construction of new homes with modern amenities inside, but the exterior must fit it to the surroundings. Owners of the homes can decorate the interior how they please; this is the uniqueness of each home allowing each home owner to have the home they want without introducing architectural anomalies to Savannah. As architects design and plan a new home build in Savannah, GA, we should approach security architecture with the same broad, yet focused vision in the enterprise.

With the previous database system access scenario fresh in our minds, what would be more of an architectural approach? First, should security architecture rigidly define how this access should be granted, or can a more flexible approach be leveraged? I think the best first step would be to back up and take a broader look at the requested access. If we can understand the criticality of the data/system based on the data or function, what type of access is needed, why the access is needed, who or what will access the data/system, then we can determine the risk and better develop an architecture that properly secures the data/system and provides the access needed to allow the business to function. The issue we most often run into is we jump right into figuring out how we are going to secure something, whether it is networks' communications, system access, or whatever, without any idea what (if any) risk is introduced. The other issue is, since we have focused so much on securing the DMZ, we haven't properly architected security further into the infrastructure, at least not more that the typical firewall, IDS/IPS, and maybe some system security products, so we are forced to either make expensive purchases or compromise on security.

Unless we develop a new security architecture—an architecture that addresses all facets of security and provides a realistic picture of the risk posed by any implementation—the secure enterprise will never be realized. The new approach to security architecture takes into account data, processes, applications, user roles, and users, in addition to the traditional network security mechanisms to provide end-to-end security from entry to the network to the data resident within the enterprise. The following diagram shows a more comprehensive approach to security based on risk of the entire interaction with enterprise data:

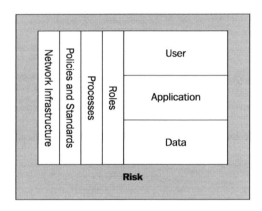

Enterprise security pitfalls

The challenging responsibility of leading security within an enterprise can be successful or disastrous. Security in principle is black and white, however, implementation and the real world is gray. When security personnel operate from a binary perspective on security principles it fosters a false perspective of an ideal enterprise security posture. It does not exist and will frustrate security objectives. We as security personnel are charged with understanding how the enterprise functions so that we can provide the desired security direction and expertise as a business enabler. We can then more effectively determine risk associated with implementation, and risk identification will determine investment is securing the implementation.

Many times the security conversation is nothing more than just that, a conversation, because the security team is unable to speak in a language the business or other IT teams can understand, let alone in a compelling manner to influence change if a solution will introduce risk or undermine security. If we are insisting that certain technologies must be implemented, then we must be able to bring this full circle and tie this position to supporting processes, policies, standards, business needs, and risk.

Application developers are a great example of a team that typically steers clear of point solutions and looks for options that easily insert into their existing processes and are repeatable. Working closely with other IT teams will prove to be fruitful and help achieve security-focused goals when collaboration and cooperation are encouraged to collectively decide on security solutions.

Shortcomings of the current security architecture

The current security architecture is not meeting the current enterprise trends such as **bring your own device (BYOD)** and cloud initiatives; it also does not address the internal network facet of information security. This gooey, soft inside has traditionally been neglected because the current security architecture deemed internal assets, employees, contractors, and business partners as trusted. The same security controls are typically not mandatory for the internal communications as in the perimeter, however, this is where an enterprise's most sensitive and critical systems and data typically exist.

Example shortcomings of the current security architecture are:

- It fails to secure internal assets from internal threats
- It remains static and inflexible; small deviations circumvent and undermine intended security
- All internal users are equal, no matter what device is used or if the user is a non-employee
- Security is weak for enterprise data; access is not effectively controlled at the user level

We have done what the security industry vendors want us to do, buy security appliances and software and implement them, regardless of whether it actually increases the security posture of the organization. Some trends indicating we are doing it wrong are the significant increases in data breaches and more moves of security implementation to the cloud and other managed security services. This is indicative of implementing point solutions with little to no integration, limited in-house expertise and/or staff, and the overwhelming amount of data produced by the solutions. So while we have done all the correct surface things, we have in fact produced little positive impact, while complicating security.

What do we do when an implementation cannot be implemented per this current "security" architecture, or access that is requested causes the architecture to be broken? We compromise; not only on the architecture, but on the security of the enterprise. New security architecture must be developed to address the issues outlined. The remainder of this book presents a methodical approach to better positioning security in the enterprise and looks at how to implement flexible and agile security architecture to enable the business to take advantage of the latest trends.

Communicating information security

The zealous security professional will often focus so intently on the responsibility of securing the enterprise that they miss the business objective. This leads to security personnel having tunnel vision and only seeing one set of methods to secure an enterprise. This tunnel vision can be detrimental to the success of the security team overall and can have a negative influence on design and purchasing decisions.

Because security is not a commonly and generally understood IT function, it can be difficult to get upper management and other IT teams to give buy-in. This is evident when security is asking them to make costly network changes, or change the way a solution is to be implemented and the security team has failed to provide a compelling rationalization to do so. Why is this? I think, because we have not spent the time to understand how the business functions and we do not always have representation at the highest levels to present our case. In my experience, organizations that are missing a security focused executive-level sponsor are at a significant disadvantage of successfully implementing a security practice that really reduces the risk to business. What an individual at this level can achieve far exceeds the capability of management at a lower level because of the position of influence. It is much easier to influence laterally and downward, but very difficult to influence upward.

Discussions at lower levels within an organization tend to be more shortsighted, specific to an implementation, and more emotional. For example, when security becomes a topic during an initiative, the implementation of this initiative may be an individual's or team's vision, and now security is seen as threatening to complicate the implementation or halt it, maybe at an additional expense. Often, security is an afterthought, and is therefore not well received. Having a security-focused senior management position or having a security architect (team if needed) that is responsible for the overall security architecture of an organization can avoid or lessen the burden of this scenario. It should be noted that all enterprise employees are responsible for security and must embrace the integration of security into all applicable IT and business processes. The security of the enterprise is only as good as the weakest link.

The cost of information security

If security is communicated as an enterprise priority and is generally understood, we might think that we should be able to do whatever it takes to secure the enterprise. However, this is not necessarily always the case. At some point the cost valuation has to be determined before an enterprise makes a decision to take on additional expense to implement security controls. The difficulty in providing quantifiable data to back up the cost and request for security-related purchases is significant; we must learn to operate smarter according to more intelligent security architecture.

Let's think of it like this. If an intangible is presented such as if we buy security product "X" we reduce our risk of being hacked costing the enterprise a high-dollar figure and another team is presenting an expense that is tangible and quantifiable, where do you think the money will go? An example is: the security team wants to spend $150, 000 on a web application firewall; there is no data on current attacks against the enterprise, just the latest report on the Internet showing the trends in data breaches associated with web application security. Another IT team needs to buy servers because the current servers are at capacity and without the purchase, several key IT initiatives will be impacted. This is not to say the latter is not valid, but this budget contention will always exist with the server team or some other IT team. Again, I ask, where do you think the money will go?

It is rather predictable because security has become a bit of a cat-and-mouse game, and we are losing. So the next best thing to winning is detecting and mitigating last year's threat. This makes the security budget every year a bloated figure that leaves the security team vulnerable to not being able to properly secure the enterprise and fighting for every cent to do so.

The overall reason why this is the case is due to the failing security architecture of yesteryear that we keep trying to shoehorn everything into. There are methods to reduce the security spend by making more intelligent business-focused decisions, that allow the business to be agile without compromising security, or at least with reduced risk.

The conflicting message of enterprise security

We as a security industry are too focused on one thing, "numero uno". That is to say that no one apparently in information security seems to be interested in actually solving the issues we face, but just to profit by keeping the well-oiled machine running. We have factions within security that say "do this, don't do that", while other groups are saying the opposite. This leads to teams of security personnel having very different ideas and views on how to implement security for the enterprise, determine risk, and handle day-to-day security operations.

An example of this conflicting message is the great debate on the subject of penetration testing and the false sense of security some believe it produces. There is great benefit to be had by consistent testing of enterprise security. The issues as observed are the lack of business justification, "value-added" when there is a lack of quantifiable findings, and knee-jerk reactions of buying something that probably won't fix the real problem identified.

Our trusted security vendors generally develop other conflicting messages on what the real issues are and how only their product or service is the solution. Remember, each has the best solution for you, choose wisely. One will recommend their file integrity monitoring, another their whitelisting application, and yet another will recommend their next-generation firewall. What is management to do? The best solution will have to be determined once the proper security architecture has been developed and accepted at the highest levels of the enterprise. Execute to this, not the latest marketing slicks.

Enterprise security is truly a risk-centered balancing act between business initiatives and security. The vendors will sell their products and experts will have their opinions. However, ultimately the enterprise security professional will need to decipher how each impacts the security posture of their respective enterprise. Once this logic is applied, the message is no longer conflicting because you, the professional, have made sense of the messages for your application of security. It may be difficult to get other IT teams to see the same perspective. Communicating security tool effectiveness and the expected impact to risk reduction and securing the enterprise will be the best way to decipher the sometimes-confusing messages communicated by the security industry.

Proving a negative

One of the most significant challenges in information security is proving a negative. This is to say for example, if specific steps, or actions are taken or a specific technology purchased, we are preventing what would be successful network intrusions. This is in part because there is no technology deployed that will give us this information and in part because we only learn of a small portion of breaches. Even if breaches are reported they may not happen in the same industry vertical or may lack pertinent details, and therefore do not provide any meaningful statistical data to justify security expense.

It is a challenge to get the executive board or other IT management excited about information security, and the price tags of the line items on the annual security budget. The traditional approach to information security decision making will fall flat on its face without a well-defined security architecture that is understood and adopted by those who will ultimately approve information security spend. This will have to be carefully approached using any and all applicable data that can support the position of the security team.

Ultimately, you can never prove the negative or convince senior management that changes need to be made in order to properly secure the enterprise without compelling data. A feasible method may be a well-written business presentation of applicable threats, assessed risk, and a recommended mitigation strategy for the enterprise. Also, providing a road map can be very useful if significant cost is associated with getting the enterprise to a proper security posture. Realizing this is an ever-evolving and moving target, a roadmap can allow for flexibility in strategy implementation over a period of time.

The road map to securing the enterprise

The road to a risk aware secure enterprise does exist; it is challenging, but tangible. In this section, I will lay out a road map to developing flexible security architecture as the foundation to securing the enterprise. It is not the only method, but it is sound and will hopefully serve as an exercise to challenge enterprise security teams to rethink the current architecture and security methods being implemented.

Road map components

There are several exercises that must be completed to obtain an accurate representation and definition of the enterprise assets (systems, data, and so on), communication methods, users, roles, business processes, policies, and standards. Each will need to be defined in extreme detail to be most effective, but if this is the first attempt a more generic definition of each can be the starting point, with a gradual increase in detail, until everything is defined and all possible combinations identified. The road map provided is an introduction to the detailed approach in the next chapter.

Starting with user groups may be the easiest, however, you can focus on systems and data in the beginning phases, especially if there has been absolutely no data classification or critical system identification. All of this data will serve as input to the trust models we will develop in the next chapter. Here we will provide an overview of what should be collected for each defined component. It should be noted that all components need periodic review, and recertification should be built into the process. A simple diagram of the process at a high level is provided as follows:

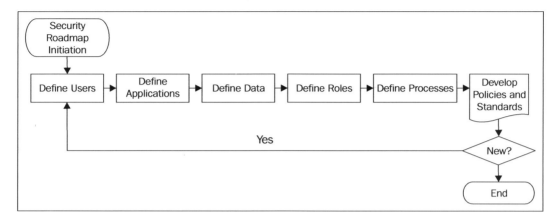

Defining users

All users within the enterprise and those that interact with the enterprise, such as contractors and business partners, must be identified and their relationship with the enterprise determined. This data will provide input to roles and start tying the relationship of an individual or group of individuals to data.

Defining applications

Define all applications in the enterprise, their purpose, and what data they are used to access. It is also important to understand what systems the applications are installed on to determine scope when identifying risks associated with application access.

Defining data

This may seem very simple, but it can prove to be a difficult task even for the smallest enterprise. Each department may have different data, and subjectively valued, it may not be defined in the perspective of overall value to the enterprise. Additionally, identifying where the data resides, such as which systems or physical locations, is a key issue. Things to consider are duplication and backups of the data. Data may reside in desktop applications such as Microsoft Access with databases duplicated many times over for each user that needs access residing on the user systems. Additionally, data should have a classification assigned per policy that dictates the required security for the identified data and may need to be in compliance to HIPPA, SOX, PCI, and other regulatory requirements. Data is the focus, as typically systems have no value aside from the expense of the physical hardware and the data that is contained within them.

Defining roles

Once users and data sets have been identified, the purpose of the access must be defined. For instance, basic user access versus administrator access. There are also data custodians; perhaps our trust model will have additional monitoring requirements based on the level of access to critical data. These roles can start as generic, but the more defined the user group and roles are, the better the user interaction will be understood and the more granular the controls that can be implemented.

Defining processes

Defining business processes will often lead to identification of the business critical data and systems. Understanding the processes that make the enterprise function can also identify additional users and roles not previously identified. Examples of processes are automation, change management, and third-party oversight.

Defining policies and standards

Once all users, roles, and processes have been defined, there must be some policy that dictates what is permitted use of the authorized access, and defines what is unauthorized behavior while using the enterprise assets including but not limited to: network, applications, systems, and data. Standards by which users are to be provisioned, access to applications, data, and systems to be handled should be standardized to ensure consistency. Standards will also include items such as system builds and security, security configuration of applications, and security monitoring.

It is important that the enterprise is willing to take action if there is a violation of policies and standards because it is implied that deviation from these will introduce risk to the enterprise and possibly undermine security, resulting in a data breach or other negative impact to the enterprise.

Defining network infrastructure

This process requires understanding what has already been implemented to facilitate business partner communications, external access via website, VPN access, and so on. Having defined the network "zones" and the users, both internal and external, that use them will drive the required security monitoring and protection mechanisms. In some cases once this exercise has been completed, it may be determined that a new zone needs to be created and implemented to support the security initiative of the organizations.

A layered approach to security that includes network infrastructure is critical to an end-to-end secure enterprise. Ultimately, the preceding component definition should drive much of the network architecture, where applicable, requiring the network and security teams to work closely in these areas of the infrastructure. There must be consistent standards, especially for the network infrastructure, as it provides all the connectivity for business network communications.

Defining application security architecture

Applications are the preferred method for accessing enterprise data. Understanding how security is integrated into applications through a formal **Software Development Life Cycle (SDLC)** will not only provide useful data for trust models, but may also highlight other areas that need additional security implemented to meet the standard of the application. Standards for data protection can be gleaned from the secure development processes that can be used in other areas of IT.

Summary

We as security professionals have become used to the idea that security is a state to reach, but it is unattainable. In part, because the old security architecture no longer meets the enterprise needs, and because we have not adopted a more intelligent architecture that is focused on enterprise data and risk. There are several challenges that the enterprise security teams must navigate. This chapter introduced concepts that will be further explored in this book and that will address these challenges and provide a methodical approach to securing the enterprise with the adoption of a new, flexible, and agile security architecture.

2
Security Architectures

As the enterprise evolves by leveraging new technologies such as **bring your own device (BYOD)** and the cloud, security architecture needs to be redefined to remain effective. Many services are moving out to the network edge and beyond. There are security issues that must be considered, as often these are tied to internal systems. These significant changes to the traditional network and security architecture results in the need to go back to the blueprints and develop an agile architecture. Understanding the complex data interactions in the enterprise by developing trust models is a requisite exercise, and will be explained in detail in this chapter.

We will cover the following topics in this chapter:

- The evolution of networks and why the security architecture must change
- Introduction of the data-centric security architecture
- Developing trust models and mapping data interaction
- Considerations for developing trust models for BYOD initiatives

Redefining the network edge

The enterprise network edge has been an evolving infrastructure, as many applications have become web-enabled in addition to the increasing demand for enterprise data from business partners and other third parties. The requirement for access to enterprise data is being driven by the need for the enterprise to outsource portions of their provided services, an example being the calculation of shipping costs for an e-commerce transaction. Traditionally, the sources of enterprise data may have resided in the internal trusted segments of the network, but this is changing with new opportunities provided by cloud-based offerings and collapsed virtualized DMZ implementations.

A newer internal network trend is a "**trust no one**" model, where the internal data systems are firewalled and protected at the same level as a typical DMZ implementation. In order for the internally secure zone to maintain restrictive access policies, a virtualization technology may be implemented to further control and prohibit direct access to the data. This approach essentially defines the internal user population as untrusted, moving the network edge further into the core of the internal network. A serious consideration of the implementation caveats is recommended, as cost and application complexity may be significant challenges. Let's take a closer look at the business drivers that have changed the definition of the network edge.

Drivers for redefinition

There are many reasons for the changes observed in the network edge. Generally, the observed changes are due to new services that require access to enterprise data for both internal and external sources. If we take a step back and think about the evolution of the DMZ, we can recognize the shift from providing a basic Internet presence to providing feature-rich Internet accessible applications, and complex network connections to business partners for sharing enterprise data. An increase in the use of cloud-based services and capital expense savings of BYOD initiatives further complicate and gray the lines of network boundaries. Each of these introduces unique security challenges that stretch our current network-based security architectures.

Feature-rich web applications

In order to provide a full-featured web application, permission to access the enterprise data stored in an internal database infrastructure may be required. The typical implementation of an Internet accessible web application positions the presentation and logic tiers within the DMZ infrastructure with the backend data located in the internal network or in a segmented portion of the DMZ. Due to the database relationship, web applications are the primary target for exploitation.

A common attack called **SQL injection** is used as a method for exploiting a web application misconfiguration, which can lead to direct access to the data resident in the database infrastructure. It is generally understood how SQL injection is carried out, but if reliance is solely on the network security appliances to protect data, it will quickly be realized that this approach to security architecture is flawed. Simply implementing the web application infrastructure within the current standard network and security architecture does not properly address this security issue, however, an architecture focused on data interaction ensures that secure access to data is implemented.

A typical deployment of a web application is two to three logical tiers comprising the web, application, and database components. There are also some implementations where the web and application tiers are collapsed into a single tier. In the latter case, we start to see a deviation from the generally accepted security architecture practices, because there is confusion on where this hybrid web and application instance should reside in the DMZ. To date we have used our network design to determine our security architecture and limit the value of it to restricting protocols and network communication direction.

The hybrid solution could reside in the web tier, bypass the traditional second tier, and connect directly into the database tier, typically located in the core internal network. This type of implementation usually makes the security team cringe. The other option is to place the hybrid instance in tier two of the architecture, but now we have the untrusted Internet and semi-trusted business partners accessing the application tier directly; this again is not ideal. The benefit of user input sanitation, validation, and protocol enforcement is minimized by the lack of firewalled and segmented tiers.

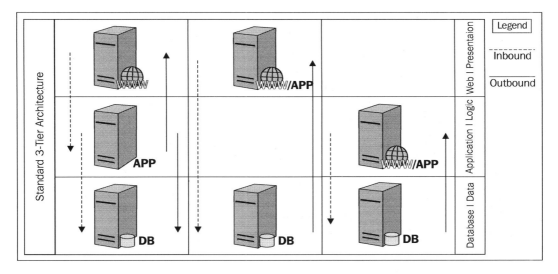

To help facilitate these types of implementations, we often find ourselves making hard decisions to get something to work. We may even decide to move the database into the DMZ or try some method of segmentation with a stateful firewall. Either way, we should be able to discern that we are only manipulating the network aspect of the implementation.

The protocols and communication methods are not modified in this design even though the architecture is. This deviation from the architectural standard circumvents the intended security and leaves us unsure of the risks associated with the deviation. This unknown is counterintuitive to risk reduction; risk is what we are trying to limit with well-developed security architecture.

Business partner access

Another driver for redefining the network edge is business partner access to the enterprise data. Some enterprises have developed unique network zones to handle the network connectivity, but haven't really solved the data location issue because the security architecture is still network driven. Common access is provisioned to the same highly-sensitive segment of the network, where the most critical enterprise data resides to facilitate access requirements. The end result is an internally segmented network that is secured from internal users, but accessible directly from an offsite network that circumvents the internally deployed security mechanisms. This example is extraordinary, as the secure internal segment in this example does not exist across the traditional enterprise landscape.

Here are a few examples of a standard business partner connectivity that enforce a simple security architecture:

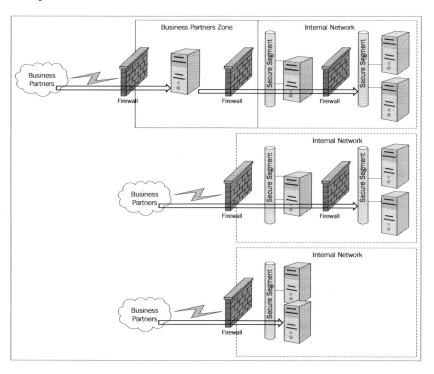

The business partner architecture shown in the preceding diagram may look very similar to the DMZ architecture; in concept they are the same. It may be a micro architecture within a tier of the macro architecture of the enterprise. Variations of this architecture may include allowed protocols, destination systems, communication directions, and types of required security mechanisms implemented based on a calculated risk that defines a level of trust. It can be assumed that a business partner will have a higher trust than an anonymous user on the Internet. There are many ways to facilitate the business partner connectivity. I have given an example of a common network architecture where the security of the implementation is an overlay. There are issues with this logic where risk cannot be measured individually for the connections permitted, and appropriate security mechanisms are implemented to differing degrees for risk mitigation.

Access to the enterprise data is many times unavoidable; it may be needed for the enterprise to perform some business critical function or to provide a service enabling function, by allowing the business partner to access the enterprise data. The primary issue is that the enterprise may not have a method where data can be fed to multiple destinations, allowing the data to be served to a solution for business partners. This forces the enterprise to allow access to the most critical systems and network segments, where even the internal users do not have access permissions.

If the scope of a compromise is being considered, I am not sure this is where I would want to connect my business partners into my network. If the business partner is compromised and the threat is propagated over the business connection then the threat can have a heyday in the most secured part of the network. A proper implementation of a security architecture built on a well-defined trust model is the key to a successful implementation of any connectivity to the network, including business partners.

Miscellaneous third-party services

In order for the enterprise to thrive in the global economy, it has become increasingly important to leverage services provided by third parties who specialize in the desired service. As I mentioned earlier, one example is the shipping cost calculation for an e-commerce website. Of course, the enterprise could create a solution to generate this data and store it in a database, but there is an associated overhead cost with this method. Not only would the enterprise have to purchase the infrastructure, build the database, and secure the data, but there is also a significant total cost of ownership based on the operational aspect of the implementation. If the enterprise is not specialized in the desired area, the cost will be significantly more. Having a third party provide the service(s) in a canned manner with an interface into the enterprise application makes much more sense.

The most impactful consideration here is not only the type of data but also where it resides. Because the third-party service connections are much like business partner connections, the same challenges exist with trying to implement per a standard security architecture.

Cloud initiatives

Cloud service offerings are extending the enterprise network to hosted virtualized infrastructure. Enterprise data literally can reside anywhere within the global network of the cloud service providers. Due to cost savings and high availability offerings, a service several enterprises are moving to the cloud is their e-mail implementation. With this relocation of services comes a significant concern over the security of the hosted data.

Enterprises must consider this reality when they consider what data gets moved to the cloud and how it will be protected, not only in transmission but also in storage. An example would be providing data loss prevention capabilities for services that are provided in the cloud. Typically, this would occur on hosts and possibly the DMZ zone of the enterprise network, both of which are no longer in the control of the enterprise in the typical cloud implementation. Information security teams must provide secure access for data, along with providing a flexible architecture to handle the hooks into the enterprise network from the cloud solution. The scope of protection in a cloud solution is well beyond what the enterprise has ever had to solve.

Security architecture models

The typical security architectures range from a generic layered approach, where only connected layers may communicate with each other, to complex source and destination zones, allowed protocols, and specific communication channels permitted per endpoint type to advanced models based on data risk. **Data risk** is comprised of understanding what data needs protection including from whom and what, based on loss probability.

The data-centric security architectures emphasize enterprise data, where it is stored, how it is transmitted, and the details of any data interaction. Once all pertinent enterprise data and associated systems are identified, the required security mechanisms can be designed and implemented. Placement of the systems may not be a concern if the security mechanisms are based on the risk profile built by the previously learned information. The next sections will cover how the components of the security architecture are developed.

Defining the building blocks of trust models

In the previous chapter, we looked at a roadmap for securing the enterprise. To begin the process of properly securing the enterprise, a security architecture needs to be defined. The nature of architecture is principle based, therefore there is not a single one that fits into all security architecture concepts. Do not confuse architecture and design as they are fundamentally different disciplines. We have seen monumental shifts in how business is being conducted. The architecture(s) must consider these methods and be agile enough to provide security while enabling the business.

In order to sufficiently satisfy security interests and meet the needs of an ever-evolving enterprise, trust models need to be developed in such a way that they encompass all the interactions with the data they are designed to protect. It is important to note that the focus of a security architecture is not the network segment or the system; it is the data, which is the purpose for the network, and the system. As we look at the characteristics of the data access and determine who, what, why, and so on, patterns will emerge that will show the flexibility of a data-centric architecture versus the traditional network-based approach. We will then be able to drop a trust model on top of a network segment, system, and data type; do you see the pattern yet?

First, we will dive into defining each step in securing the enterprise roadmap presented in *Chapter 1, Enterprise Security Overview*. We will then present sample trust models that can be used as is or tailored to a specific situation. The next image depicts the determination of trust and hos risk dictates trust and trust influences policies and standards.

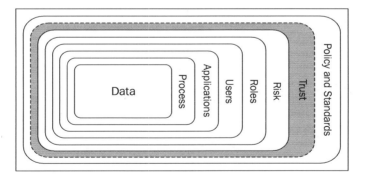

Defining data in a trust model

The typical security architecture will look at the data in the last step to decide how to securely provide access to it. This often occurs well after a significant investment has been made to enable the business function that requires data access. This is also where we see compromise of the intended security architecture, because security will have technically been an after thought.

The lack of flexibility offered by network-centric architecture is the Achilles heel of the model. An enterprise must understand what data exists, why the data exists, data sensitivity, and data criticality. This can all be assessed without thinking about the data location. Data is the "what" portion of the data interaction. If it is determined that the data or "what" being accessed has little value or risk associated with it, then security mechanisms may be reduced or become non-existent. Enterprise data may be processed, stored, and transmitted during its lifecycle. The following image is a simple depiction of typical enterprise data interactions:

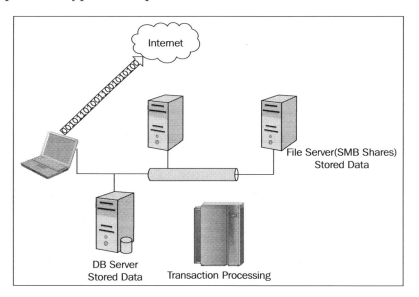

Data locations

Typical locations of data can be determined by understanding business processes — another phase in the roadmap. But if they are not well defined, then an enterprise can begin by looking at databases and network shares for data at rest. This process should identify a majority of the enterprise data. Some applications may have a local database and this needs to be identified, but a few outliers will not impede proper data identification and classification to build the trust models.

During the discovery of enterprise data, be sure to include end-point devices to look for local database instances and data stored in typical desktop processing applications. Laptops are one location that has been a significant cause of data breaches, because critical and high-risk data was stored on a laptop with no protection, and was stolen.

Data types

Essentially, there are two states data can be: **transient** and **stored**. Transient data is the data that is processed by an application on a system and transmitted over a network. Stored data resides in a database or a network share for a period of time beyond a single transaction. Depending on the type of business, the industry vertical will directly relate to the expected data types. For instance, a clothing retailer will more than likely have credit card numbers as a form of data in both transient and stored network locations, whereas a technology firm may have patented trade secrets. Risk associated with the data types may come from business criticality (in relation to impact), regulatory compliance, and legal mandates. Once the risk is understood, appropriate security mechanisms can be implemented.

Typical data loss prevention solutions have data discovery capabilities. These tools can aid in the discovery of stored data across all enterprise systems. Data may be stored in text files, spreadsheets, log files, and databases, to name the most common file types. Similar tools exist to capture data in transit on the network, alerting security personnel when a triggered event has occurred.

Defining data types, value, and regulatory responsibilities per industry				
Industry	Data type	Data purpose	Data value	Regulatory/legal responsibility
Retail	Credit card numbers	Product sales	High	PCI
Healthcare	Patient information	Patient care and billing	High	HIPAA
	PII			
Banking	Credit card numbers	Service Offerings	High	PCI, FTC, and SEC
	PII			

The preceding table gives examples of data types for common industries, including possible purposes of the data, perceived data value, applicable laws, and regulatory responsibilities for the data.

> If the enterprise is responsible for meeting the requirements of a regulatory body, it is imperative to fully understand the requirements and what is expected as proof of compliance. Requirements should then be integrated into the developed trust models and an effective security architecture.

Defining processes in a trust model

How does the enterprise conduct business? This will start the discovery necessary to understand the systems of highest criticality and require the most attention when it comes to securing the infrastructure. The previous section covered defining the enterprise data that needs protection. If the data is unknown, start with the current business processes; this should lead you to the most critical data. I highly recommend using a discovery tool to find data in storage, as the most sensitive data seems to find its way into the most insecure locations of the network.

A defined process may be the method to take an online payment for a product or service, or some other "method" used by the enterprise to conduct business. This is the "why" of the data interaction. Something as simple as an e-mail is also a process. The user uses an e-mail application to access messages, some containing attachments, which is all data.

Interviewing system and application owners is an affective method to identify business and technical processes, if not commonly known. Identification of data transfer systems such as, **extract, transform, load** (ETL), and **Enterprise Information Integration** (EII) are a good starting point for finding automation and critical business processes within the enterprise. Once processes have been identified, opportunities should be taken to correct any process that introduces risks to the enterprise, as processes are primarily data-centric with direct data access and manipulation capabilities.

> When using scripts for automation in an enterprise environment, never store passwords, make sure to remove interactive login for Windows, and restrict shell access on Linux. This mitigates CLI and GUI access if the script credentials are compromised.

Defining applications in a trust model

Now that we have defined the enterprise data and processes, we need to define the applications that transmit, process, or store the defined data. As we build our definitions, we will begin to see the picture of "use and access", I sometimes call interactions, which will serve as our guide to determine the proper security mechanisms for implementation. Applications can literally be any application in the enterprise from e-mail clients to complex sales processing applications.

In a retail environment, the point of sale application would need to be defined as a method to interact with enterprise data, possibly used by a person or other automated methods, such as scripts. The methods in which the applications interact with the data become the factors defining users, roles, and ultimately the security mechanisms required.

In some cases, applications and protocols can represent the same thing as in the e-mail example. We are not looking to necessarily define the different e-mail clients that the user is running to access e-mails. Rather, POP3 and SMTP are the protocols leveraged to access the e-mails in the enterprise e-mail servers. The e-mail client in the previous scenario may come into play based on the features that define the enterprise data interaction by the user.

Defining users in a trust model

A user interacts with an application that has access to data; the user may be a person, script, system, or another application. Not all users will require the same level of access. It is critical to identify as many users as possible and also the types of interactions with the enterprise data that is required for each user. Users can be discovered by thoroughly defining the processes in the enterprise.

Assessing enterprise job functions, such as departmental affiliation, will help to define more granular groups. For instance, a user may be in the Information Technology department, and also a UNIX administrator within this department. This is not the same as defining a role, which is applying the user's interaction with enterprise's data for a specific purpose. If the UNIX administrator was to perform backups of data, this may be a role associated with this user for that specific set of data. What is to be accomplished at this stage is to know that the UNIX administrator exists.

There are also high-level distinctions for users such as:

- **Internal (employee)**: This individual uses employee-owned equipment to interact with enterprise data. This may be blurred with a BYOD implementation; this will be addressed in the BYOD section.

- **External (non-employee)**: This individual uses some non-enterprise system to interact with the enterprise applications and/or enterprise data.

- **Business partner**: A contractual relationship binds the enterprise and the business partner for the purposes of conducting business. Access to enterprise data may be significant to the business relationship and from systems not owned by the enterprise.

- **Contractor**: A person or business entity that is hired contractually to work for the enterprise in the capacity of an internal employee. They may use some combination of employee-owned assets, personal assets, or issued assets by their direct employer (contractor firm).

Each user type should influence at some level the trust applied to the interaction with enterprise data. This cannot be the primary factor but should be a good and generic indicator of trust on an objective scale from "no trust" to "trusted".

The outcome of this exercise will have significance when we begin the trust decision process for each high-level user type, taking into consideration the type of data and access level to the data. An enterprise may have as many user definitions as necessary to complete this exercise.

Defining roles in a trust model

An important part of defining users is to identify the interactions that the users will have with the data including how the access will be facilitated—whether through an application, shell, script, or direct. This is where roles come into the picture and must be defined.

Using our example of the UNIX administrator, what does the user need access to, why is the access needed, and how is the access facilitated? We should know this information by now if we have properly defined the data, processes, applications, and users. If the role of the UNIX administrator is to simply perform system support and not interact with the data on the system, then it is possible to state that access to enterprise data must be denied and access attempts to the data should be monitored. This is a simple example of defining user roles based on information learned versus simply by departmental role. Interviewing users and teams may provide more information for granular role definition.

High-level user roles:

- **Application user**: Users of an application may input data, read data, and modify data through the application.

- **Application owner**: Responsible for the functional and operational aspects of the application, maybe coding the application if homegrown.

- **System owner**: Provides operation support for the underlying operating system and the hardware where the application and data reside.

- **Data owner**: Responsible for data input, read, modified, or processed by enterprise applications, systems, and users. The data owner may use the data for various functions or simply provide the data to other functions within or outside the enterprise.

- **Automation**: These include scripts and applications that run with no human interaction to process, transfer, and manipulate data for the purpose of business operations.

Each defined role may have requirements to interact with the same data, however, in differing methods. The roles listed are the most generic containers and common to most enterprises. Using these high-level roles is the starting point for defining user roles within your organization. I only caution you from creating too many user roles as this can lead to confusion, and more than likely the duplication of roles. If this is the case, reconsider making the role more generic to truly meet the needs of the enterprise.

Defining policies and standards

The last components that must be defined are the policies that will guide a secure access and use of the enterprise data, and the standards that ensure a consistent application of policy. There typically are no lack of policies and standards in most enterprises, but the application and enforcement of both are the challenges that most enterprises fail. If there are no policies, the second component, standards, becomes what policies should we have been.

Fortunately, compliance bodies such as the PCI Council require the creation and implementation of a security policy, acceptable use policy, operational security policy, and so on. This can serve as a good place for the start of policy development. There are also other resources available on the Internet to help develop the relevant policies for your industry, see *Appendix B, Risk Analysis, Policy and Standard, and System Hardening Resources*, for further information.

Think of policies and standards as the law and enforcement of the security architecture. They may be written in response to a new business process or request, and are a requirement to communicate the security strategy and safe computing expectations to the employees, business partners, and anyone else doing business with the enterprise.

Enterprise trust models

We have identified all the components that will help us define our trust models, which can be overlayed wherever necessary in the network—on systems, in the cloud, in applications, or anywhere applicable, as determined by the enterprise. Trust models may comprise more than the human element of data interaction as exhibited in the process definition section. Depending on the trust that is given to each combination of data, process, application, and user, determination of the required security mechanisms can be defined. It is important to understand this is not a simple trust/no trust approach. There are going to be degrees of trust depending not only on the user type, but also on the criticality of the data and associated risk. Another way to think of this is to assign allowed trust levels depending on roles. Any user type with a certain assigned trust level can access data according to the permissions associated with that assigned trust level. To make the determination manageable, it is recommended to use a small scale, such as 1 to 3—1 as not trusted, 2 as median trusted, and 3 as trusted.

We will cover the following trust models:

- Application user (external)
- Application owner (business partner)
- System owner (contractor)
- Data owner (internal)
- Automation (scripts, non-human interaction)

Let's build a table to correlate the data that we have gathered about the types of users that may exist along with the other building blocks of a trust model, such as data types, processes, applications, and roles. I will be using sample data, but you can input real data from your discovery exercises. The more time spent on these discovery and documentation exercises, the better developed and applicable the trust models will be for the enterprise. This can be repeated until an accurate representation of what exists is documented and understood. This should be an iterative process whenever a change occurs. I recommend running each new implementation through these exercises.

Sample trust model building blocks

Data	Process	Applications	Users	Roles	Policies and standards
Credit card numbers	Application for a new service	Web application	External, non-employee	Application user	Acceptable use Secure access
Credit card numbers	Fraud detection	Fraud software	Business partner	Application owner	Data protection standard
Credit card numbers	Storage	Database	Contractor	System owner	Data protection standard
Credit card numbers	Loyalty tracking	Business intelligence	Internal, employee	Data owner	Data protection standard
Credit card numbers	Order processing	Credit authorization and settlement	Automation	Automation	Data protection standard

Application user (external)

Defining a trust model for an external user should focus on the fact that the enterprise does not know the security posture of the end system. Generally speaking, external users should be the least trusted. An enterprise is not for example responsible nor in the position to update the anti-virus signatures on the external system or make sure that the end system is patched. The point here is that the enterprise scope of responsibility starts wherever the end system is connecting to it. So, the level of trust should be none with the highest level of monitoring and protection implemented.

User type	External
Trust level	1: Not trusted
Allowed access	Tier 1 DMZ only, least privilege
Required security mechanisms	FW, IPS, and Web App Firewall

Application owner (business partner)

In a scenario where a third party has access to a system on the internal network and the data it processes, there must be a level of trust. After all, the enterprise more than likely signed a business contract to enable this relationship. Because there is a mutual relationship in place, the enterprise has some level of influence for how the business partner is to interact with their systems and data. With a contract in place, there are legal protections provided for the enterprise.

User type	External
Trust level	2: Median trusted
Allowed Access	Tier 1 and 2, least privilege
Required security mechanisms	FW, IPS, Web App Firewall, and data loss prevention

System owner (contractor)

This scenario is similar to a business partner, however, the contractor may seem more like an employee because they reside on-site and perform the job functions of a full-time staff member. In this case, a contractor is the same as an associate; however, notice that the more access granted, the more security mechanisms must be in place to reduce the risk of elevated privileges.

User type	External
Trust level	3: Trusted
Allowed access	Least privilege
Required security mechanisms	FW, IPS, Web App Firewall, and file integrity monitoring

Data owner (internal)

The data owner has a significant level of access to the enterprise data. As an internal employee, the trust level is 3—the most trusted. With this access level, there is great responsibility not only for the data owner, but also for the enterprise. If the data is decided to have little value, then the security mechanisms can be reduced.

User type	External
Trust Level	3: Trusted
Allowed access	Anywhere, least privilege
Required security mechanisms	FW, IPS, and Web App Firewall depending on the type of data that is being interacted with

Automation

Automation through scripts and applications are unique, since there is no human interaction. In this implementation, however, many times the permissions are incorrectly configured and allow scripts the ability to launch interactive logons, and shell access equivalent to a standard user. Another contributing factor to their uniqueness is if authentication is required the credentials are sometimes embedded in the script. These factors contribute to the trust level of the script and automation. Scripts can be trusted, but not like an internal user.

User Type	Automation
Trust level	2: Median trusted
Allowed access	Least privilege
Required security mechanisms	FW, IPS, Web App Firewall, file integrity monitoring, and data loss prevention depending on the data that is being interacted with

Micro architectures

A micro architecture is architecture within architecture. An example may be the logical three-tier DMZ architecture implemented within a single layer of the standard three-tier architecture. This type of architecture is more network-centric, but can play a part in the overall data-centric security architecture of an enterprise.

This method may be used in a cloud-based solution, where an enterprise desires to maintain the three-tier approach, but the cloud solution itself is some shade of gray in the standard three-tier model. It is trusted, but coming from a semi-trusted source, traversing the untrusted Internet, possibly landing in the web/presentation layer of the enterprise DMZ. Micro architectures may reside on a single system, especially if we consider cloud-based virtualized solutions. A simple representation of a micro architecture is as follows:

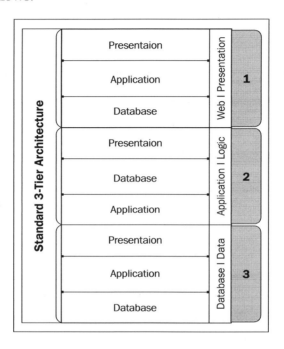

Virtualization has had a unique effect on the security architecture implementation. In order to enforce the correct presentation, application, and database tiers, there should essentially be three distinct physical systems segmented by a firewall. Now, with the ability to host all three hosts on a single physical system, the lines of segmentation have been blurred. The segmentation happens at a lower physical hardware layer below the virtualized system's operating system, yet above the traditional physical network segmentation of network switches, routers, and firewalls. In some cases, the aforementioned segmentation cannot occur below the virtualized infrastructure. This limitation requires a separation of hardware and implementation of security appliances as separate virtual systems leveraging routing to force traffic through the required security mechanisms. This is suboptimal, as the cost benefits of virtualization cannot be realized if more physical systems need to be deployed for separation.

Another common use of micro architectures are in the DMZ, when there are collapsed tiers of the three-tier model. This may literally be implemented in a single system. The challenge then becomes properly segmenting the tiers, securing them, and limiting the scope of compromise. Feature-rich web applications are sometimes implemented in a collapsed-tier model to reduce system overhead and to increase performance.

Data risk-centric architectures

I have already introduced the concept of risk as a key factor of any security architecture. Ultimately, systems and applications exist because there is data to be generated, processed, transmitted, and stored. The risk introduced in an enterprise is significantly data-driven. Therefore, we as security architects must consider this as the primary reason to implement a security solution. This does not mean that we only protect enterprise data; we still need to protect the network that makes data access possible.

What does data risk-centric mean? To answer this question, let's understand how a business functions and what information is used to make the business a business. If I were a retailer, then I have a product to sell, market to reach my buyers, and store customer data including credit card numbers. Of these items a few are data, and of these the most important would be top-secret marketing data and the customer data including credit card numbers. From the perspective of the security architecture, I need to focus on the data with the most risk to the business; meaning, if the data is lost, stolen, or manipulated, it would cause adverse implications for the enterprise. The risk could equate to fines, lost sales, marred reputation, or worse; business failure.

I presented trust models as a generic method of placing certain user types in buckets. These buckets should be further defined by a risk assessment. The risk rating for the data interaction should be based on the defined data, business value, regulatory compliance, user type, and user role. Understanding enterprise processes and applications will serve as a source of knowledge that can be leveraged to properly implement and maintain the security of the data and implementation.

BYOD initiatives

Bring your own laptop, cell, and tablet are a few of the new initiatives that are throwing security teams for a loop on how to properly secure not only the device, but also the network it connects to and the data that it will have to access and possibly store. Thanks to the incredible marketing of manufacturers and decent functionality of the new portable consumer products, such as tablets, rapid consumerization of corporate networks is occurring at a faster rate than the time required to properly secure them. This model, being used by some enterprises to reduce the IT budget, has introduced some challenges not only to security but also to the legality of properly securing the devices while connected to the enterprise network.

Data access typically occurs through systems owned by the enterprise. Some of the data is day-to-day seemingly benign data, such as an e-mail discussing lunch plans. However, an e-mail can contain very important information in its body. We can also add attachments to an e-mail. Literally, any type of file can be attached to an e-mail, such as a customer list, compensation spreadsheets, acquisition documents, credit card numbers, and social security numbers. The use of non-employer assets changes the game when the data that is being interacted with has a real value.

A challenge faced with securing the "bring your gadgets" is that the enterprise does not own the endpoint, the phone, laptop, tablet, or whatever the end user has brought to work that day. The data that we allow the user to access must be protected, but where are the ownership lines drawn and how is protection enforced? There have been several security manufacturers developing products to "secure" these devices, but each seems to fall short of meeting acceptable enterprise security requirements, while allowing the functionality expected by the end user. Data is either intertwined with everything else on the device or is completely compartmentalized to the point of extremely limited use.

Let's look at some of the common BYOD initiatives and discuss considerations when applying trust models and to attempt securing the data accessed, transmitted, and stored on these consumer end points.

Bring your own mobile device

One of the first bring in your own plans was based on allowing the end user to bring their own cell phone. Of course, there are few plain cell phones; we also have smart phones with the ability to e-mail and manage calendars among other things. In fact, this was the first thing the end users started to configure, so everything could be managed and accessed from one device. The primary benefits for the enterprise are no more cell phone hardware expense and management, and policing to keep the bills reasonable.

It is hard to find a cell phone that is just a cell phone. Mostly, every brand and model available is a smartphone with significant processing capabilities. I know this seems like a known fact but I am emphasizing the need to treat the cell phone as a computing device that has an always on Internet connection through 3G, 4G, GSM, or wireless. Would you rethink connecting the device to the network if it did not have to traverse any of the implemented security mechanisms, such as proxy servers, Firewalls, data loss prevention, and intrusion prevention; probably not.

In most cases, cell phones just showed up at work as the cell phone owner learned about all the cool applications that could be used for work; they even figured out how to get the device on the network. The already strained security team in the typical enterprise environment did not anticipate this, so it went undetected. It is next to impossible to know what data the users are putting on the devices and what online services they are uploading enterprise data to without a management solution in place.

The security team must assess the capabilities and use cases for consumer technology products that are or can be connected to the network, and interact with data they must protect. A quick and easy fix is to throw a mobile device management solution at the problem; however, this does not address the security architecture that should serve as the framework for securing this access.

A common **mobile device management (MDM)** solution will generically solve the security issues of having a consumer, employee-owned device on the network. However, determining what exact data the device has access to will be up to you to solve. Keep in mind that some cell phone platforms require the devices and the MDM solution to communicate with their data centers. Let's take a look at a common MDM implementation:

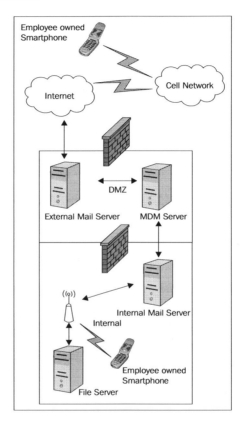

There are levels of application control and security policy that can be enforced with most MDM solutions. However, these are focused more on the device itself than the data the device is accessing. From a network perspective, this implementation is not a real deviation except for the fact that the smartphone can be dually connected to the cell network and the internal trusted wireless infrastructure. While on the internal wireless network, the smartphone would have access to any network asset available to an employer owned asset. The diagram depicts the most common feature requested, which is e-mail and calendar. Eventually, the end user will want to do more with enterprise data because there are several options for word processing and other business functions.

The enterprise will have to map the interaction to a defined trust model or develop one to meet this request. If the access is too risky, the enterprise needs to support the correct security posture based on the risk. I focused on the cell phone, but this will also cover tablets that are running the same operating systems as smartphones. The next section will cover "bring your own computer" type initiatives.

Bring your own PC

Bring your own PC is a slightly more complicated initiative to secure though still a BYOD initiative. Enterprises are realizing the tremendous cost savings of allowing employees to bring their laptops to work to perform their jobs. The issue with securing the devices and protecting the network are a challenge, because maintaining a device by the enterprise that is not owned by the enterprise may cross some privacy and/or technical boundaries. The lines of responsibility are easily blurred and many times not worth the idea.

In order to mitigate the obvious security issues, some enterprises are leveraging virtualization in a "trust no one" model where the only way to access anything is through a virtual desktop environment. This model is very secure, but comes at a cost to build a robust enough infrastructure to support.

Some enterprises are allowing employees to bring their own PCs to access enterprise assets, with no virtualization and balancing access with risk. This must be implemented very methodically with the utmost attention paid to the data interaction, to properly assign a realistic risk to the model, providing a trust model to which the policy can be applied. In this scenario, the best solution is to limit the access to all the data that has been assessed at a risk level of high and above, or to a level the enterprise's risk tolerance will allow.

Summary

In this chapter, we presented the idea of building a trust model constructed from building blocks of information. Once the trust model is built and enterprise risk has been assessed, the model can be applied to various types of data and data interactions. Agility in security can be achieved if data is the center of the analysis, providing determination of the required security mechanisms to reduce risk and support business initiatives. The next chapter will cover security as a process, supporting the developed security architecture.

3

Security As a Process

Security is a process that requires the integration of security into business processes to ensure enterprise risk is minimized to an acceptable level. This chapter will introduce the concept of using risk analysis to drive security decisions, and to shape policies and standards for consistent and measurable implementation of security. Ensuring the security team is involved in IT policies and standards development, and the enterprise change management process is key to reducing risk to the enterprise, especially when changes include firewall policy modifications, business partner connectivity, changes to network architecture, and defined policies and standards. Additionally, exceptions to defined standards and policies must be managed by a method that requires remediation so that the end solution becomes compliant. Security as a process is an approach that highlights the integration of security and business initiatives to reduce the security impact of implementations and changes to the enterprise environment. Resources for topics covered in this chapter can be found in *Appendix B, Risk Analysis, Policy and Standard, and System Hardening Resources*.

This chapter will cover:

- An introduction to risk analysis
- Developing IT policies and standards
- Processes for reducing enterprise risk through change review and exception handling

Risk analysis

In the previous chapter, I introduced risk as a factor of building trust models that ultimately define the security architecture in an enterprise. First, we must understand what risk is, how it is calculated, and then implement a solution to mitigate or reduce the calculated risk. At this point in the process of developing agile security architecture, we have already defined our data. The following sections assume we know what the data is, just not the true impact to the enterprise if a threat is realized.

What is risk analysis?

Simply stated, **risk analysis** is the process of assessing the components of risk; threats, impact, and probability as it relates to an asset, in our case enterprise data. To ascertain risk, the probability of impact to enterprise data must first be calculated. A simple risk analysis output may be the decision to spend capital to protect an asset based on value of the asset and the scope of impact if the risk is not mitigated. This is the most general form of risk analysis, and there are several methods that can be applied to produce a meaningful output. Risk analysis is directly impacted by the maturity of the organization in terms of being able to show value to the enterprise as a whole and understanding the applied risk methodology. If the enterprise does not have a formal risk analysis capability, it will be difficult for the security team to use this method to properly implement security architecture for enterprise initiatives. Without this capability, the enterprise will either spend on the products with the best marketing, or not spend at all. Let's take a closer look at the risk analysis components and figure out where useful analysis data can be obtained.

Assessing threats

First, we must define what a threat is in order to identify probable threats. It may be difficult to determine threats to the enterprise data if this analysis has never been completed. A **threat** is anything that can act negatively towards the enterprise assets. It may be a person, virus, malware, or a natural disaster. Due to the broad scope of threats, actions may be purposeful or unintentional in nature adding to the absolute unpredictability of impact. Once a threat is defined, the attributes of threats must be identified and documented. The documentation of threats should include the type of threat, identified threat groupings, motivations if any, and methods of actions.

In order to gain understanding of pertinent threats for the enterprise, researching past events may be helpful. Historically, there have been challenges to getting realistic breach data, but better reporting of post-breach findings continues to reduce the uncertainty of analysis. Another method to getting data is leveraging existing security technologies implemented to build a realistic perspective of threats.

The following are a few sample questions to guide you on the discovery of threats:

- What is being detected by the existing infrastructure?
- What are others in the same industry observing?
- What post-breach data is available in the same industry vertical?
- Who would want access to this data?

- What would motivate a person to attempt unauthorized access to the data?

  ° Data theft

  ° Destruction

  ° Notoriety

  ° Hacktivism

  ° Retaliation

A sample table of data type, threat, and motivation is shown as follows:

Data	Threat	Motivation
Credit card numbers	Hacker	Theft, Cybercrime
Trade secrets	Competitor	Competitive advantage
Personally Identifiable Information (PII)	Disgruntled employee	Retaliation, Destruction
Company confidential documents	Accidental leak	None
Client list	Natural disaster	None

This should be developed with as much detail as possible to form a realistic view of threats to the enterprise. There may also be several variations of threats and motivations for threat action on enterprise data. For example, accessing trade secrets by a competitor may be for competitive advantage, or a hacker may take action as part of hacktivism to bring negative press to the enterprise.

The more you can elaborate on the possible threats and motivations that exist, the better you will be able to reduce the list to probable threats based on challenging the data you have gathered. It is important to continually challenge the logic used to have the most realistic perspective.

Assessing impact

Now that the probable threats have been identified, what kind of damage can be done or negative impact can be enacted upon the enterprise and the data. **Impact** is the outcome of threats acting against the enterprise. This could be a denial-of-service state where the agent, a hacker, uses a tool to starve the enterprise Internet web servers of resources causing a denial-of-service state for legitimate users. Another impact could be the loss of customer credit cards resulting in online fraud, reputation loss, and countless dollars in cleanup and remediation efforts.

There are the immediate impacts and residual impacts. Immediate impacts are rather easy to determine because, typically, this is what we see in the news if it is big enough of an issue. Hopefully, the impact data does not come from first-hand experience, but in the case it is, executives should take action and learn from their mistakes. If there is no real-life experience with the impact, researching breach data will help using Internet sites such as DATALOSS db (http://datalossdb.org). Also, understanding the value of the data to the enterprise and its customers will aide in impact calculation. I think the latter impact analysis is more useful, but if the enterprise is unsure, then relying on breach data may be the only option.

The following are a few sample discovery questions for business impact analysis:

- How is the enterprise affected by threat actions?
- Will we go out of business?
- Will we lose market share?
- If the data is deleted or manipulated, can it be recovered or restored?
- If the building is destroyed, do we have disaster recovery and business continuity capabilities?

To get a more accurate assessment of the probable impact or total cost to the enterprise, map out what data is most desirable to steal, destroy, and manipulate. Align the identified threats to the identified data, and apply an impact level to the data indicating if the enterprise would suffer critical to minor loss. These should be as accurate as possible. Work the scenarios out on paper and base the impact analysis on the outcome of the exercises.

The following is a sample table to present the identification and assessment of impact based on threat for a retailer. This is generally called a **business impact analysis**.

Data	Threat	Impact
Credit card numbers	Hacker	Critical
Trade secrets	Competitor	Medium
PII	Disgruntled employee	High
Company confidential documents	Accidental leak	Low
Client list	Natural disaster	Medium

 Enterprise industry vertical may affect the impact analysis. For instance, a retailer may have greater impact if credit card numbers are stolen than if their client list was stolen. Both scenarios have impact but one may warrant greater protection and more restricted access to limit the scope of impact, and reduce immediate and residual loss.

Business impact should be measured in how the threat actions affect the business overall. Is it an annoyance or does it mean the business can no longer function? Natural disasters should also be accounted for and considered when assessing enterprise risk.

Assessing probability

Now that all conceived threats have been identified along with the business impact for each scenario, how do we really determine risk? Shouldn't risk be based on how likely the threat may take action, succeed, and cause an impact? Yes! The threat can be the most perilous thing imagined but if threat actions may only occur once in three thousand years, investment in protecting against the threat may not be warranted, at least in the near term.

Probability data is as difficult, if not more difficult, to find than threat data. However, this calculation has the most influence on the derived risk. If the identified impact is expected to happen twice a year and the business impact is critical, perhaps security budget should be allocated to security mechanisms that mitigate or reduce the impact. The risk of the latter scenario would be higher because it is more probable, *not possible*, but probable. Anything is possible. I have heard an analogy for this to make the point. In the game of Russian roulette, a semi-automatic pistol either has a bullet in the chamber or it does not, this is possible. With a revolver and a quick spin of the cylinder, you now have a 1 in 6 chance on whether there is a bullet that will be fired when the firing pin strikes forward. This is oversimplified to illustrate possibility versus probability. There are several variables in the example that could affect the outcome such as a misfire, or the safety catch being enabled, stopping the gun's ability to fire. These would be calculated to form an accurate risk value. Make sense?

This is how we need to approach probability. Technically, it is a semi-accurate estimation because there is just not enough detailed information on breaches and attacks to draw absolute conclusions. One approach may be to research what is happening in the same industry using online resources and peer groups, and then make intelligent estimates to determine if the enterprise could be affected too. Generally, there are outlier scenarios that require the utmost attention regardless; start here if these have not been identified as a probable risk scenario for the enterprise.

The following are a few sample probability estimation questions:

* Has this event occurred before to the enterprise?
* Is there data to suggest it is happening now?
* Are there documented instances for similar enterprises?
* Do we know anything in regards to occurrence?
* Is the identified threat and impact really probable?

The following table is the continuation of our risk analysis for our fictional retailer:

Data	Threat	Impact	Probability
Credit card numbers	Hacker	Critical	High
Trade secrets	Competitor	Medium	Low
PII	Disgruntled employee	High	Medium
Company confidential documents	Accidental leak	Low	Low
Client list	Natural disaster	Medium	High

Based on the outcome of the probability exercises of identified threats and impacts, risk can be calculated and the appropriate course of action(s) developed and implemented.

Assessing risk

Now that the enterprise has agreed on what data has value, identified threats to the data, rated the impact to the enterprise, and the estimated probability of the impact occurring, the next logical step is to calculate the risk of the scenarios. Essentially, there are two methods to analyze and present risk: **qualitative** and **quantitative**. The decision to use one over the other should be based on the maturity of the enterprise's risk office. In general, a quantitative risk analysis will use descriptive labels like a qualitative method, however, there is more financial and mathematical analysis in quantitative analysis.

Qualitative risk analysis

Qualitative risk analysis provides a perspective of risk in levels with labels such as Critical, High, Medium, and Low. The enterprise must still define what each level means in a general financial perspective. For instance, a Low risk level may equate to a monetary loss of $1,000 to $100,000. The dollar ranges associated with each risk level will vary by enterprise. This must be agreed on by the entire enterprise so when risk is discussed, everyone is knowledgeable of what each label means financially. Do not confuse the estimated financial loss with the more detailed quantitative risk analysis approach; it is a simple valuation metric for deciding how much investment should be made based on probable monetary loss. The following section is an example qualitative risk analysis presenting the type of input required for the analysis. Notice that this is not a deep analysis of each of these inputs; it is designed to provide a relatively accurate perspective of risk associated with the scenario being analyzed.

Qualitative risk analysis exercise

Scenario: Hacker attacks website to steal credit card numbers located in backend database.

Threat: External hacker.

Threat capability: Novice to pro.

Threat capability logic: There are several script-kiddie level tools available to wage SQL injection attacks. SQL injection is also well documented and professional hackers can use advanced techniques in conjunction with the automated tools.

Vulnerability: 85 percent (how effective would the threat be with current mitigating mechanisms).

Estimated impact: High, Medium, Low (as indicated in the following table).

Risk	Estimated loss ($)
High	> 1,000,000
Medium	500,000 to 900,000
Low	< 500,000

Quantitative risk analysis

Quantitative risk analysis is an in-depth assessment of what the monetary loss would be to the enterprise if the identified risk were realized. In order to facilitate this analysis, the enterprise must have a good understanding of its processes to determine a relatively accurate dollar amount for items such as systems, data restoration services, and man-hour break down for recovery or remediation of an impacting event. Typically, enterprises with a mature risk office will undertake this type of analysis to drive priority budget items or find areas to increase insurance, effectively transferring business risk. This will also allow for accurate communication to the board and enterprise executives to know at any given time the amount of risk the enterprise has assumed.

With the quantitative approach a more accurate assessment of the threat types, threat capabilities, vulnerability, threat action frequency, and expected loss per threat action are required and must be as accurate as possible. As with qualitative risk analysis, the output of this analysis has to be compared to the cost to mitigate the identified threat. Ideally, the cost to mitigate would be less than the loss expectancy over a determined period of time. This is simple return on investment (ROI) calculation. Let's look again at the scenario used in the qualitative analysis and run it through a quantitative analysis. We will then compare against the price of a security product that would mitigate the risk to see if it is worth the capital expense.

Before we begin the quantitative risk analysis, there are a couple of terms that need to be explained:

- **Annual loss expectancy (ALE)**: The ALE is the calculation of what the financial loss would be to the enterprise if the threat event was to occur for a single year period. This is directly related to threat frequency. In the scenario this is once every three years, dividing the single lost expectancy by annual occurrence provides the ALE.

- **Cost of protection (COP)**: The COP is the capital expense associated with the purchase or implementation of a security mechanism to mitigate or reduce the risk scenario. An example would be a firewall that costs $150,000 and $50,000 per each year of protection of the loss expectancy period. If the cost of protection over the same period is lower than the loss, this is a good indication that the capital expense is financially worthwhile.

Quantitative risk analysis exercise

Scenario: Hacker attacks website to steal credit card numbers located in backend database.

Threat: External hacker.

Threat capability: Novice to pro.

Threat capability logic: There are several script-kiddie level tools available to wage SQL injection attacks. SQL injection is also well documented and professional hackers can use advanced techniques in conjunction with the automated tools.

Vulnerability: 85 percent (how effective would the threat be with current mitigating mechanisms).

Single loss expectation: $250,000.

Threat frequency: 3 (how many times per year; this would be roughly once every three years).

ALE: $83,000.

COP: $150,000 (over 3 years).

We will divide the total loss and the cost of protection over three years as, typically, capital expenses are depreciated over three to four years, and the loss is expected once every three years. This will give us the ALE and COP in the equation to determine the cost-benefit analysis.

This is a simplified example, but the math would look as follows:

$83,000 (ALE) - $50,000 (COP) = $33,000 (cost benefit)

The loss is annually $33,000 more than the cost to protect against the threat. The assumption in our example is that the $250,000 figure is 85% of the total asset value, but because we have 15% protection capability, the number is now approximately $294,000. This step can be shortcut out of the equation if the ALE and rate of occurrence are known.

When trying to figure out threat capability, try to be as realistic about the threat first. This will help us to better assess vulnerability because you will have a more accurate perspective on how realistic the threat is to the enterprise. For instance, if your scenario requires cracking advanced encryption and extensive system experience, the threat capability would be expert indicating current security controls may be acceptable for the majority of threat agents reducing probability and calculated risk. We tend to exaggerate in security to justify a purchase. We need to stop this trend and focus on what is the best area to spend precious budget dollars.

The ultimate goal of a quantitative risk analysis is to ensure that spend for protection does not far exceed the threat the enterprise is protecting against. This is beneficial for the security team in justifying the expense of security budget line items.

When the analysis is complete, there should still be a qualitative risk label associated with the risk. Using the above scenario with an annualized risk of $50,000 indicates this scenario is extremely low risk based on the defined risk levels in the qualitative risk exercise even if SLE is used. Does this analysis accurately represent acceptable loss? After an assessment is complete it is good practice to ensure all assumptions still hold true, especially the risk labels and associated monetary amounts.

Applying risk analysis to trust models

Remember our trust models from the previous chapter? Well, now we can apply our risk methodology to our trust models to decide if we can continue with our implementation as is, or whether we need to change our approach based on risk. Our trust models, which are essentially use cases, rely on completing the risk analysis, which in turn decide the trust level and security mechanisms required to reduce the enterprise risk to an acceptable level. I provided some of this in the previous chapter when we generically assigned a trust level to a user category and the scenario of the user group's interaction with the enterprise data.

It would be foolish to think that we can shove all requests for similar access directly into one of these buckets without further analysis to determine the real risk associated with the request. After completing one of the risk analysis types we just covered, risk guidance can be provided for the scenario (and I stress *guidance*). For the sake of simplicity an implementation path may be chosen, but it will lead to compromises in the overall security of the enterprise and is cautioned. I have re-presented the table of one scenario, the external application user. This is a better representation of how a trust model should look with risk and security enforcement established for the scenario. If an enterprise is aware of how it conducts business, then a focused effort in this area should produce a realistic list of interactions with data by whom, with what level of trust, and based on risk, what controls need to be present and enforced by policy and standards.

User type	External
Allowed access	Tier 1 DMZ only, Least privilege
Trust level	1 – Not trusted
Risk	Medium
Policy	Acceptable use, Monitoring, Access restrictions
Required security mechanisms	FW, IPS, Web application firewall

The user is assumed to have access to log in to the web application and have more possible interaction with the backend database(s). This should be a focal point for testing, because this is the biggest area of risk in this scenario. Threats such as SQL injection that can be waged against a web application with little to no experience are commonplace. Enterprises that have e-commerce websites typically do not restrict who can create an account. This should have input to the trust decision and ultimately the security architecture applied.

Deciding on a risk analysis methodology

We have covered the two general types of risk analysis, qualitative and quantitative, but which is best? It depends on several factors: risk awareness of the enterprise, risk analysts' capabilities, risk analysis data, and the influence of risk in the enterprise. If the idea of risk analysis or IT risk analysis is new to the enterprise, then a slow approach with qualitative analysis is recommended to get everyone thinking of risk and what it means to the business. It will be imperative to get an enterprise-wide agreement on the risk labels. Using the lesser involved method does not mean you will not be questioned on the data used in the analysis, so be prepared to defend the data used and explain estimation methods leveraged.

If it is decided to use a quantitative risk analysis method, a considerable amount of effort is required along with meticulous loss figures and knowledge of the environment. This method is considered the most effective requiring risk expertise, resources, and an enterprise-wide commitment to risk analysis. This method is more accurate, though it can be argued that since both methods require some level of estimation, the accuracy lies in accurate estimation skills.

I use the Douglas Hubbard school of thought on estimating with 90 percent accuracy. You will find his works at his website `http://www.hubbardresearch.com/`. I highly recommend his title *How to Measure Anything: Finding the Value of "Intangibles" in Business, Tantor Media* to learn estimation skills. It may be beneficial to have an external firm perform the analysis if the engagement is significant in size.

The benefits of both should be that the enterprise is able to make risk-aware decisions on how to securely implement IT solutions. Both should be presented with common risk levels such as High, Medium, Low; essentially the common language everyone can speak knowing a range of financial risk without all the intimate details of how they arrived at the risk level.

There are several risk methodologies that exist somewhere between these two fundamental methods. See *Appendix B, Risk Analysis, Policy and Standard, and System Hardening Resources* for a list of risk analysis resources.

Other thoughts on risk and new enterprise endeavors

Now that you have been presented with types of risk analysis, they should be applied as tools to best approach the new technologies being implemented in the networks of our enterprises. Unfortunately, there are broad brush strokes of trusted and untrusted approaches being applied that may or may not be accurate without risk analysis as a decision input. Two examples where this can be very costly are the new BYOD and cloud initiatives. At first glance these are the two most risky business maneuvers an enterprise can attempt from an information security perspective. Deciding if this really is the case requires an analysis based on trust models and data-centric security architecture. If the proper security mechanisms are implemented and security applied from users to data, the risk can be reduced to a tolerable level. The BYOD business model has many positive benefits to the enterprise, especially capital expense reduction. However, implementing a BYOD or cloud solution without further analysis of risk can introduce significant risk beyond the benefit of the initiative.

Do not be quick to spread fear in order to avoid facing the changing landscape we have worked so hard to build and secure. It is different, but at one time, what we know today as the norm was new too. Be cautious but creative, or IT security will be discredited for what will be received as a difficult interaction. This is not the desired perception for IT security. Strive to understand the business case, risk to business assets (data, systems, people, processes, and so on), and then apply sound security architecture as we have discussed so far. Begin evangelizing the new approach to security in the enterprise by developing trust models that everyone can understand. Use this as the introduction to agile security architecture and get input to create models based on risk. By providing a risk-based perspective to emerging technologies and other radical requests, a methodical approach can bring better adoption and overall increased security in the enterprise. I will be providing strategies of securing various facets of technology and security implementation in coming chapters.

Security policies and standards

Enterprise policies and standards are meant to be the written law on how to implement, use, and monitor a technology, process, and other HR and legal scope items. For the purposes of the book, we will focus on IT policies and standards. These "laws" also serve as a warning to consequences if there is a violation of the policy. For instance, an employee cell phone policy may be created in response to the business request to use personal phones for business. However, with the ability to use a personal cell phone, there may be restrictions on using the "smart" features to access enterprise data, or a requirement to load a mobile device management application on the cell phone. The standard in this scenario may be a requirement of a certain smart phone operating system type and version level. This may be driven by management and security capabilities of the platform.

Policy versus standard

These two document types are different and commonly confused. In an effort to simplify the understanding of the two, they can be categorized by the intent of the document. A policy's intent is to address behaviors and state principles for IT interaction with the enterprise. Standards focus on configuration and implementation based on what is outlined in policy. Lastly, tools need to be implemented to measure compliance and provide enforcement of policies and standards. When writing policies and standards, refer back to these definitions to ensure effectiveness of content and reduce the common confusion of the two.

A quick note on wording

When writing policies and standards, the words "must" and "should" have specific meaning. Something stated as a "must" is non-negotiable and can be measured and enforced, whereas the word "should" indicates a guideline and can either be implemented or not based on various factors. Be careful to use these words correctly to set the proper expectations for the intent of statements in policies and standards.

Let's take a more detailed look at security policy development and focus on standards to ensure the acceptable security posture of the enterprise. The next several sections are meant to be a general guide for development of IT security policies and standards.

Understanding security policy development

When security policies need to be developed for an enterprise, there is typically an outside driver such as regulatory compliance, industry certification, or business driver. In the case of compliance and certification, the requirement is usually the general security domain and is prescriptive as to what must be included in the policy. An example is the **Payment Card Industry Data Security Standard** or **PCI DSS**. While its policy requirements were developed to protect cardholder data, they are focused on the general security domain. What happens though when new technology use cases such as bring your own device are the topic of discussion? We can apply general principles, but the enterprise position on the use of the device will need to be specific to address the capabilities and risks introduced by approved devices. If the enterprise has adopted a risk-based security architecture model, developed trust models, and assessed risk, then the approach to new technology initiatives must follow this same process. When enterprises do not follow this approach there is fear and uncertainty driving the decision to implement, commonly without written policy or standards to enforce and guide the enterprise.

Common IT security policies

There are several policies that every enterprise needs to have. Of course there are shades of gray and applicability, but there are some policies that are a must. Not only must they exist as a formality, but they must also have actionable content for times when policy adherence is an issue. The list provided is not exclusive, however, is the "typical" set of policies written.

The following is a list of standard policies:

- Information security policy
- Acceptable use policy
- Technology use policy
- Remote access policy
- Data classification policy
- Data handling policy
- Data retention policy
- Data destruction policy

Each of these policies is written for a specific purpose; a holistic approach to reduce risk to the business by outlining the appropriate use or implementation of technology, and the acceptable interaction with enterprise data. The exact number of policies really is insignificant, in fact, the simpler the process the easier to implement, enforce, and measure. The intent is to have the IT security position on what is being asked of the business in a policy and/or standard that is approved and accepted by senior leadership. Policies are living documents, so be sure to regularly assess their effectiveness, especially when faced with the implementation of an emerging technology.

Information security policy

This general policy should address all the security-specific requirements that may or may not be addressed in other policies. The policy should outline what is expected from employees to ensure technology implementations and use are on par with what has been required for the enterprise to maintain a certain security posture. This might include verbiage on the use of only secure protocols, logging requirements of systems, up to a position on risk analysis, and a requirement for regular risk analysis. The PCI DSS and SANS are great resources for information on writing policies. Additionally, the SANS Security Policy Project has templates that can serve as a base or be used as is with little modification. All other policies pertinent to IT should be referenced in the information security policy to ensure there is a logical connection and single point of reference for applicable policies.

In addition to stating the enterprise position on IT security-related requirements, the policy in effect makes known that IT security exists. This policy provides the basis for the security team to protect the enterprise data. This includes giving the right to monitor employee use of systems and data access and install software to do so.

The following are some questions to start building the information security policy:

- What are common security requirements across the enterprise?
- What technologies are used in the enterprise?
- What regulatory requirements does the enterprise need to comply with externally?
- Is there anything unique in the enterprise's industry that needs to be policy?

Acceptable use policy

The acceptable use policy is usually technology generic but may include items such as the network, employer provided equipment, website access, e-mail, and other use-based technologies where a code of conduct needs to be established, with consequences communicated for failure to comply. The primary focus of this policy is to reduce not only security risk to the enterprise but legal liability too. For instance, if an employee decides to use an employer-owned server system to host illegal downloads on the premise of the employer, this introduces both security and legal risks. To ensure this does not happen without consequence, the acceptable use policy must dictate that the equipment must be used only for employer-sanctioned activities, and this should be applicable for applications too.

The following are a few considerations when developing the acceptable use policy:

- What services are employees permitted to use that need parameters?
- What services can be abused and introduce risk to the enterprise?
- What is the consequence for violating the policy?

Technology use policy

This policy may be developed separately from the acceptable use policy to call out specific technologies allowed and their approved use, including access to the enterprise network and data. This policy could be used to capture items such as BYOD initiatives versus writing new policy on the subject. If the enterprise has the controls in place to completely enforce policy, then there may be some coverage in this policy. Specific BYOD or cloud technology use policies can be written to capture specifics not covered in the general technology use policy. Consider using the developed trust models to serve as input to the technology use policy to increase applicability and adherence.

The following are a few questions to consider for this policy development:

- What is the technology?
- How can it be used within the business for better productivity, and so on?
- What types of data can the technology access?
- Who will be permitted to use the technology?
- How will the technology be secured?
- How will the technology be monitored?
- How will the technology be managed?
- How will data and network access via the technology be managed?
- How is the policy enforced?

Remote access policy

This policy is self-explanatory for the most part. The remote access policy should indicate what types of devices and who may connect to the enterprise network remotely. It may also include the appropriate authentication methods such as two-factor or simple username and password. Remote access should be restricted to only known devices, and have least privilege access to network resources. Though this is generally written in the policy, the typical access afforded to successfully authenticated remote access users is cart blanche access to the internal network. We as a security community need to address this issue, especially with the emerging technologies that are being requested for the same access level. One trust model that might affect this policy more than others is the "trust no one" model. All systems will be protected as if the source, no matter whom, is at zero trust by default. Some enterprises are very strict on employer-owned devices being the only method to use a VPN connection to the employer network. Not only is the device that is making the VPN connection important, but equally so is who is permitted to use the technology.

The following are a few questions to consider for this policy development:

- What devices will be permitted to be used for remote access?
- Is remote access permitted for employee- and employer-owned devices?
- How is remote access to be secured?
- How is remote access to be monitored?
- Who must approve remote access requests?

Data classification policy

As we are moving towards a data-centric model for security architecture and overall guidance in security control selection, data classification is an absolute. We must know what data exists, where it resides, and how to protect it. As part of that discovery, the data should be mapped to a classification model that outlines its sensitivity and high-level protection requirements. Anytime new data is generated or old data discovered, it should go through the process of classification.

The following are a few discovery questions to begin data classification:

- What data is present?
- What value does the data have to the business?
- What is the purpose of the data?
- Are there external requirements for identified data?
- How do we protect the data?

Once discovery questions are answered, a process can be developed to classify all enterprise data into manageable data types. Typically, data types will follow standard enterprise data labeling such as, confidential, restricted, and public. Each one of these labels should indicate exactly what data falls into the category, and the data protection required.

	Restricted	**Confidential**	**Public**
Data type	Customer: - Credit card number, PII Employee: - SSN number, PII Company: - Merger plans - New product	Customer: - PII Employee: - PII Company: - Internal documents	Anything not in the previous sections are items considered in the public domain.
Data protection	Encryption	Restricted access permissions	None

Data handling policy

The data handling policy should be very prescriptive on approved interactions with enterprise data. Interactions may be people, applications, or automation. A closely integrated policy would be the data classification policy. Once the enterprise has identified all data and data types while in transit, being processed, and being stored, it should be classified based on importance to the business as assessed during the business impact analysis. This was input to our trust models. This policy will be the basis for standards implemented to perform appropriate data handling procedures. Data protection may also be included within this policy in an effort to reduce the overall number of policies. In practice, there should be a policy indicating what is expected for data protection. This may also be located in the information security policy.

Items in this policy may include:

- Acceptable storage for enterprise data
- Enforcement of secure handling of appropriately classified data
- Access and authorization procedures for sensitive data

Data retention policy

An area of risk often overlooked is data retained for long periods of time, beyond the time when access to the data is required. A data retention policy simply states the length of time to retain data in the enterprise. The general rule is to only keep data as long as needed for data recovery and regulatory requirements. Maintaining data for long periods of time significantly increases the risk of data leakage; you can reduce possible damage to the enterprise by enforcing data retention limits. This policy is tightly related to the data destruction policy and both should be mentioned in each policy.

Items in this policy may include:

- Acceptable data types to be retained
- Length of time allowed for each data type to be retained
- The business reason for retaining data for the approved amount of time
- Relationship to the data destruction policy

Data destruction policy

It is common to hear of residual data on second-hand computer equipment discovered by the new owners. Often the amount of effort put into protecting data is not given to the proper destruction of it when no longer in use or of value to the enterprise. A data destruction policy provides an enforceable and measurable method to ensure data is properly destroyed. The data destruction policy is the reminder policy that says, "Hey! We need to sanitize these hard drives before we trash them." In some cases, where the equipment is not being trashed but resold, this has even greater risk associated with the transaction. The failure to properly destroy data on used or malfunctioning equipment is negligence when there are exceptional commercial products, free tools, and paid-for services that perform data destruction. Some enterprises have a scorched earth policy when it comes to data destruction, this ensures absolutely no data is recoverable regardless of whether it is sensitive or in the public domain. The cost associated with this method should be considered before taking a formal position, as the hardware cannot be reused.

We must ensure the data destruction policy includes:

- Requirement to securely wipe all functioning hard disks
- Requirement to physically destroy non-working hard disks, tapes, and so on
- If completed by third party, a formal process developed with verification
- Labeling of systems with data that require destruction
- Clear consequences for negligent data leakage

Policies for emerging technologies

Technology used in the enterprise has traditionally been employer-owned technology, and therefore policy has been focused on enterprise assets. We've tried to use our existing policies and trust models for new initiatives such as BYOD and cloud, but we struggle to make the current paradigm work. This is one limitation enterprises run into when approaching emerging technologies. The mind-set is how do we approach this new technology the same way we have approached everything in the past? The new trends are becoming game changers for how enterprises are doing business. The same old approach is not going to work.

The focus with any new technology introduced to the enterprise has got to be who, what, how, and why, to assess the feasibility of allowing the technology to interact with enterprise data. A relative risk can be associated with the initiative and implementation can occur if the risk is deemed acceptable. The next two sections cover how to approach policy development for emerging technologies.

Policy considerations

When considering if a technology will be allowed and how it will be permitted, lines in the sand can be drawn quickly without much thought. A step back to properly analyze the request and develop a strategy is recommended to show the business that security can be an enabler, not a perceived road block. In order to help determine the best way to approach the acceptance and use of a new technology in the enterprise, there are several questions that need to be answered and at least a basic risk analysis completed.

The following are some guidelines and questions to help guide the discussion around the acceptance and use of a new technology. This list is not exclusive; one must modify appropriately for the unique enterprise environment:

- What is the new technology (BYOD, tablets, smartphones, cloud, and so on)?
- What value does it provide to the business?
- How will it be used?
- What does it need access to (data, systems, and so on)?
- What needs access to it?
- Who will use it?
- Who will manage it?
- What are the boundaries of responsibility?
- Do we have the ability to manage the technology?
- Can the technology be secured?
- Is risk introduced?
- How much risk is introduced?

Once the business and IT leaders have gone through a series of assessments, policy can be drafted to begin establishing the framework of integration.

Emerging technology challenges

The challenge with introducing a technology that is not under the control of the enterprise is *trust*. This is a basic understanding with simple security architecture that drives the security mechanisms required to permit the technology use and access. If the administrative control is within a separate entity from the enterprise, how does it get secured and how is the security posture verified? This line of questioning is most important regardless of a BYOD or cloud initiative.

Solutions such as network access control are starting to make a greater introduction in the enterprise, though it has been a slowly adopted technology due to the administrative overhead. Some challenges associated with permitting a device on the network that is not enterprise managed are malware (viruses, Trojans, botnets), online storage services, and data leakage through these technologies, and also the use of encrypted tunnels out of the network. Policy must be drafted to include boundaries of responsibility, but more importantly, acceptable use within the enterprise. Once this is stated, the enterprise must have a method to enforce it. It is becoming common for the enterprise environment that personal tablets and smartphones have overrun IT security and are being used in daily business with no management or effective policy. If there is no policy written, communicated, and enforced, there is no recourse available to information security. Controlling this access has to be a priority of upper management, above the security manager, to be effective. The bottom line is, the infiltration of these devices puts the business at some level of risk that has to be assessed and mitigated to an acceptable level.

When it comes to hosted solutions such as cloud services, the enterprise may have a different set of questions specific to using the technology. Certainly, there may be an overlap if, in addition to using the cloud service, it is also accessible by employee-owned devices. Hosted solutions pose unique challenges for enterprises that seek to store, transmit, and process sensitive data in an environment they have little control over. Currently, the standard security architecture would consider this remotely-hosted environment as some shade of trusted, but not wholly trusted. This is the correct logic but must be addressed through thorough review of the service contract and implementation of security mechanisms. The enterprise should provide policy communicating what is acceptable use of the cloud, including what, if any, business functions are able to be moved to the cloud, what type of data is permitted, and let's not forget how to get the data back out of the cloud when no longer using the service.

One unique challenge to the cloud that is a great benefit of the technology is high availability and resilience. The data in a cloud solution can reside anywhere within the global network of the provider; this may suggest enterprise data resides on servers in hostile or high-risk nations at any given time. Doing homework and knowing how the specific service works is an absolute and will be a significant source for policy material. For instance, if it is learned that the data loaded to the cloud may reside in a hostile nation, the enterprise may reconsider the data type that is permitted in the cloud service. If the data is permitted then protection methods may be required. This should be driven by policy and the policy must provide a method of action if there is a lack of compliance. Also, be prepared to hold the service provider responsible by involving your legal team to review terms of service, protection methods implemented, and server locations. You may be able to restrict your data to a specific set of geographic locations.

The point here is, a lot of the service offerings in the cloud space are being driven by client demands. Focusing on enterprise data and risk associated with new technologies like cloud is a requirement for securely leveraging the services.

Developing enterprise security standards

A quick note on the difference between a policy and a standard is, that the policy dictates what must be done, whereas the standard states how it gets done. An example is a data handling policy stating that all confidential data at rest must be encrypted; the data encryption standard will state what level and type of encryption is acceptable such as Advanced Encryption Standard 128-bit (AES-128). Individual teams would then create specific procedures to implement the encryption on systems or wherever policy states it must be implemented. The PCI DSS is an excellent example of a good information security standard.

The best way to approach development of standards is to focus on meeting the written policy for the enterprise. If a policy calls for encryption, then research the encryption needs of the enterprise; if data is at rest, learn what it would require to encrypt the different types of data at rest and on the pertinent operating system where it resides. This will help the team determine what is feasible. Once the options for the type of encryption are narrowed, then a standard can be developed to ensure all data at rest can be encrypted and this will be consistently implemented across the enterprise.

Common IT security standards

There are few things that define information security requirements uniquely across industry verticals. The business, data, systems, and charter may be different, but the shared goal is securing a business or provider of a service. There may be a few unique threats based on the enterprise or entity, but the basic security issues will need to be addressed. I have provided several common IT security standards that play an important part in our security architecture. Each standard should be driven by a risk-based approach developed from defined trust models.

Wireless network security standard

Wireless networking is as common as typical wired Gigabit Ethernet network segments in today's enterprise. The primary security concern with wireless networking is that it extends the network outside of the physical bounds of the brick-and-mortar enterprise. This is a legitimate concern, but it must be only a component of the risk analysis to best implement the wireless network. Let's first look at the basic security requirements, and then apply logic from our trust models that will guide us to a secure and standard method to approach this flexible technology.

Trust model building block for wireless network security standard

We will assume that a wireless network type has already been decided; the network team has implemented 802.11n and brand X. Technically, these do not matter much from a security perspective.

First, we need to understand the reason for the wireless network and other information to determine trust, assess risk, and apply security mechanisms:

- What will the wireless network be used for?
- What type of data will be accessible via wireless network?
- Who will have access to the wireless network?
- What type of data access will be permitted?

These questions should seem familiar or at least you should see the relationship to the trust model building blocks. Based on this exercise, a risk level needs to be assigned to all defined use cases. If it is decided that because of the data type that will be traversing the network only employees are permitted to access the wireless network, then the policy and standards must support this stance.

A risk assessment may be initiated with questions such as:

- What are the threats introduced with the wireless network?
- What is the impact of threats to or through the wireless network?
- What is the probability of impact?
- What risk is introduced with the wireless network implementation?

We now need to assess the trust of not only the wireless network but also those using it. The trust of the network itself may be influenced by a standard such as PCI DSS, which states how a wireless network can be implemented in a network with cardholder data present. The trust level is directly derived from the risk analysis and the use cases leveraged for the analysis:

- What is the trust level of the wireless network?
- What are the trust levels for the user types using the wireless network?

Applying trust models to develop standards

Once the trust models have been developed, not only should policy be developed, but also the security standards can be written.

User type	Internal
Allowed access	Internal assets
Trust level	3 – Trusted
Risk	Medium
Policy	Technology use, Acceptable use, Wireless access policy, Wireless network security standard
Security mechanisms	FW, IPS, Monitoring, Two-factor authentication

At first glance it may appear we are stating the obvious, but building a highly secure wireless network for guest-only access that will never interact with enterprise data makes no sense. We have been trained that we must first secure, then make solutions functional. It is actually a balancing act that has to be properly assessed. The trust model example we just saw is for an internal user that is trusted, and introduces medium risk to the enterprise based on risk analysis. We can reach into our toolbox of policies and determine which make sense to apply, but we need to also develop a standard based on identified use cases. Standards require some research and thought to figure out what can practically be implemented versus simply stating the latest buzzwords.

The following are a few examples of wireless network standards:

- Implementation of WPA2-Enterprise
- Two-factor authentication using certificates (policy would state two-factor requirement)
- Wireless client configured to deny dual connection on wired and wireless networks

Enterprise monitoring standard

The enterprise must broaden the scope of security monitoring of systems, networks, and users, as it is necessary for both policy enforcement and as an implemented security mechanism. It may be decided that certain types of connections to the network or data access must be monitored for malicious activity or simply to provide an audit trail. Having a standard that the IT personnel can reference to ensure consistent implementation of the enterprise monitoring strategy is important and should be assessed regularly. Recently more breaches can be attributed to lack of proper monitoring and support functions on the backend to take action.

Observing what has been compiled for user types and interaction with enterprise data, a framework for monitoring can be developed. An example would be access to customer credit card data must be monitored and specific information collected on the interaction to provide a complete audit trail including who, when, what, and where in explicit detail. Solutions should be carefully evaluated to make sure they are capable of providing the required data.

The following are the recommended audit data to capture:

- Timestamp (date and time)
- User
- Event type
- Source IP address
- Source port and protocol
- Destination IP address
- Destination port and protocol
- Actions taken (that is add, delete, modify data, and so on)

This is the standard list of audit trail information and there are many methods available to gather. The more information relative to a transaction, the more useful the data will be.

The following are examples of locations to monitor:

- Network boundaries (business partner zones, DMZ, M&A zone)
- Critical systems
- Critical applications
- Privileged users and privileged user systems

The following are examples of monitoring tools and methods:

- Intrusion detection/prevention
- Firewalls
- Anti-virus
- File integrity monitoring
- Operating system logging
- Application whitelisting

Enterprise encryption standard

If encryption is required within the enterprise, there is a lot to consider and assumptions cannot be made, as this will probably involve more business input on data types, their use, processes, and technologies implemented. Data encryption required for data in transit, storage, or being processed may pose some unique challenges. In fact, several enterprises are moving to solutions where they reduce or remove their need to encrypt data where it is enforced by regulation, law, or a standards body to reduce the TCO of encryption implementation.

For enterprises that need to implement a method to encrypt data, a standard must be written to provide guidance and consistency across the enterprise.

The following are the areas to focus on to standardize encryption:

- Whole disk encryption
- Database encryption
- File-level encryption
- Secure transport encryption

Before jumping head first into an encryption project, fully understanding how the data is used within the enterprise is required for successful implementation. A significant pain point may be rewriting or adding additional code in applications to encrypt and decrypt as it is interacting with the data. How the data will be used after encryption may be an issue, an example is tracking payment activity of a customer to a specific credit card number. In order to track this info, the application must either decrypt the credit card number or find another method such as format-preserving encryption or tokenization where the value remains constant.

Key management is probably the most involved and difficult task with encryption; after all, the *key* is the most significant component in encryption. The following tasks comprise key management:

- Key creation
- Key dissemination
- Key storage
- Key rotation
- Key destruction

When standardizing on a solution or solutions to implement encryption, be sure to understand how to implement key management. One issue is handling data encrypted with a previous key and maintaining access to the data after key rotation or destruction. This process can be a disruption to business and requires extensive planning and testing before and after the rotation or destruction activity. Encrypted backups may pose a challenge too; sometimes the position taken by the enterprise is if access to the encrypted data is not desirable after the crypto period, the lifespan of an encryption key and the key is rotated and the original key deleted. There are cases when the key must be rotated prematurely, so this desire may not always be realistic, especially if not in sync with data retention timelines. Other items to consider are key length, crypto period, and who will be responsible for key management in its entirety. Consistent adherence to the standards developed for the key management process will ultimately ensure consistent security and the benefit of encryption.

System hardening standard

System hardening is a passionately debated topic in some enterprises; in others it is well understood and adheres to one of the many available standard resources. The need for system hardening is comprehended by most in IT, but to what degree of hardening and where is it mandatory become the points of contention. Typically, **hardening** involves reducing the attack surface of a system by turning off unnecessary services, patching the operating system and software, and enabling attack mitigation features such as iptables for Linux and Windows Firewall for Windows.

There are several hardening guidelines and standards available by NIST, NSA, and most product vendors. The challenge is which makes the most sense for the enterprise and where should enforcement be most stringent. It is ideal for the security team and system owners to agree on the approach since each team is responsible for their respective role expectations. There may be differing standards for network locations such as where the system resides, who is using the system, and what data is on the system. I caution that this method can backfire if not well thought through. It is very common to make the standard for development systems rather lax and place them in the same network segment as critical production systems. The development systems make great targets for compromise, and once compromised they are leveraged against other internal assets. There should be at least a base set of hardening standards, and additional specific standards developed for unique instances. We will now look at high-level areas to cover in the standard and a few resources on system hardening. Not everything presented in these resources will be applicable or advisable; the examples from NIST and the NSA provide guidance to the government, not private enterprises, but can be used as they are best practice approaches to security.

The following are the items that should be included in the hardening standard:

- Operating system hardening
- Software hardening
- Required attack mitigation software and configuration
- Unique hardening requirements for specific scenarios (DMZ, critical assets, and so on)

The following are a few hardening guide sources:

- NIST (`http://csrc.nist.gov/groups/SNS/checklists/`)
- NSA (`http://www.nsa.gov/ia/mitigation_guidance/security_configuration_guides/operating_systems.shtml`)
- Microsoft (`http://www.microsoft.com/en-us/download/details.aspx?id=16776`)

 Microsoft has guides but all the guidance is now also available in the *Microsoft Security Compliance Manager* by going to the previous link. I have not listed all sources, but there is plenty here to get started on developing your hardening standards. More can be found in *Appendix B, Risk Analysis, Policy and Standard, and System Hardening Resources.*

Hardening systems is a small but crucial component of the overall security of the enterprise. This exercise should have priority, as many breaches are simply an exploitation of the operating system or the running applications. If the enterprise is not security conscious or does not see the value in this phase, be diligent but patient. Provide resources for the system owners to educate and ensure you have the support of the senior leadership. At the end of the day, no one single person has the authority to accept risk for the enterprise, there is an obligation to ensure security and IT in general are doing the best to secure enterprise data. We will go into more detail on this subject in *Chapter 5, Securing Systems*.

Security exceptions

Indeed, if we have policies and standards we will have exceptions too. Let's face it; it is hard to implement everything by the letter of the law due to complexity, costs, and limitations of software and hardware. There are two schools of thought on policy implementation, one school, only put in policies on what is currently being done or with little effort, the other, write a policy that the enterprise should be implementing. The first school of thought may not be ideal, but upper management may not want to hear that the enterprise is dismally implementing a policy that has been written. On the other hand, upper management that understands security will want to push the enterprise to a higher standard and push for the best feasible policy.

In either case of policy creation and enforcement, there will be exceptions. Exceptions are not necessarily a bad thing, but they must be documented with a path to resolution and a timeframe to do so. Without an acceptable timeframe with accountability the exceptions, which are a security shortcoming, may be introducing unnecessary risk to the enterprise. Assigning a risk level for the exception and developing required remediation timelines is crucial for exceptions to serve their purpose while ultimately getting in adherence to policy. Indefinite exceptions cannot be an acceptable practice as this undermines the intent of policy and maintains a revolving door of risk.

Security policy exceptions require proper documentation not only to make it clear what the exceptions are, but when audit time comes around, due diligence, through following a formal process will reduce the impact of identified exceptions.

The following items should be documented for security policy exceptions:

- Exception number
- Date and time
- Exception requester
- Exception owner (responsible party for remediating the exception)
- Exception approver
- System, application, configuration (which has the exception)
- Cost, complexity, limitation (cause of the exception)
- Portion of policy not met (what part of the policy the exception is for)
- Exception remediation date (when the exception expires and remediation is required): Cannot be indefinite, and exceptions must be remediated
- Next review date

Ideally, exceptions would be managed in a system that can be used to track the progress of each exception and provide an overview of all open, closed, and in progress exceptions. Exception systems can also send notifications to owners or preferably roles (in case of personnel changes) as a friendly reminder to get their open exception in compliance with written policy. Additionally, providing a searchable repository allows for better reporting and metrics on open exceptions that may indicate a trend that needs addressing at the policy tier.

The primary focus for exceptions is not only opening and closing them, but also analyzing patterns of exceptions. Are the same portions of the security policy creating multiple exceptions again and again? This may be an indicator that the policy is either identifying a serious issue within the organization or that the policy may need to be tweaked to better fit how the enterprise is functioning.

Security review of changes

A formal change management process is not only a requirement for many regulatory and standards bodies, but in general a good practice of due diligence. In the typical implementation of change management there is a process followed to ensure all affected parties are aware of a planned change. This allows the various business units and IT to fully understand impact and properly set the risk level for the change. What happens many times though is the security team is not made aware of the changes in the environment. Sometimes this lack of review is due to reducing the workload for the team and not overburdening them with reviewing countless changes. This can be a serious misstep because teams may not be aware that a change has security implications.

Another issue is intentional bypassing of security because security is seen as a road block. Information security should be involved in changes that affect the security posture of the enterprise, introduce risk, involve a modification to an existing implementation, or a net new implementation. There are approaches to IT service management such as ITIL that provides an excellent road map for proper change management implementation and process flow. The following process flow diagram is from Cisco's *High Availability Change Management: Best Practices* site `http://www.cisco.com/en/US/technologies/collateral/tk869/tk769/white_paper_c11-458050.html`, and is also available via download in PDF form from `http://www.cisco.com/en/US/technologies/collateral/tk869/tk769/white_paper_c11-458050.pdf`:

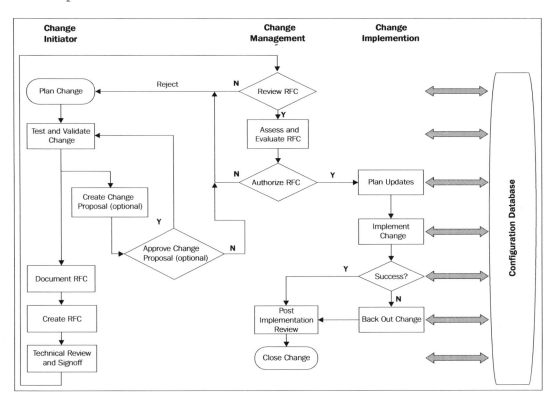

Ideally, the security team would be involved in technical review and post-implementation review phases of the change management process. This will allow the security team to halt a change if it is assessed as too risky, or provide another solution to meet the business needs without increasing risk. The security team should thoroughly document their review of the change for audit purposes and for historical documentation.

Perimeter security changes

The **perimeter**, whatever and wherever it is, is the area where the first line of defense is positioned to protect assets within the perimeter. Types of security mechanisms deployed at the perimeter include, but are not limited to firewalls, intrusion detection and prevention, data loss prevention, Internet proxy, and advanced malware mitigation. Therefore changes to this infrastructure can have a significant impact on the security provided at the perimeter. Changes in this area of the network should by default always include the information security team to assess the security implications of the change and assign a risk value to the proposed change. Though the perimeter is typically not the scope of attack if there is a weakness introduced, it can be detected and exploited. A recent large-scale breach was the result of the data loss prevention technology being configured only to detect not prevent, as it is capable of doing. The implementation may have always been in this manner, but changes like this can happen with a lack of due diligence and oversight by the information security team.

The following are a few questions to determine if IT security should review a change:

- Does the change involve a perimeter network or security solution?
- Does the change provide more access than previously permitted?
- Does the change affect traffic flow at the perimeter?
- What type of access is being provisioned?
- What systems and data are being accessed?

If this process is implemented, it is critical that there is absolutely no change implemented without the explicit documented approval of the information security team. The other side of this equation is that the information security team must involve themselves in the process and when presented with a change, understand it, analyze it, and if it is not a sound security change, provide an alternative solution to the requester. This last step not happening is what usually gets the security team bypassed. Other times the security operations team who run the security infrastructure such as firewalls are simply aggressively entering firewall policy changes in order to reduce a ticket queue with no regard to the security implications of the request.

Data access changes

All data within the enterprise ideally is classified, and the handling of all data types is communicated and understood by all those who will handle enterprise data. The challenge that is typically the undoing of data classification is enforcing the policy. What happens over time is data is put where it is not supposed to be and not protected properly; it either sits there unnoticed or it falls into the wrong hands. What we attempt to do is protect at the system level, but in reality this method is no less than useless.

Implementation of the trust models applied to enterprise data should get us to the protection mechanisms required to enforce the trust level we have for who and what is accessing the data. Once we have implemented these mechanisms, we need to closely monitor any and all changes to the protection mechanisms. Changes will most likely be location of the data or modification to access permissions.

With data protection the primary concern of auditing bodies, permissions for all locations of data whether a file, file share, database, or ETL, will be heavily scrutinized to ensure that only those individuals, processes, and applications that need access to the data are permitted it. The access level will be audited as well. Ideally, data access changes are few and far between and when it does occur, the process is well documented. The documentation should include all the information necessary for both internal and external resources to make a proper risk decision and be able to attest to the business reason for the access creation or access modification. Including data access modifications and additions in the formal change management process will ensure the previously mentioned documentation and approvals occur. If the enterprise loses sight of the value their data represents, then the IT security team has some work to do!

The following are a few questions to ensure review of data access changes:

- Is the data business critical?
- Are there internal and/or external regulatory requirements for protection?
- Is the access method secure?
- What trust model does this access fall within?

Network architectural changes

Great! A new network segment was created. The new zone was undoubtedly in reaction to a business unit request. Should information security have been made aware of the request before implementation? Absolutely! The network itself is the infrastructure that provides connectivity to business partners, third parties, the Internet, and enterprise assets so it is important when it undergoes a modification that IT security is able to analyze any risk and make suggestions or provide solutions to reduce the impact to the enterprise.

Communicating network changes to other IT teams will help identify when security mechanisms implemented may not be in place where the change is occurring to provide the correct security protection. The security team usually thinks more from a data position and network teams about how to get traffic from point A to point B. Both are correct, but they need to work together to ensure the long-term protection and availability of the enterprise data.

As networks become more complex to support emerging technologies and updated protocols, the relationship between network and security becomes less of a non-functional requirement but an intertwined and joint venture. IPv6 is an example where there are many security implications when assessing the implementation of the upgraded protocol. Various enterprise implementations seem to be eluding the traditional wisdom of network and security architecture and are putting a strain on current solutions. Therefore, network teams are sometimes forced to make bad decisions to meet a business request. Reaching out to the ally security team may be the best option to save the enterprise from itself.

A benefit of engagement across both network and security teams is an evaluation of current network and security technologies implemented at each phase of change. Significant cost can be attributed to increasing security hardware required to protect each perimeter connection. This is leading to a shift in integrated solutions where a firewall, IPS, and proxy server is one physical device providing the protection of the traditional three separate solutions. Security spend can be more intelligent by simple cooperation and collaboration with other teams. Business benefits can be realized with a simple step in the change management process to include IT security.

Summary

In this chapter we took a detailed look at security as a process. First, we took a look at analyzing risk by presenting quantitative and qualitative methods including an exercise to understand the approach. We moved on to getting security expectations documented and the power to enforce them by developing policies and standards. Applying these items to use cases provides the data needed to build the enterprise trust models. When policies and standards cannot be met, we have exceptions to track deviations and develop a remediation plan. We noted that if the same exceptions are raised consistently, a review of the policy or standard might be required. Lastly, we covered when to involve the security team in the change management process for review and approval of change requests and properly documenting the review. The overall goal of security is to be integrated into business processes, so it is truly a part of the business and not an expensive afterthought simply there to patch a security problem. The next chapter begins a series of chapters on securing the various components of the enterprise, starting with the network.

4

Securing the Network

Defense in depth is a foundational concept of information security. Each tier of the enterprise network needs to be secured to mitigate attacks against assets at each tier. This chapter will introduce multiple technologies that can be implemented in the network to secure enterprise infrastructure, network services such as e-mail, DNS, file transfer, and web applications. Advancement in firewall technologies that provide more in-depth inspection and protection capabilities will be covered as a method to consolidate solutions and increase visibility into the network traffic.

We will also cover intrusion detection and prevention, and how this technology can protect against simple and the most advanced attacks across applications, systems, and network services. Last, this chapter will cover increasing security through network segmentation while reducing the scope for regulatory and compliance initiatives.

We will cover the following topics in this chapter:

- Introduction to network security solutions
- Securing network services
- Securing web applications
- Network segmentation

Overview

When developing an enterprise security strategy, a layered approach is the best method to ensure detection and mitigation of attacks at each tier of the network infrastructure. Although it is changing, the enterprise network perimeter to the outside world remains the same and the basic network security mechanisms still have their purpose. In general, the same types of security mechanisms need to persist, however, where they are implemented may change slightly depending upon the network architecture. Our approach to securing the network will not focus much on where the network perimeter is, but on what needs to be protected.

In *Chapter 2*, *Security Architectures*, we discussed how emerging technologies are playing a fundamental role in the paradigm reset of the network and security architecture, design, and implementation. Bring your own device (BYOD) initiatives and the increase in need to share business critical data require network and security architects to be agile and find unique ways to properly secure not only the data, but also the network infrastructure itself.

We have seen a significant increase in the attacks targeted at the network hardware and the low-level operating systems that make these devices function. In addition to this, continued vendor source code leaks equate to the need to implement proper perimeter security and relentless monitoring of the network infrastructure.

The next sections will provide a detailed description of the design and implementation considerations, leveraging our trust model paradigm to secure the network, network services, and web applications.

Next generation firewalls

Firewalls have been an interesting evolution. They not only provide the most basic protection, but are also able to understand the traffic inspected and look for the applications being used. This may seem insignificant at first glance, but to have a device that can tell if the traffic traversing the firewall is legitimate or not, and be able to mitigate malicious traffic masquerading as legitimate, can be the difference between a breach and a non-event. An example may be the DNS traffic as inspected by a standard firewall, which looks like legitimate DNS traffic, but in reality has DNS packets that are padded with data that is being exfiltrated from the network.

A **next generation firewall (NGFW)** would be able to detect the anomaly behavior in such network transactions, alerting security staff of a potential network breach. The standard firewall would simply check for the policy allowing the source IP, destination IP, and TCP/UDP port, without a further deep packet analysis to ensure that the traffic is in fact DNS related. This is the primary distinction between an NGFW and a stateful firewall. The following image is taken from the Palo Alto networks website (`http://media.paloaltonetworks.com/documents/Content_ID_tech.pdf`). It shows how an NGFW inspects traffic for data, threats, and web traffic:

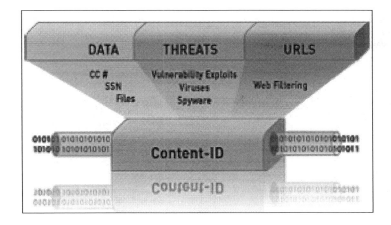

Over the years, there have been many names given to firewalls with the ability to identify application traffic. Most recently, it is called the NGFW. Each vendor has developed a trademarked name along with unique offerings. There are leaders in this space, such as Palo Alto Networks. Where the firewall industry is headed is still unclear, as the path of software development blazes with more features and the firewall role is becoming gray. This is partly because the value of a one-trick pony technology doesn't uniquely distinguish the vendors enough, nor does it drive better mitigation technologies for the buyer.

With next generation firewalls, new technologies become a part of the firewall tier, including intrusion prevention, user authorization, application awareness, and advanced malware mitigation, further expanding the role of the next generation firewall in a network.

This shift in firewall capabilities may add confusion to the role the appliance plays in the overall network protection in comparison to web application and database firewalls. While the next generation firewall provides some coverage across these areas today, the available platforms do not have the advanced capabilities of purposefully designed web application firewalls or database firewalls. An NGFW is capable of basic detection and mitigation of common web application attacks, but lacks the more in-depth coverage provided by web application firewalls with database counterparts. It is important to note that implementing a NGFW in addition to web application and database firewalls provides the most comprehensive coverage for a network. A more detailed coverage of web application firewalls with database protection capabilities will be covered later in this chapter.

Benefits of NGFW technology

The most significant benefit of the NGFW is **awareness**. I know, this sounds like a sci-fi artificial intelligence concept. In a way, it is. The NGFW no longer makes packet permit and deny decisions using only the simple network portions of the communication, such as source and destination IP and port pairings; it can look into the traffic flow and decode the exact application that makes up the communication flow. This is rather special from a security perspective. The technology is aware of what the traffic is, and not just how the traffic is communicating. For years, malware has been able to invade and evade by simply masquerading as well-known legitimate traffic.

The NGFW makes evasion much more difficult, requiring malware writers to leverage encryption and complicated encoding methods to evade the firewall. While this constitutes an evasion method, there are methods to mitigate unwanted traffic with obfuscated malicious payloads within the NGFW and other perimeter security mechanisms. Two more significant features of the NGFW include intrusion prevention technology and user awareness.

The firewall can now detect and mitigate attacks typically analyzed by an intrusion prevention system while reducing the complexity of a DMZ implementation. In the common DMZ design there may be a firewall in addition to an intrusion prevention system in order to enforce permitted traffic and mitigate threats over acceptable ports and protocols. This separation in systems, while effective at segregation of duties, further complicates the network implementation and presents another point of failure. Having IPS functionality within the firewall makes sense, as the appliance is already in-line and inspecting network traffic. Potential downsides may be the maturity of the feature in a, NGFW, effective segregation of duties, and performance loss with feature enablement.

User role-based access facilitates separation of duties for policy administration, reporting, and troubleshooting. With the ability to authorize a user as a part of a rule, access is no longer based solely on a valid IP address and port pair, but also on who is attempting the access. User awareness also makes the firewall an excellent choice within the network to secure various segments, by authorizing access based on user and network information.

These features add significant layers of security to the traditional firewall. We will look at each feature in depth to help realize the benefits of the next generation firewall.

Application awareness

This feature alone provides the most value in an NGFW platform. Application awareness has for years been implemented poorly and to the point where the feature was typically turned off, reducing the firewall to the most basic mitigation through access control list logic.

The shortcoming in the area of application awareness has allowed undetected unauthorized access at staggering levels. This is evident as longtime breaches take one to three years to finally detect, because the data exfiltration was happening over accepted ports and protocols with no application awareness. The firewall manufacturers were right when they moved in the direction of application detection. This provides intelligent decision factoring, based on more than network level information that can be easily spoofed, allowing evasion.

Traditional firewalls only look at the source and destination IP addresses and the TCP or UDP port to make a decision to block or permit a packet. Here is a simplified version of a TCP packet with an IP header to only show the fields that a basic non-NGFW will inspect for the permit or deny decision. These fields are indicated by the dotted line:

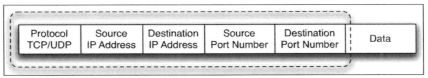

Simplified TCP packet with IP header with header inspection only

Having the application awareness capability, NGFW is able to perform deep packet inspection to also decode and inspect the application data in network communication.

The thought leaders in this technology area have made application awareness a must have. We have seen this feature mature rapidly. Some firewall manufacturers, such as Palo Alto Networks, are able to identify over 3000 unique applications as traffic traverses the firewall. An example benefit of this capability is detecting and mitigating protocol misuse. This method of attack would typically be passed ignorantly through a basic firewall. Additional examples are applications such as torrent clients, anonymous proxy services, and tunneled connections back to a home, office, or other unapproved destinations. The ability to identify and take action on network traffic that violates security policy or in other ways introduces risk to the enterprise reduces the enterprise threat surface significantly.

It is highly recommended to do your research when assessing what technology to purchase. There are well-known testing services, such as NSS Labs (`https://www.nsslabs.com/`), that can provide objective effectiveness testing results. Understanding the purpose of the device in the network is critical to product selection. Leveraging a trusted third-party integrator may also be a method to test the validity of vendor claims and observe the solution in the environment prior to a purchase.

The following questions may influence a purchase decision:

- What is the perceived need for the technology?
- What protection capabilities are required?
- How does the product integrate with existing infrastructure and technologies?
- Will the technology be used to augment other solutions?
- What is the level of expertise required to operate the solution?

Intrusion prevention

Another benefit of the NGFW is the inclusion of intrusion prevention technology. This is significant, because one challenge the security team must face is providing intrusion prevention coverage for every connection to the enterprise network. With the average cost of an IPS being over $40,000, this adds up quickly in addition to the support and maintenance costs. The balance of available budget and protection requirements increases the acceptance of relatively similar protection from a software feature of the firewall that is already inline. It is not a bad gamble as firewall manufacturers have taken this new responsibility seriously and are providing undeniable intrusion prevention protection according to industry-accepted lab tests results.

Simplifying the security implementation at the perimeter provides several gains that must be taken into consideration when replacing the traditional standalone intrusion prevention system. First, removing a device and the related management components simplifies management of IT security and the skillsets required to operationally support the solution. Second, one less appliance in the DMZ or inline inspecting traffic increases the performance and removes one layer of failure probability.

Here is a diagram depicting an example of the benefit of simplification using a next generation firewall IPS feature-set. There are fewer devices in the network perimeter, reduced management requirements, and less points of failure.

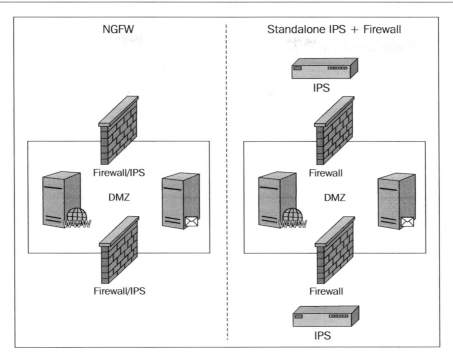

Advanced malware mitigation

The newest addition to the features that NGFWs are offering is advanced malware protection in the form of botnet identification along with malware analysis in the cloud. Botnets, such as Zeus, have been a painful reminder that end point protection and security awareness training alone will not thwart the more persistent malware writers. A few products have come to market to address advanced malware detection and mitigation, but with significant cost to purchase and the additional skillset needed to properly use the tools. With a solution built into the firewall, where the malware is examined in the cloud, protection developed and mitigation implemented by the manufacturer, all without any work by the customer or additional operational costs, make this an attractive option.

There are standalone solutions for **Advanced Persistent Threat (APT)** detection and mitigation at the network perimeter, but there is a learning curve and additional analysis required. This may not be an issue for an organization that can get the skillset needed, but it is not attainable for smaller IT organizations. Another consideration for standalone solutions is the high price tags of the top products in this space.

When evaluating a solution, look for opportunities to simplify implementation and operationalizing. Where there are expertise gaps, there may be features built into the solution that provide the benefits of advanced analysis and mitigation that would take additional time and money to equal the value.

An example is malware analysis, detection, and mitigation. This is a highly specialized skillset. If this can be done in an automated fashion, value can be realized quickly.

Malware mitigation at the perimeter is not the ideal implementation, however, it does provide an additional layer of protection needed before the malware can make a successful connection back to the initiator. It is assumed that if the detection and mitigation happens at the network perimeter, internal hosts get infected and current endpoint protection becomes insufficient. If the firewall can provide this last layer of malware communication disruption, it is a worthwhile investment. While the next generation firewall implementation is less mature than the standalone solutions, leveraging the cloud and the vendor's entire customer base to provide samples will increase the effectiveness and value of the feature at an accelerated rate.

Intrusion detection and prevention

Intrusion detection and prevention technology has remained a mainstay at the network perimeter, though predicted to be a dead technology by security experts five to seven years ago. The IPS market is thriving, and enterprises are finding value and regulatory compliance in the platform used to stop malicious attacks at the perimeter. While several firewall technologies are integrating intrusion prevention into their offerings, there has not been a complete shift to this implementation. As with other security areas, there are multiple perspectives that drive technology theory and practice. Typically, the shift to an integrated solution becomes more of an consideration when the network segments requiring protection increase to the extent that it is simply cost prohibitive to deploy standalone intrusion prevention.

Larger enterprises seem to be interested in this capability to reduce cost on a grand scale. Smaller enterprises look at the integrated solutions for reduction in operational expense with some financial savings. A primary reason for keeping the technologies separate is the separation of duties where network and security teams may jointly manage technologies in the network perimeter infrastructure. It is a clear separation when the devices are homogeneous solutions that have a clear management ownership by one team or the other

Both intrusion detection and prevention continue to be deployed at various points within the enterprise network, but the shift to purely threat prevention has become a standard. There are a few pure intrusion detection technologies available, but to provide detection on an IPS is a simple flip of a switch to not mitigate a detected attack. In some cases, the desire not to mitigate may be driven by the sensitivity of the environment monitored, where a false-positive block may be detrimental to the enterprise. Simply knowing that an attack is occurring and the benefit of traffic analysis has value on internal segments, though not typically deployed in this manner at the network perimeter. These two approaches of detection versus detection and mitigation are covered in the following sections.

Intrusion detection

Intrusion detection is simply a method for detecting an attack but taking no action, such as blocking the malicious traffic. For the most part, this has been abandoned at the network perimeter when a breach is undesirable. Intrusion detection seems to still have a significant implementation in the internal network server segments where custom applications may be blocked due to non-adherence to a protocol RFC. Typically what happens is a developer uses a TCP port in an application that is already used for something malicious like a Trojan, therefore triggering the IDS; in this case, detection versus mitigation would be desired to reduce the impact on the enterprise. Intrusion detection has all the detection logic of intrusion prevention but without the ability to actively mitigate a threat.

Another benefit of deploying intrusion detection in the internal network is to passively observe the behaviors of internal network users. Significant intelligence can be gathered by monitoring the network activities of internal users that can lead to a better indication of areas that need to be secured. This knowledge can also trigger an investigation into internal malicious actors and lead to additional targeted monitoring of the user. An investigation can determine whether the behavior is intentional or if malware is running on the user's system. This can highlight potential areas of weakness and the fact that an internal user does not necessarily imply trustworthiness.

Intrusion prevention

Intrusion prevention is similar to intrusion detection, but has the capability to disrupt and mitigate malicious traffic by blocking and other methods. Using an IPS in front of an external firewall is a great way to detect and block port scanning that may otherwise use up the available connections on the perimeter firewall. Many IPS devices have purposefully built denial of service mitigation technology, which is ideal to protect Internet accessible infrastructure including systems and network equipment.

Intrusion prevention can be deployed at the network perimeter with greater confidence that legitimate traffic will not be impacted due to the limited number of services that should be Internet accessible. However, IPS should be considered for implementation in the internal network to protect the most critical assets within the organization. Because IPS technology is looking for patterns, legitimate network communication may be impacted due to non-compliant coding practices and seemingly odd network operating system behaviors. Some organizations will opt to just detect and alert. This method may prove to be inefficient in scenarios where there is a lack of constant monitoring, and an attack may go unnoticed.

Detection methods

Today's IDS/IPS devices use a combination of three methods to detect and mitigate attacks; behavior, anomaly, and signature, to gain most of the benefits of packet analysis. Though it is rare to find a detection method without the others, initial IDS/IPS systems were specialized in one method or another. Additionally, attacks are not always as simple as protocol misuse or a known Trojan signature. As the attacks have become advanced, there is debate on the overall advantage of the IDS/IPS implementation and it is enough to protect the network. Though it can be argued that advanced malware has ended this debate, a defense in-depth strategy is best including IDS/IPS as an essential network protection mechanism.

Behavioral analysis

Behavioral analysis takes some intelligence from the platform to first gain an understanding of how the network "normally" operates, what systems communicate with other systems, how they communicate, and how much. Any deviation from this baseline becomes an outlier and triggers the IDS/IPS based on this behavioral deviation. This method can be very effective for detection of a system compromise at both the network perimeter and internal critical network segments. If a system is compromised and, for example, the connection rates exceed what is common for the system, the IDS/IPS will detect the outlier traffic and alert or mitigate. Typically, behavioral analysis alone is not sufficient to determine if there is an imminent threat. However, this information in combination with protocol anomaly and signature-based detection, creates a solid approach to attack detection and mitigation.

The primary caveat with this technology is the mistake of baselining malicious traffic within standard network traffic as "normal". This common and almost unavoidable mistake requires the other detection methods to bring real value. If and only if "normal" network traffic, which is more than likely a combination of good and bad anomaly traffic, exceeds a defined threshold will this detection method trigger an alert. This weakness is the primary reason to leverage other detection methods to augment network behavioral analysis.

Anomaly detection

Understanding the RFC specifications for every protocol is a daunting task, but knowing when a communication is violating how a protocol is supposed to be used can be a great indicator that something is wrong. It is common for malware writers to attempt to masquerade their application as a legitimate application that would have access to the network and preferably be permitted outbound from the protected network.

To evade detection by IDS/IPS and firewalls, this method is commonly employed by chat clients, bit torrent, and other P2P applications. These examples are typically violations of the information security and or acceptable use policies and not permitted, so developers have written the application to look harmless and appear like other typical Internet traffic on the network.

Anomaly detection at the network perimeter can be extremely effective in analyzing inbound HTTP requests where the protocol is correct, but there has been some manipulation to the packet in an effort to identify vulnerabilities in the web application. An anomaly-based IDS/IPS would detect or mitigate this attempt while saving cycles on firewalls and systems serving the web application.

Signature-based detection

Signature-based detection has been a consistent method to detect known malicious attacks. The IDS/IPS looks for known patterns in the packets being inspected. When a signature or pattern match is found, a predetermined action is taken. The primary annoyance with this method is the high rate of false positives, which can be the difference in effective security monitoring or status quo. Tuning IDS/IPS is absolutely essential. Otherwise, compromise will be difficult to detect, because it will be amongst all the garbage-in-garbage-out traffic and alerts.

While signature-based detection may not be most effective, it will detect the most common, generic attacks. Without the ability to inspect encrypted payloads, it proves mostly ineffective for the more sophisticated attacks. With a majority of attacks targeted at the network being Distributed Denial of Service (DDoS) and SQL injection (SQLi), signature-based IPS can be very effective in mitigating these attacks and continue to provide value at the network perimeter.

Advanced persistent threat detection and mitigation

Advanced persistent threats (APTs) are complicated and well disguised malware infecting internal systems and have become the coin phrase of late, due to there being no better way to describe the capabilities of this more recently observed sophisticated malware. The anti-virus software companies have done a good job at eradicating the most common malware such as the "I Love You" virus and others. What has not been easy to eradicate are the malware types that use complicated zero-day vulnerabilities, multi-encoded malicious payloads, encryption, obfuscation, and clever masquerading techniques that are infecting networks at an all-time high.

The approach taken by APT mitigation solutions is providing a safe environment; usually virtualized instances or sandboxes of operating systems, such as Microsoft Windows, are employed, where malicious software can run and infect the operating system. The tool then analyzes everything the malicious software did, and decodes the payload to identify the threat and create a "signature" to mitigate further exploitation. Some tools are appliance-based. This decoding and analysis happens on the box and some vendors provide the service in the cloud. Some other capabilities of these tools include tracking infections and detecting whether a connection has a successful callback to the malware host.

Technology in this space is new and it is unknown at this point in time how today's solutions will ultimately advance in the future. A significant consideration when assessing products in this area of technology is what skillsets are required to effectively maintain the solution and gain the most benefit of its use. They do a lot of the work for the IT security staff, but some level of malware analysis knowledge and techniques may be required to use the solutions. Leveraging a cloud solution may be better for less experienced teams or simply to reduce the operational overhead of using an advanced technology that analyzes some of the most complicated application code today.

Several manufacturers in the IDS/IPS and NGFW technology areas have made significant progress in providing APT detection and mitigation, both on the box and in the cloud. The benefit of leveraging one of these technologies would be that the devices are already inline and the feature is usually a software component of the solution. This keeps the management interface consistent and can provide operational efficiencies not afforded by many specialized appliances.

Securing network services

It is a common requirement for enterprises to provide and leverage Internet services such as DNS, e-mail, and file transfer. How the services are used and properly integrated into the enterprise network infrastructure remains a constant challenge for enterprises in addition to implementing security. The latest malware threats utilize these common services in order to redirect internal hosts to Internet destinations under the control of the malware writers. In a network with correctly implemented architecture, this scenario would mostly be a mute point, and with additional security mechanisms, a rare occurrence.

DNS

Domain Name Service (DNS) is in my opinion one of the greatest inventions, saving all of us from memorizing 32-bit and soon 128-bit IP addressing to browse to our favorite Internet websites. DNS provides a mapping of an IP address to a fully qualified domain name, an example is `www.google.com`, at IP address `173.194.75.106`, one of the many web servers that serve the website. It is much easier to memorize a name versus a string of numeric characters. A system can be directed anywhere on the Internet with DNS, so the authenticity of the source of this information is critical.

This is where **DNS Security Extensions (DNSSEC)** come into play. DNSSEC is a set of security extensions for DNS that provide authenticity for DNS resolver data. In other words, the source of DNS data cannot be forged and attacks like DNS poisoning, where erroneous DNS is injected into DNS and propagated, resulting in pointing hosts to the wrong system on the Internet is mitigated. This is a common method used by malware writers and in phishing attacks.

Another area of security in regards to DNS implementation are DNS zone transfers—the records that the DNS server maintains for the domains it is responsible for. A lot can be learned from the records on the DNS server, including hidden domains used for purposes other than general Internet use and access. The extremely insecure practice of storing information in TXT records on DNS servers can be detrimental if the document has sensitive information contained within, such as system passwords. We will take a more detailed look into securely implementing DNS using some ideas from our trust models.

DNS resolution

DNS resolution can make for easy exploitation of victim hosts if there is no control on where the internal hosts are getting this mapping information from on the Internet. This has been the main method used by the Zeus botnet. Hosts are pointed to maliciously controlled Internet servers by manipulating DNS information. With complete control of how a host resolves web addresses, this ensures that the victim hosts only go where the malicious hackers want them to venture. The method also relies on compromised or specifically built DNS servers on the Internet, allowing malware writers to make up their own, unique and sometimes inconspicuous domain names that, at a glance, do not spark the interest of the IT security team and can remain undetected.

Here is an example of an incorrect DNS resolver implementation. This highlights that internal hosts are able to resolve DNS names from anywhere on the Internet.

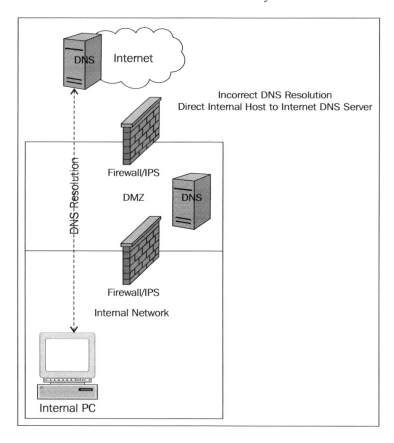

DNS should be configured and tightly controlled to ensure that DNS resolution information is sourced from an enterprise maintained DNS infrastructure for internal hosts. In this implementation, the internal hosts rely on a trusted DNS server owned and maintained by the enterprise. The enterprise DNS infrastructure is configured in such a way that resolution of domain names is tightly controlled and will leverage only trusted Internet sources.

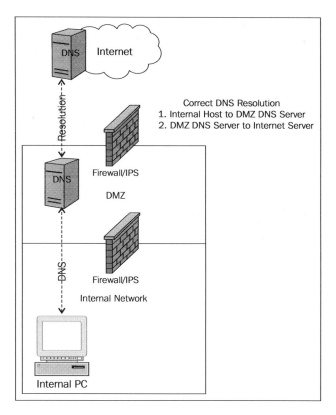

DNS zone transfer

A DNS zone transfer is the mechanism used in DNS to provide other DNS servers with what domains the DNS server is responsible for and all the details available for each record in the zone. A DNS zone transfer should be limited to only trusted partners and limited to only zones that need to be transferred. The next screenshot provides information that is gathered with a DNS zone transfer using the Domain Information Groper (DIG) tool.

The command used to get this information is:

```
dig axfr @ns12.zoneedit.com zonetransfer.me
```

Typing this command at the command prompt will produce the following output:

```
 ; <<>> DiG 9.7.3-P3 <<>> axfr @ns12.zoneedit.com zonetransfer.me
 ; (1 server found)
 ;; global options: +cmd
 zonetransfer.me.         7200    IN      SOA     ns16.zoneedit.com. soacontact.zoneedit.com. 2012179462 2400 360 1209600 300
 zonetransfer.me.         7200    IN      NS      ns16.zoneedit.com.
 zonetransfer.me.         7200    IN      NS      ns12.zoneedit.com.
 zonetransfer.me.         7200    IN      A       217.147.180.162
 zonetransfer.me.         7200    IN      MX      0 ASPMX.L.GOOGLE.COM.
 zonetransfer.me.         7200    IN      MX      10 ALT1.ASPMX.L.GOOGLE.COM.
 zonetransfer.me.         7200    IN      MX      10 ALT2.ASPMX.L.GOOGLE.COM.
 zonetransfer.me.         7200    IN      MX      20 ASPMX2.GOOGLEMAIL.COM.
 zonetransfer.me.         7200    IN      MX      20 ASPMX3.GOOGLEMAIL.COM.
 zonetransfer.me.         7200    IN      MX      20 ASPMX4.GOOGLEMAIL.COM.
 zonetransfer.me.         7200    IN      MX      20 ASPMX5.GOOGLEMAIL.COM.
 zonetransfer.me.         301     IN      TXT     "Remember to call or email Pippa on +44 123 4567890 or pippa@zonetransfer.me when making
 DNS changes"
 zonetransfer.me.         301     IN      TXT     "google-site-verification=tyP28J7JAUHA9fw2sHXMgcCC0I6XBmmoVi04VlMewxA"
 testing.zonetransfer.me. 301     IN      CNAME   www.zonetransfer.me.
 164.180.147.217.in-addr.arpa.zonetransfer.me. 7200 IN PTR www.zonetransfer.me.
 ipv6actnow.org.zonetransfer.me. 7200 IN AAAA     2001:67c:2e8:11::c100:1332
 info.zonetransfer.me.    7200    IN      TXT     "ZoneTransfer.me service provided by Robin Wood - robin@digininja.org. See www.digininja
 .org/projects/zonetransferme.php for more information."
 owa.zonetransfer.me.     7200    IN      A       207.46.197.32
 office.zonetransfer.me. 7200     IN      A       4.23.39.254
 canberra_office.zonetransfer.me. 7200 IN A       202.14.81.230
 dzc.zonetransfer.me.     7200    IN      TXT     "AbCdEfG"
 dr.zonetransfer.me.      300     IN      LOC     53 20 56.558 N 1 38 33.526 W 0.00m 1m 10000m 10m
 alltcpportsopen.firewall.test.zonetransfer.me. 301 IN A 127.0.0.1
 www.zonetransfer.me.     7200    IN      A       217.147.180.162
 staging.zonetransfer.me. 7200    IN      CNAME   www.sydneyoperahouse.com.
 deadbeef.zonetransfer.me. 7201   IN      AAAA    dead:beaf::
 vpn.zonetransfer.me.     4000    IN      A       174.36.59.154
 _sip._tcp.zonetransfer.me. 14000 IN      SRV     0 0 5060 www.zonetransfer.me.
 dc_office.zonetransfer.me. 7200  IN      A       143.228.181.132
 zonetransfer.me.         7200    IN      SOA     ns16.zoneedit.com. soacontact.zoneedit.com. 2012179462 2400 360 1209600 300
 ;; Query time: 120 msec
 ;; SERVER: 209.62.64.46#53(209.62.64.46)
 ;; WHEN: Sat May 19 13:52:09 2012
 ;; XFR size: 30 records (messages 30, bytes 2124)

 Aarons-MacBook-Pro:~ aaron$
```

This is a specially created DNS instance configured by **DigiNinja** as the **ZoneTransfer.me** project to show the dangers of allowing zone transfers to any anonymous system on the Internet. The project along with an excellent write-up can be found at the project site: http://www.digininja.org/projects/zonetransferme.php.

With a quick glance, you are able to determine the DNS structure of this server and the possible avenues of attack if you were a penetration tester or malicious hacker. An enterprise may have several domain names for various services they provide to business partners and employees that are not "known" by the general public. While the fact remains that if the service is available on the Internet, it can be found, a simple zone transfer reduces the discovery process significantly. This specific example shows office-specific records, a VPN URL, SIP address for VoIP, and it looks like there might be a staging system with potentially poor security. That is a lot of information about the enterprise services available on the Internet.

Depending on the DNS structure within the enterprise, there may be internal and external DNS implementations with records specific to the areas of the network they service. For instance, the internal DNS server may have records for all internal hosts and services, while a DNS server in the DMZ may only have records for DMZ services. In this type of implementation, there will be some dependencies across the DNS infrastructure, but it will be critical to keep the records uncontaminated from other zones. If the DMZ server somehow receives the internal zone information, then any system that can initiate a zone transfer with the DMZ server will also get the internal network DNS information. This could be a very big problem if anonymous users on the Internet could study the internal DNS records.

We will talk more about the TXT records discovered after the zone transfer in the next section.

DNS records

DNS records are the mapping of IP addresses to fully qualified domain names of systems, services, and web applications available either internal or external to a network. The **Request for Comments (RFC)** 1035 for DNS indicates the resource types that a record specifies. The standard resource records are A, NS, SOA, CNAME, and PTR. We will not cover DNS in detail as it is out of scope for this book. To learn more about DNS, start with the RFC: http://www.ietf.org/rfc/rfc1035.txt.

Using DNS is a great way to provide access to a service using an easy to remember name. If the IP address mapped to a name changes, it is no big deal; it is a simple DNS change. In most cases, this would be an invisible change to the user of the system or service. Records can be created for services such as VPN, web e-mail, and special sites for specific users. In the ZoneTransfer.me example, we not only see these types of services, but also a record for a staging system and FQDNs that would probably never be guessed and would remain unknown to those not seeking them.

With a closer examination of the resource record types from ZoneTransfer.me, there are a few records that stick out, the TXT resources.

```
zonetransfer.me.  301  IN  TXT  "Remember to call or e-mail Pippa on
+44 123 4567890 or pippa@zonetransfer.me when making DNS changes"
zonetransfer.me.  301  IN  TXT  "google-site-verification=tyP28J7JAUHA
9fw2sHXMgcCC0I6XBmmoVi04VlMewxA"
info.zonetransfer.me.  7200  IN  TXT  "ZoneTransfer.me service
provided by Robin Wood - robin@digininja.org. See www.digininja.org/
projects/zonetransferme.php for more information."
dzc.zonetransfer.me.  7200  IN  TXT  "AbCdEfG"
```

As you can see from the output, there is specific information contained in these `.txt` files that probably should not be public. It looks like the owner of DNS is Pippa and we can also see all the contact information for Pippa to request changes to DNS. This could easily be used maliciously if it was real data. Initially, the assumption by the DNS administrator is that no-one will see this information and this is a relatively safe location to put the information.

The important thing to note about the usage of TXT records is that the data leakage may give too much information that can be used in a malicious manner against the enterprise. Information provided in this example not only provides system administrator information but also information for Google site verification and could lead to exploitation by creative means.

The DNS server administrator was probably not thinking a zone transfer would give up so much information that could be used to attack the organization. DNS records should only contain information needed to resolve IP addresses to domain names.

DNSSEC

Security extensions added to the DNS protocol make up the **Internet Engineering Task Force (IETF) DNS Security (DNSSEC)** specification. The purpose of DNSSEC is to provide security for specific information components of the DNS protocol in an effort to provide authenticity to the DNS information. This is important, because some of the most well known hacks of recent times were actually DNS attacks and systems were never hacked as clients were simply redirected to another website. However, if clients can be directed to a site that resolves a domain name they entered, then they have reached a compromised website in their minds. This is **DNS poisoning**, where the DNS information on the Internet is poisoned with false information, allowing attackers to direct clients to whatever IP address on the Internet they desire.

The importance of DNSSEC is that it is intended to give the recipient DNS server confidence in the source of the DNS records or resolver data that it receives. Another benefit is users of DNS, have some protection that ensures their information is not altered or poisoned, and users intending to access their systems will get to the correct Internet destination.

E-mail

An essential method of communication for the enterprise today is e-mail. The requirement to send and receive e-mails with the expectation to respond to it as instantaneously as instant messaging makes this service a critical business function. With the increased growth and acceptance of cloud-based services, e-mail is amongst the first to be leveraged. Some enterprises are taking advantage of the low cost option to move their e-mail implementation to the cloud. This, however, introduces some challenges for not only the control of the e-mail and data within, but filtering unwanted e-mails. While some cloud services have impressive SPAM detection and mitigation, the enterprise may want to augment this with a solution they have some control over. The next sections will cover common e-mail threats and present methods to secure e-mail from SPAM and SPAM relaying.

SPAM filtering

E-mail is one of the most popular methods to spread malware or lead users to malware hosted on the Internet. Most often, this is the single intent of unwanted e-mails in the form of SPAM. Threats from e-mail SPAM range from annoying and unsolicited ads to well-crafted socially engineered e-mails that steal credentials and install malicious malware.

Methods to protect the enterprise from SPAM include cloud-based and local SPAM filtering at the network layer and host-based solutions at the client. A combination of these methods can prove to be most effective at reducing the risk and annoyance of SPAM. Receiving SPAM and becoming the source of SPAM while being used as a relay are two sides to the same coin, and the challenge most focused on by e-mail administrators and IT security.

SPAM filtering in the cloud

Cloud-based solutions offer an attractive option for protecting the enterprise from this nuisance. The service works by configuring the DNS **mail record** (**MX**) to identify the service provider's e-mail servers. This configuration forces all e-mails destined to e-mail addresses owned by the enterprise through the SPAM solution filtering systems before forwarding to the final enterprise servers and user mailbox. Outbound mail from the enterprise would take the normal path to the destination as configured, to use DNS to find the destination domain email server IP address.

With this solution, there can be a significant cost depending on how the service fee structure is designed. The benefits include little-to-no administration of the solution, reduced SPAM e-mail traffic, reduced malware and other threats propagated through e-mails. Some caveats include lack of visibility into what filters are implemented, what e-mail has been blocked, service failure can mean no e-mail or undesirable delay, and potential cost associated with the service.

Here is an example of what an email SPAM filtering solution looks like in the cloud:

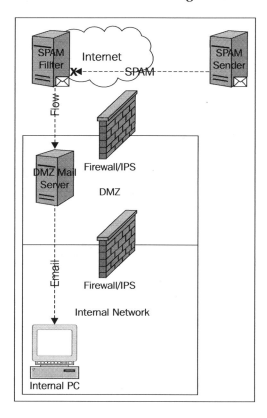

The following questions should be answered when making a decision to select a cloud-based SPAM service:

- Is there a cost benefit of using the solution? (Consider capital and operating expense including people and processes that must be in place.)
- How will the enterprise be informed if an e-mail is blocked? Will there be a list of e-mails to ensure there are no false positives?

- What happens if the service fails? Is there an internal SLA on the e-mail service?

- Are there contract restrictions, forcing the use of the service for a defined period of time?

- What is the reputation of the provider? Is there a low false-error rate?

Local SPAM filtering

The enterprise may decide to perform SPAM filtering locally to maintain complete control over this critical communication method. There are several solutions that are able to provide SPAM filtering and e-mail encryption in one appliance. This may play a role in the enterprise data loss prevention and secure file transfer strategies, providing more than just SPAM filtering. However, if the enterprise opts to leverage a cloud-based e-mail solution, local e-mail security mechanisms may have no place in the new e-mail communication flow.

In the case of web-based e-mail hosting, the SSL connection would be from the user's browser or e-mail client to the hosted e-mail servers. SSL decryption could be possible, but the overhead and privacy implications should be weighed carefully to ensure that additional cost is not incurred with little benefit to the enterprise. There are differing views on SSL decryption. Technically, decrypting SSL by presenting a false certificate in order to snoop, breaks SSL theory and is considered a man-in-the-middle attack. The position taken by each enterprise must be based on the risk determined by the enterprise based on users, data, and access level.

Local SPAM filtering leverages an appliance that receives e-mails from Internet sources, and then analyzes incoming messages and attachments for offenses to configured policies, and forwards e-mails to local e-mail servers if assessed as safe to forward. In order to maintain the best protection against emerging SPAM threats, the vendor will continuously update the appliance to include new block list updates and signatures. An additional benefit of having the service locally is the ability to also own the DNS infrastructure that tells other e-mail systems where to send e-mail. In the event of appliance failure, e-mails can be routed around the failure using DNS to maintain the e-mail service.

An assessment for operational feasibility should be completed prior to making the decision to locally detect and mitigate SPAM.

The following diagram is a depiction of what local SPAM filtering may look like for an enterprise:

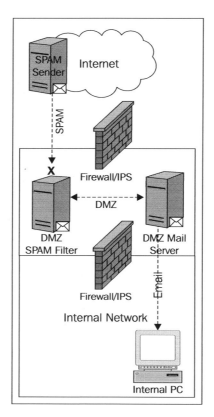

The following questions should be answered when making a decision on local SPAM protection:

- Can the solution provide a user-controlled quarantine? (Users can remove erroneously blocked e-mails.)
- Does the solution have a bypass feature?
- How often is the appliance updated?
- How easy is it to view blocked or quarantined e-mails?
- Are there additional email security features available such as encryption?

SPAM relaying

Misconfiguration of the enterprise mail servers may lead to exploitation in the form of using the servers as a SPAM relay. This method uses the server's lack of sender authentication and capability to send e-mails from domains which it does not have authority to send e-mail. Unfortunately, this misconfiguration is common for Internet facing e-mail systems where the only authentication would need to be the internal mail relay. It is common for internal servers to have misconfiguration due to the requirement of non-human processes that must be able to send e-mails, such as the alerting mechanism on a security system.

Instead of creating accounts for every possible system that would need this authorization, it is easier to allow anyone to send e-mails through the mail server. The internal server should still have restrictions on sending domains, to avoid the system being misused to send SPAM or other spoofed e-mails.

To test the enterprise mail servers for relaying capability, use telnet and connect to the mail server on port 25. Once connected, use the available commands and attempt to send an e-mail from an e-mail domain that the enterprise does not have authority to send e-mail from; for example test@acme.com. If this is allowed, the server is misconfigured and relaying is possible. Once this server is identified on the Internet, it is likely to be exploited for this capability. The enterprise may be at risk of becoming the source of SPAM and can therefore be blocked by services such as SPAMHAUS. To check for blocked status, visit the SPAMHAUS Block List page at http://www.spamhaus.org/lookup/.

Another method to reduce the enterprise's likelihood of ending up on a SPAM block list is to ensure that only the enterprise e-mail servers are permitted to send e-mails via TCP port 25 outbound from the enterprise network. Some malware is specifically designed to blast e-mail SPAM from the infected system, thus getting the enterprise blocked by services such as SPAMHAUS.

The following diagram presents the correct and incorrect methods to implement e-mail controls at the firewall to ensure that only the internal mail servers are able to directly send e-mails to the Internet. This method reduces the potential impact of end system malware, designed to send SPAM from inside the network, potentially getting the enterprise blocked on SPAM lists.

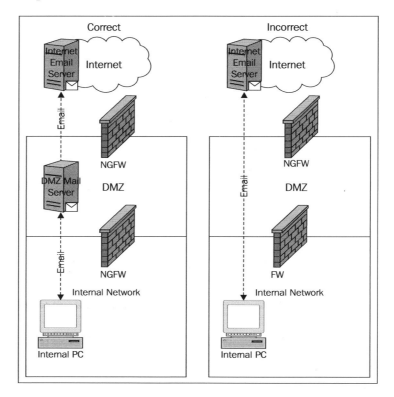

File transfer

Getting data to and from the enterprise network is not only a convenience, but also many times is a necessity to facilitate business operations. There are many protocols and methods that are viable options; FTP, SFTP, FTPS, SSH, and SSL to name a few standard protocols with many more proprietary options available too.

The migration to secure protocols has been driven primarily by security standards such as PCI DSS, ISO 27001, and NIST, though adoption has been dismal for enterprises that lack a third-party audit requirement. One of the challenges with file transfer is secure implementation. Not only should the protocols be secure, but the design must also adhere to network and security architecture, to ensure that any compromise is limited and to enforce control over file transfer.

Implementation considerations

Imagine what security challenges may be inherent with the ability to use uncontrolled encrypted file transfer from a user's desktop to any Internet destination. Essentially, an implementation, as described, would circumvent most network-based security controls.

A method to ensure secure communication and the ability to control what is transferred and to whom is to implement an intermediary transfer host. The ideal location of the host would be the DMZ to enforce architecture and limit the scope of compromise. The solution should also require authentication to be used and the user list audited regularly, for both voluntarily and involuntarily terminated employees.

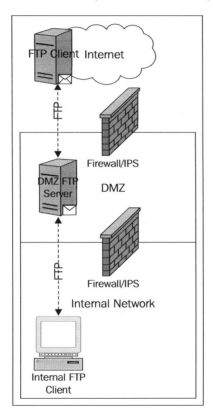

Secure file transfer protocols

Not all enterprises that have implemented secure protocols use a secure file transfer. In some cases, this is by design such as credit card authorizers, where the risk has been accepted due to the overhead and complexity of managing secure communications for a high number of clients. Design may have nothing to do with the lack of secure communication capabilities. It may not be a priority as the enterprise may not have to perform any type of risk analysis on the business process or may remain ignorant to the idea of risk associated with the use of insecure file transfer and business critical data.

It can be challenging to implement a secure transfer solution, especially if not using an SSL implementation where encryption can be managed by certificates, which are both inexpensive and easy to implement. Not to mention, almost everyone knows how to use a browser to upload a file. In instances where SSH or SFTP is used, this can be more complicated to provide authentication and encryption.

User authentication

For SSH, SFTP, and other such protocols, there are two methods of authentication, namely user credentials and keys. For user authentication, the enterprise must configure either locally or using directory services, such as Windows Active Directory for users that can access the service. Both have security implications. For local accounts, the fact that they are locally stored on the server may leave them vulnerable to compromise even if hashed in the Linux /etc/shadow file or SAM on Windows. The system administrator will also have to manually manage user credentials on each and every system configured.

For systems that rely on a central user directory, the implementation must be thought out to ensure that any compromise of the system does not lead to a compromise of the internal user directory. Some enterprises implement a unique user directory to be used for services in the DMZ to enforce segregation of directories, with the ability to limit the scope of a compromise while centralizing administration for multiple systems and services.

An alternate method for authentication is to use **Simple Public Key Infrastructure (SPKI)**. This method is used with PGP. The design of the SPKI is based on trust determined by the owner, and if the owner chooses to trust another, then the other will be given a public key that is mathematically related to the owner's private key. This private-public key combination can be used for authenticating systems, applications, and users.

In our example, a user is issued a key that provides user authentication. When the SSH session is started, the receiving system checks to see if there is a trusted key for authentication being presented. If there is a match, the authentication is successful. The keys must be protected on the system that generated the private key. The benefit is that the key can be used in an application and referenced in a script where using credentials in this case should be avoided.

User Internet access

Internal user access to the Internet is probably deemed a much more critical service than even e-mails. Calls to the helpdesk will happen faster if access to Facebook is down versus a critical business application. With so much focus on the use of this technology, it must be secured and monitored to provide a safe use of the Wild West Internet, reducing the risk this threat vector presents.

In order to provide some level of security and monitoring, the use of Internet proxy technology is required. A proxy accepts a connection from a client, such as an internal host, and makes the connection to the final destination on behalf of the client. This allows the true identity of the client to be protected and provides the ability to filter Internet traffic for inappropriate sites, for example.

There are standalone proxy solutions and the aforementioned NGFWs have this feature, which allows for URL filtering based on category and known malicious destinations. Depending on the implementation, various features can be utilized with the NGFW that are not an option with some standalone proxy solutions; for example, features such as advanced application inspection for Internet threats and malware. If an NGFW is implemented, providing Internet proxy at this control point may be desirable to reduce complexity and gain features including user authentication.

Standalone proxies typically have the option to perform user authentication, but lack more advanced security features. It should be noted that proxy solutions without the ability to inspect Internet traffic for advanced threats typically have a mechanism to send traffic to a third-party system for inspection prior to sending the traffic to the Internet destination.

There are cases that require a purpose built proxy solution to provide advanced proxy capabilities, such as **Proxy Auto-Configuration (PAC)** files that control which connections use the proxy and which are routed directly. This is a feature that is lacking today in most NGFW solutions. To make the best selection, understand the requirements for Internet access, protection, and monitoring to ensure that the solutions considered are capable of meeting the defined requirements.

The following diagram presents the incorrect and correct method to providing Internet access to internal systems:

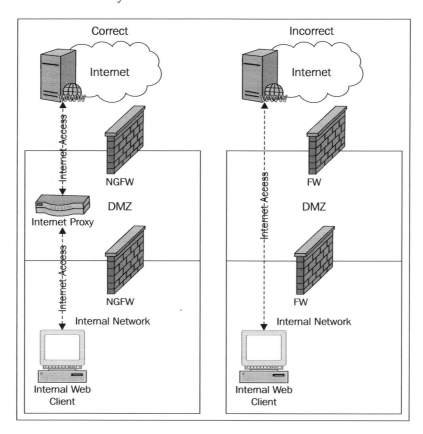

Some enterprise networks do not have a proxy solution, and Internet access is facilitated directly from the client to the Internet destination. These implementations are typically where most malware is successful, purely due to the lack of security and monitoring. Using SPAM and leveraging social engineering techniques, internal users can be directed to websites that automatically install malware, some of which can go undetected by anti-virus installed on end systems.

At a minimum, an Internet proxy is recommended to monitor and block access to known malicious sites and sites that may introduce varying levels of risk to the enterprise. It is recommended to have a layered approach to Internet access, where data is inspected not only for malicious content but critical enterprise data that may indicate a compromise.

Websites

Internet accessible websites are the most targeted asset on the Internet due to common web application security issues, such as SQL injection, cross-site scripting, and cross-site request forgery. There are several approaches to securing websites, but it is truly a layered security approach requiring a combination of secure coding, web application firewalls, and other security mechanisms that will provide the most benefit. We'll take a look at methods to secure Internet accessible websites.

Secure coding

The website would not exist without the web application. Technically, a website does not constitute a web application, but even the simplest one has a contact form, or search function. These are examples of web applications that perform a function to collect and store visitor data when the contact form is completed and submitted, and the **search** function searches the web content stored in a database, such as MySQL, Oracle, or MSSQL. The web application is the link between the user and the data where it is stored, and any mistake or security oversight in the development of the web application can have grave consequences.

Secure coding is not a natural tendency for developers as they are mainly tasked with developing applications with business requested functions and features. Without a security check during the development phase, critical security vulnerabilities may be coded in the final product. Utilizing a **secure software development lifecycle (S-SDLC)** is the best method to ensure that secure coding practices are being followed. Essentially, the life cycle provides a framework for how the coding process is to be completed with testing and validation of the code. This process is iterative for each new instance of code or modified portions of code.

During the iterative SDLC, developers can and should test their code for security vulnerabilities either in the development or quality assurance phase to ensure that no vulnerabilities or at least only low risk vulnerabilities make it into the code release.

There are several open source and commercial products available for testing not only web applications via web scanning, but source code analysis as well. The tools typically are designed for developer use, but it is helpful to have IT security personnel who understand development and common web application programming languages. IT security involvement can help remediation efforts if the development team is unclear of the tool's output and how to remediate vulnerabilities.

When using tools to test web application code for vulnerabilities, the reporting capabilities should be tested to determine which product meets the requirements of the enterprise by first understanding how the data is to be shared and with whom. Ownership of the tool should technically reside with the development team but with oversight from the IT security team to ensure that the SDLC process is being followed and to independently assess the effectiveness of the SDLC. Ultimately, vulnerabilities identified should be documented and tracked through remediation within a centralized vulnerability or defect management solution.

Secure coding must be the focal point of the security strategy for securing web applications; if not, there must be a shift to this model to have a truly layered defense against cyber attacks. There is a limit to the protection of using only third-party solutions versus securing the code. Any misconfiguration of these other tools exposes the vulnerable application where the vulnerability should have been fixed.

Next generation firewalls

We have already covered the next generation firewall (NGFW) earlier in the chapter, but this section warrants further discussion, as it pertains to leveraging the NGFW to protect Internet-facing enterprise websites and applications. Threats within seemingly benign connection attempts to the web servers can be detected and mitigated with the application aware firewall. By enforcing strict access to applications necessary to provide the service to Internet users, risk is greatly reduced for other applications running on the server and the underlying operating system. A benefit of using a next generation firewall is that access can be provisioned by applications, such as web browsing, and is not restricted by TCP port. This requires more intelligence and a deeper inspection of communication.

Filtering all inbound traffic at the firewall can also alleviate system resource consumption from bursting traffic loads on the web servers, by inspecting and mitigating all illegitimate traffic, such as denial of service attacks, before they reach the web servers. This implementation, in addition to secure coding, will provide additional protection for Internet-facing web servers and applications. It should be noted that NGFW alone is not sufficient for protection for web applications, but a layer in the security protection mechanism is. There is a lack of in-depth application capability and detection beyond basic attack types with no protection for database interaction.

IPS

Intrusion prevention may also be implemented at the network perimeter to mitigate known attack patterns for web applications and the underlying operating system. Typically, IPS detection and mitigation engines have limited intelligence apart from the typical patterns found in the malicious payload of SQL injection attacks and other popular attacks. The lack of in-depth web application behavior and accepted communications can lead to a high number of false positives, however, IPS can provide excellent denial of service protection and block exploit callbacks.

 With the capabilities found in NGFW, a standalone IPS may not be a viable protection mechanism investment to protect the web infrastructure if the capability is enabled in the NGFW. There are various schools of thought on standalone or integrated IPS and there are logical reasons for each. This book does not purposely attempt to endorse one method over the other.

Web application firewall

Web application firewalls are designed to specifically mitigate attacks against web applications through pattern and behavioral analysis. The primary detection and mitigation capabilities include attacks against known web application vulnerabilities, such as SQL injection, cross-site scripting, command injection, and misconfigurations. More advanced web application firewalls use another component at the database tier of the web applications, which is either installed on the database server or proxies inbound connections. This is important for a couple of reasons.

First, it is hard to determine if a detected threat warrants further investigation, if it is unknown whether the threat was able to interact with the database. The database is key as it serves as the data repository for the web application and may house sensitive information such as customer information, credit card numbers, and intellectual property, for example, product information. All this important data must be accessible to the web application for the service being provided.

Second, attacks that do get past the first layer of the web application firewall can be mitigated at the database tier of the network architecture. The database team may not detect a successful database attack through the web application if the team is not trained to identify a successful exploit. Some web application firewall solutions are able to leverage both the tiers of protection to control the alerting of attacks, reducing false positive alerts and meaningless data to manually analyze attacks by the security team.

The most significant benefit of database protection using a web application firewall is the ability to enforce security controls for database access initiated not only by the web application but also by database administrators. This allows strict control of the queries sent to the database whether from the application or a database administration tool. Any deviation from the expected can be blocked, therefore mitigating common database attacks through incorrectly written and configured web applications or misuse. A commercial product leader in this space is **Imperva** (http://www.imperva. com). Their solutions provide comprehensive web attack mitigation and database security through database access and activity management capabilities.

There may be confusion with the difference in protection capabilities of NGFW and a specialized web application firewall. An NGFW will perform very basic mitigation of common web application attacks at the perimeter; there is no database protection. Additionally, the NGFW typically is not capable of advanced customization and configuration specific to the environment where it is deployed. This is where the web application firewall exhibits the benefit of a specialized solution designed for web application and database protection.

Web application firewalls should be considered as an important layer in the defense strategy to mitigate web application threats and provide the much needed database security in the enterprise.

Network segmentation

A network can have the most sophisticated security mechanisms implemented, but without network segmentation, their value will be greatly undermined, if not invalidated. Internal segmentation is often overlooked, because focus is on the external threat. Unfortunately, the external threat is counting on weak internal network segmentation to spread malware throughout the enterprise and gain a foothold for exfiltration of critical enterprise data.

Significant investment has been made in **network access control** (**NAC**) and perimeter technologies, meanwhile the latest threat introduced to the network through a trusted host is wreaking havoc on internal client systems and the most critical systems in the enterprise. The need to segment the user base of systems from server systems is a must; or else any slight deviation of the end client security posture can put the entire enterprise at risk.

More advanced threats are introduced through infected consultant systems on the network or the unauthorized introduction of personal devices to the network and business-critical applications. In order to protect critical assets from external as well as internal threats, consideration should be given to secured segmentation within the internal network. With business initiatives, such as BYOD, more enterprises are segmenting their networks to secure critical assets and infrastructure.

Network segmentation strategy

Before any network segmentation can occur, critical data, processes, applications, and systems must be identified and thoroughly documented. Understanding what these assets are and how they communicate with other applications and systems will help determine the complexities of moving the assets to a network segment separated by a firewall. Simple VLAN separation does not provide any additional security and has only dismal advantage with the use of access control lists. Within the segmented network may be further segmentation, as network and security architecture are applied to the assets of value.

Asset identification

To determine what assets must and should be placed in the securely segmented network, assets have to be identified and prioritized based on criticality to the enterprise. We covered the need to identify all data, processes, applications, users, and roles to determine the trust level and therefore any controls that need to be implemented and enforced by policy and standards in *Chapter 2, Security Architectures*, and *Chapter 3, Security as a Process*.

It is important to identify systems and applications that will cause significant business operational impact or detriment to the existence of the enterprise if the asset is temporarily unavailable, unavailable for an extended time, or destroyed. Systems and applications that can have the most impact, if they are affected in some negative manner, should be the assets with this highest priority for segmentation and have the most security implemented to protect them.

Clearly defining and documenting the necessary network communications required for each system and application will increase the success of this significant undertaking. This exercise may also identify design weaknesses or poor implementation that can be remediated prior to moving assets into the secured segment. Once the trust model building blocks are developed, the driver for asset prioritization and security control requirements for the segmented network can be defined.

Security mechanisms

The internal segmented network (requires a firewall) is the simplest network-based security control for critical assets in the enterprise network. With this being stated, there are highly recommended security monitoring tools, such as **Security Information and Event Management (SIEM)** and **File Integrity Monitoring (FIM)**, that should be implemented to ensure that in the event of an attack or lack of availability there is monitoring for early detection and timely incident response. Because this area of the network is home to the most critical assets of the enterprise, additional security tools, such as intrusion prevention, should certainly be a consideration for implementation either standalone or within an NGFW.

In some cases, leveraging data loss prevention tools may be ideal to protect against data leakage due to unauthorized access or misuse of privilege. This segment should be treated as if the enterprise depends on its security and availability. Selection of protection methods may vary and complexity is limited by network design and internal politics. Be sure to perform risk analysis and security testing to validate the design and implementation.

Applying security architecture to the network

The shift of security architecture to a data-centric model versus a network access-centric model confuses the method in which we have continued to approach securing the network perimeter. We have marched to the same wisdom of a DMZ sandwiched between firewalls or now the same firewall with multiple interfaces. This network design addresses network connectivity and is non-important for real data protection. While it is true, the basic low skill attacks will be stopped, but we have seen that this design does not thwart even the semi-sophisticated attack methods. The reason is because the data is not protected, but the network perimeter is.

While it is important to protect the network and implement segmentation via firewalls, we cannot stop here to protect our network assets. If we approach the systems as storage for data, we can overlay our trust models to enforce authorized access methods that can be much more agile than the typical DMZ, business partner zone, or remote access network architecture. Do you recall the section in *Chapter 2, Security Architectures*, where I suggested that security architecture has been robbed of its individuality by basically working only within the confines of network architecture? Security architecture is a distinctly different practice with differing rationale and therefore needs to be aware of the network design, but the network is merely transport; let's not elevate it to be the primary defender of our network and assets.

Security architecture in the DMZ

Typically, the DMZ access is tightly restricted for inbound connections; however, outbound connections can be a little more lax. This is because from the network architecture perspective, traffic leaves and does not pose the risk of a possible inbound attack. From a security perspective, the concern may be more about what is leaving than what is coming in, after all, a firewall and IPS protect the majority of the inbound network at the perimeter.

Firewall policy, however, does leverage security architecture if closely examined. An example is HTTP connections inbound to a web server. First, the firewall rule typically will have an "any" as the source; this is an untrusted source, per our trust models. The second configuration will be a specific destination or set of destinations that represent the web servers, and lastly the specific TCP port 80 or application HTTP will be defined. Some of what is configured at the network perimeter is inherently security architecture defined in network security appliances.

To take this a step further, let's apply this same logic to each host in the DMZ. Applying trust models at the host and services tiers is where most security-based network architectures end their application. Flexibility is lost when agile security architecture is not applied. Several instances of the same application may be stood up to support different user groups, just because the systems have to reside in certain portions of the network, based solely on the user of the system. In this case, defining all user types for the known data and applications will form the basis for the trust models to be applied; there will be a model for each user type defined.

Security architecture in the internal network

The internal network should technically not be treated any different than a DMZ from the security architecture perspective. Just because a host is on the internal network does not vouch for its trustworthiness. From my experience, the internal network is still soft and an extremely vulnerable portion of the network that gets little attention. I am not stating that the internal network has to be locked down like Fort Knox; only if proper network segmentation does not exist and a proper perspective of risk exists based on an analysis.

Internal network hosts should be treated as trusted as they can be, depending on what controls are implemented on the hosts themselves. The key to internal network security architecture is enforcement and monitoring. The initial implementation will be very clean, but over time, things get messy and, before you know it, the user groups on systems are a mess. All the restrictions and controls in place serve as nothing more than a management nightmare with no security value being realized.

This is found more on the internal network, because enterprises have a somewhat blind trust for all things on the internal network, yet we find breaches occurring through data exfiltration due to misconfiguration of security controls on internal hosts. Security must be applied uniformly to have the intended impact of securing the enterprise.

Security architecture and internal segmentation

Internal network segmentation using a firewall (only real segmentation; VLANs don't count, sorry) is a mix of the DMZ and internal network implementation of the security architecture. One significant use of internally segmented networks is that we can terminate business partner and other third-party access to services and various assets. The purpose behind this method is to limit the scope of compromise so long as the network communications are restrictive for both inbound and outbound directions.

There are some compliance standards that offer audit scope reduction through segmenting certain environments from the internal network, such as PCI DSS's recommendation to segment the cardholder data network. Other great resources that cover best practices for network security include NIST 800 series Publications, SANS Consensus Audit Guidelines, and the ISO 27001/2 standards.

The internal segment may have web, application, and database tiers much like a DMZ for critical internal business processes accessible to internal and other third-parties. The flexibility of our presented security architecture would only differentiate these user types by access level, maybe. This is the benefit of the trust model based security architecture. It doesn't matter much where the asset resides, who or what is accessing the asset, as long as there is a standard method to implement the security architecture.

Summary

In this chapter, we covered the various security mechanisms typically deployed to protect the enterprise network from threats. We also presented methods to secure the common network services e-mail, DNS, file transfer, and Internet access to avoid costly implementation mistakes. In the securing websites section, we covered leveraging a layered security approach to ensure coverage with a focus on secure coding and database encryption.

Network segmentation was presented as a method to protect internal critical assets from both internal and external threats. The flexibility of trust-based security architecture was presented for securing both internal and external access to the enterprise assets. We explored the three most common network areas, the DMZ, internal network, and internally segmented network, finding ways to simplify implementation and manage security with agile security architecture.

In the next chapter, we will cover securing systems in the enterprise from the data-centric security architecture approach.

5
Securing Systems

This chapter will introduce organization processes and methods that can be used to secure enterprise computer systems. The systems that we will focus on in this chapter are server systems that are used within the enterprise to conduct business functions. Processes and methods covered are system classification, system protection using anti-virus, host-based intrusion prevention system (HIPS), file integrity monitoring (FIM), and user account management. Additionally, challenges of implementation and opportunities to improve protection of systems will be covered. Each solution in this chapter should be independently evaluated to determine its value and suitability for purchase and implementation within the organization. There are several ways to approach system security, but to be effective, the approach must be in line with the defined security architecture based on the presented trust models. Some of the solutions provide better security advantage than others, and the consideration of layering technologies versus agile and lightweight implementation can be very effective in well-documented and mature environments. Lastly, the operational overhead of each solution has to be identified and proper staffing and supporting processes need to be put in place in order to ensure effective implementation of the solution.

This chapter will cover the following topics:

- Identifying critical enterprise computer systems
- Methods to secure enterprise computer systems
- Enforcing security policies on computer systems

System classification

In the previous chapter, we covered network segmentation and placing systems of high value and criticality to the enterprise in segmented areas of the network. In order to identify these systems, it is necessary to understand the important business processes and applications to determine what hosts maintain both. As with any classification model, there should be tiers based on criticality. There will be several "important" systems, but some are truly critical to business operations and others can be offline for a longer period before business is affected. The tiers of classification should have a criteria for each level to ensure all security and availability requirements are met as per the defined tier such as the business processes impacted. The tier classification may also include service-level agreement information based on how the system is to be connected to the network, expected recovery times, and the priority of security incidents involving the systems. The system labels applied will need to serve as an input to the overall security architecture and be referenced in other business processes such as change management, user account management, protection tool selection, monitoring, and incident response.

A system classification model may look like the following table.

Level	Classification	Process(es)/Function(s)	Requirement
1	Critical	Transaction processing, Deposit functions	Network redundancy, File integrity monitoring, User monitoring, Encryption
2	High	Payroll processing	Network redundancy, User monitoring
3	Medium	Customer e-mail promotion functions	Network redundancy
4	Low	Corporate communication processes	N/A

Individual systems will not be identified in the table, only processes or functions are. Labeling of the systems should happen in an asset management tool or a **configuration management database (CMDB)** if using the ITIL framework. The CMDB is the central database repository and the authoritative source of all assets and associated change information in a mature change management implementation. The complexity of the system classification model is dependent on the needs of the organization including any external auditing requirements. The enterprise may also decide to create a classification for systems that have regulatory compliance requirements for specific controls to be implemented. This is a good method to ensure these systems are always implemented in the same manner based on standards developed from the classification model. The model should generally mention technologies to be implemented along with required controls. Remaining non-specific is a good practice for policies and classification models; specifics can be provided in related standards.

Implementation considerations

Depending on the budget structure, required controls and network connectivity may increase the cost of implementation and should be well defined. Some considerations may include redundant network connections, additional installed monitoring tools, forensic tools, and operational expenses for security-specific capabilities. These items may not only incur additional costs to purchase, but increasing system resources for dual home connections to the network and increased memory and CPU must also be considered. The security cost of doing business should be included in every system build based on its classification.

Implementing and managing system users in adherence to the trust model and associated policies and standards should involve an identity and access management process for enforcement of user access controls. User authentication, authorization, and accounting should be implemented uniformly across all systems for complete audit data collection and post-incident forensic analysis. The more mature this process is, the easier it will be to maintain and defend during an audit if this is a required enterprise exercise.

System classification should be the basis for the location of the system within the enterprise network, security controls required, monitoring requirements, availability, and incident response priority. Though the network boundaries are constantly being redefined, there should be a segmented network to provide a more secure portion of the network for systems with high and critical classification. The segmented portion of the network may be where the most sophisticated security controls are implemented, as loss realized for other systems within the network may not have a significant risk of impact to warrant additional capital and operational expense to protect. It is important that, as in the case with data classification, system classification must be adopted by all IT groups and understood by the enterprise business units. Having a system classification will simplify implementation of security controls for important business systems and provide a solid basis for policies and standards for enforcement and consistent implementation.

System management

An important part of securing systems and properly applying security architecture is proper system management. This is the process of inventory management, system labeling indicating system classification, system owners, and required security control mechanisms. Based on the classification of a system, patching requirements can be documented and enforced through policy. System management can also play a significant role in the change management process by ensuring that the security posture of the system is maintained through all expected changes. The next two sections will cover the importance of asset inventory and proper labeling of systems for security architecture implementation.

Asset inventory labels

Once systems have been properly classified, asset inventory labels must reflect the classification to ensure the correct controls are in place and that policies and standards are enforced. Asset inventory management is critical to the overall security posture of the organization because critical systems will be properly inventoried and all pertinent information will be documented for securing and monitoring the assets. Without asset inventory there is no record of what systems exist, what data is located on the systems, and the risk introduced by the improper securing or loss of the systems. Leveraging the asset inventory function of the CMDB is critical for the change management process to ensure security controls are not intentionally or accidentally disabled or circumvented. Communication of the system classification labels must be a part of the organization's security awareness initiatives, understood by IT, and enforced.

System patching

System patching may be based on criticality of the system, the severity of the vulnerability, or impact of an unpatched software package. System classification should play a significant role in the patching cycle of systems and should be integrated in the patch and vulnerability management processes. The importance of system patching cannot be overstressed with the current threat landscape where the method of attacking dated vulnerabilities is still very successful. When systems remain unpatched and vulnerabilities continue to exist, the window is also extended for malicious actors to exploit. With other weaknesses in the network such as lack of segmentation, systems may be at greater risk when a strict patching cycle is not implemented. As with other components of the system classification model, patching requirements must be documented, communicated, and measured to be effective.

File integrity monitoring

File integrity monitoring (FIM) is one way to detect changes to a known filesystem's files, and in the case of Windows, the registry. Typically, when a system has malicious activity, either changes are made to existing files or harmful files are placed in critical areas of the filesystem. In order to detect these changes, FIM tools create a hash database of the known good versions of files in each filesystem location. The tool can then periodically or real-time scan the filesystem looking for any changes to the installation including known files and directories. Hashing is used because any variation in the file will result in a different hash value, and therefore confirm there has been a change to the file, directory, or registry. The tool will then create an event that will need to be reviewed to ensure the detected addition, removal, or modification was expected. If yes, then the reviewer can comment and accept the new hash as the new baseline. Any subsequent scan for changes will use the newly accepted artifact version as the baseline. If the change was not expected, the reviewer can investigate to determine if the source of the change was malicious or an undocumented and unapproved change by a system administrator. Some tools in this space can rollback a detected change if malicious or unapproved by an internal change management process.

An example of calculating a hash for a file is shown in the following screenshot. I have created a file and entered text, then calculated the MD5 hash with the MD5 tool using the md5 test.txt command at the command prompt. This tool is native to OSX and Linux, but may need to be installed in Windows.

```
Aarons-MacBook-Pro:~ aaron$ md5 test.txt
MD5 (test.txt) = 4221d002ceb5d3c9e9137e495ceaa647
```

I then added more text modifying the file itself so a new hash would be generated indicating the modification of the original file. You will notice that the next screenshot has a different MD5 hash for the same file because it was modified. Note that changing the filename does not affect the calculated MD5 sum; the tool only detected content changes. More complex FIM tools have the option of detecting several attributes including timestamps, name, content, and permissions.

```
Aarons-MacBook-Pro:~ aaron$ md5 test.txt
MD5 (test.txt) = 7e3fd1d231d26666538a0be78a9cdc60
```

It is plausible to assume that this type of tool would need significant tuning to reduce false positives for actions such as a login to Windows. Typically, files and directories that change frequently should not be monitored to reduce tool output. An example of a file type that is not optimal to monitor is a log file. Log files are typically written to on a frequent basis and the hash would also change causing a flag in the FIM tool. Trial and error may be used to determine the areas of the filesystem that are prone to frequent and expected changes and can be set to be ignored by the tool. Exercise some caution, however, when doing this. For example, when using Metasploit (hacking tool) persistence in Windows there are two areas affected, the registry autorun key and the Windows temp directory. It is common to ignore these areas and malicious hackers are aware of this, so this is where changes are commonly made, hoping they will not be noticed, while a foothold on the system is established. Some tools will have these areas monitored but will set them to auto accept and are available for forensic purposes. The primary use case for FIM is enforcing review of changes to business critical systems and in the case of PCI DSS to enforce a review of system changes where credit card numbers are stored, processed, and transmitted.

Implementation considerations

A caveat to using this type of tool is the accidental addition of malware or unapproved configuration added to the system baseline. This renders the protection ineffective because now the baseline is tainted and the malware may go undetected. This is also true for unapproved configurations that may be harmful to the security posture of the system. FIM is not only a security tool, but is required by PCI DSS and can determine if a system is compliant to the standard. Some FIM solutions have the capability to run checks and provide reporting for configuration compliance to PCI, SOX, CIS, and other standards, which can be a compliance benefit to running the tool.

Because this type of tool is used heavily for compliance, it is often implemented widespread without any emphasis on the critical systems, and too much data is generated to be actionable. Another challenge is that on some operating systems, a simple action such as changing permissions on a directory or adding a user to a group, will generate a very cryptic output that is not humanly understandable or actionable. Filtering out these instances, yet capturing meaningful data, is a very intensive exercise that will take time to tweak and get buy-in from system owners who are responsible for reviewing the output. It may be possible to reduce system controls through the use of FIM reducing both the capital and operational expense of securing enterprise systems.

Implementing FIM

FIM is an excellent tool to detect changes to the filesystem including installed applications. This can be ideal in scenarios that require an application folder to be monitored to make sure the application is not rooted or manipulated in some way. As stated before, the challenge to getting value out of this type of tool is the rate of change a system may go through for standard operation. This may cause a significant number of non-event alerts that will need to be investigated and deemed OK and ignored in further scans, or place a threshold to reduce alerts. It is important to think like a malicious person would and double check your logic before disabling every noisy item in FIM; this could lead to undetected compromise of a system.

The general architecture of FIM solutions is a console and an agent deployment to provide detection and policy checking. The agent can typically run in two modes, real-time and manual. In real-time mode, the local agent is constantly looking for add, delete, and modification actions on the system and will report findings to the console in near real-time. The manual mode will sit idle and when the console initiates the scan of the system, the local agent will run and report findings since the last run. Both solutions have their advantages and disadvantages. The basic architecture is depicted in the following diagram:

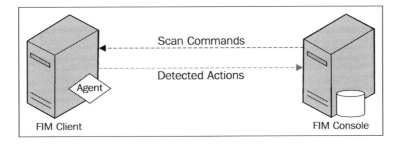

Real-time FIM

Using FIM in real-time mode has several advantages, but the constant running of the tool may be taxing to a system that is loaded with several agents for various purposes. The primary advantage to real-time mode is exactly this; all add, delete, and modification actions are detected in real time allowing for almost immediate ability to review and remediate. However, this capability must be carefully weighed to ensure the changes can be reviewed in a timely manner and that the rate of change is not so high that the alerts are overwhelming. The ability to detect actions faster can be of great benefit in the instance there is malicious action, reducing a possible malware persistence or lateral intrusion. This method will require constant monitoring or the use of another technology such as a SIEM solution to provide some intelligence, threshold, and meaningful notification of the detected changes.

Manual mode FIM

FIM in a manual mode configuration is the least taxing on the system because the scans only run when the console initiates the scan either adhoc or on a schedule. The benefit with this implementation is if scans are scheduled, then IT knows when the system may have higher memory and processor utilization and it ideally will not affect business operations. This method also provides an alert dump at the scheduled time versus spontaneously throughout the day as actions are detected. The internal processes used to process FIM output will determine the efficiency of this method. A caveat to this solution is that changes can go undetected for longer periods of time depending on how often scans are run on schedule. The organization will need to ensure that this method is within the accepted risk level and that this process is operationalized enough to meet the intended purpose of FIM. Much like how often anti-virus signatures are updated, the frequency will affect the efficiency.

Application whitelisting

A method to control what applications have permission to run on a system is **application whitelisting**. This method uses the logic that only what is permitted and trusted can run on the system; so if malicious software is installed on the system, it will not be able to execute. This model is closer to the trust model presented in *Chapter 2, Security Architectures*. Once trust is established for the applications on a system their behavior is either permitted or denied. This approach can be more effective than FIM, and with some solutions managing billions of hash baselines for trusted applications, false positives are rare.

Application whitelisting is a proactive approach to malware mitigation on end point systems such as desktops, laptops, and servers. This tool can also prevent unapproved application installs where a system user or owner may inadvertently introduce risk. If the application is not preapproved, the installation can be blocked, and if the installation is successful, the tool can block the application from running.

Due to the proactive nature of this technology, it could possibly replace an anti-virus solution and complement other advanced tools in the network such as advanced persistent threat tools and NGFW to provide a layered mitigation implementation. This protection can occur not only at the OS and application tier, but also on USB drives, and other common sources of malware can be blocked. Though this method is common in data loss prevention tools, this tool category does not analyze data type to decide what is blocked.

Implementation considerations

In order to leverage a tool that provides application whitelisting, analysis will need to occur at the frontend of implementation versus post implementation where the initial baseline occurs, and the continued process of reviewing changes is required to determine what is supposed to be a valid change. This approach alleviates the accidental baseline of malware into an accepted system baseline that would leave the system infected or misconfigured. With application whitelisting, applications will be learned and blocked according to the implemented policy and may be disruptive. The challenge of knowing every application that is permitted to run may be a hard task to accomplish in environments where application inventories are not maintained.

Host-based intrusion prevention system

The **Host-based intrusion prevention system (HIPS)** is very similar in concept to network intrusion prevention in terms of the logic of the tool. The primary difference is the network intrusion prevention tool is responsible for detecting as much as possible across multiple operating system platforms and applications while deployed on the network wire. This is a challenge even in finely-tuned environments because protection of the system asset is a configuration on the network, not the host itself. The host knows what is running, and if there is a network intrusion prevention misconfiguration, the host is still protected by the HIPS. Host-based intrusion prevention leverages being installed on the system it is protecting to actively mitigate threats against running services and applications. This additional awareness of running applications and services can reduce the footprint the HIPS requires because it will only be protecting what is running, not every possible combination, as the typical IPS is deployed. This will reduce alerts that need to be reviewed and confidence that protection moves with the system regardless of where it is moved.

Benefits of this implementation are protection regardless of the state of the network intrusion prevention system and specific protection for what is actually on the system. This reduces false positives and ensures intrusion protection. When there are multiple groups involved with implementing the security of the network and systems, misconfigurations can occur, and generally these occur in the network as the rate of change is generally greater than on a critical system. This is not to say that the network team is less competent, but the reality is security is not the focus of the network; it is moving packets as fast as possible across the infrastructure. A minor access control list tweak or route map modification can cause the complete bypass of the network-based security controls.

Host-based intrusion detection uses the same types of detection methods as the network-based counterpart, and in some cases, leverages application whitelisting techniques. The primary method is signature-based detection as this is the easiest method to implement on a host without taxing the operating system with true behavioral analysis. Though, it should be noted that a combination of methods should be employed for comprehensive protection.

Implementation considerations

In the current state of security, we have been tasked with installing several agents on systems to ensure they are secure or at least protected. Using a HIPS solution is an additional agent that must be installed unless it is a component of the anti-virus installed on the system. If this is the case, the effectiveness may need to be tested as anti-virus-based tools will only protect at a minimal-to-moderate level. This must be considered before HIPS is implemented or positioned as a primary host protection method. As with the intent of all security controls, monitoring and alerting capabilities need to be integrated into the existing response implementation. Another tool implemented requires operational considerations before implementation.

Host firewall

The host firewall can be a great method to filter traffic to and from the system. The effectiveness of this control is dependent on the operating system, location of the system, and policy configuration. For example, the implementation of Windows requires several Windows-specific ports and services to be accessible on the internal network to function within the Windows domain that expose services that may be configured in a vulnerable manner. Whereas with Linux, for instance, the host firewall (iptables) can be very effective in protecting the host and the accessible services as there is no concept of a domain. There is functionality within the Windows firewall to limit the accessibility of the Windows services and it can always be configured in an explicit manner limiting access to services.

Implementation considerations

The host firewall cannot be approached as the primary method of securing services on a system. Each service should be configured in a secure manner as the firewall may or may not provide any real protection depending on the configuration. The firewall should be considered as another layer of defense from intrusion attempts against applications, services, and the host itself. This solution is similar to the application whitelisting in regards to the requirement of knowing what applications are running and how they must communicate. In some cases, this can be very challenging when application communication ports are poorly documented, random, or are not understood. Some applications open random ports or have extremely large ranges of ports that must be used to function properly. Some host firewalls are able to allow dynamic port use, thus alleviating the need to go through the exercise of analyzing the application and observing unwanted blocks by the firewall.

Anti-virus

Anti-virus is considered as a necessary security mechanism for the low-hanging fruit, predictable malware, most of it old, easy to detect, and still dangerous. Anti-virus primarily uses two methods to detect malware:

- **Signature**: This method looks for known patterns of malware
- **Heuristics**: In this method the behavior of potential malware is analyzed for malicious actions

Depending on the sophistication of the threat, and if detected, the solution may be able to "clean" the virus from the system. With encoding and encryption methods the norm for malware and hackers, detection is near impossible.

A common method to exploit systems with malware is to bypass anti-virus using simple techniques. Methods include encoding, encryption, obfuscation, and random language compiling, all of which confuse anti-virus and the malware goes undetected. A quick search on the Internet will provide several sources on methods to evade and bypass anti-virus on a system. One example is the method provided within Metasploit, a freely available exploitation tool:

```
http://www.offensive-security.com/metasploit-
unleashed/Antivirus_Bypass
```

Typically, anti-virus solutions will install an agent on the endpoint, run scans continuously, and any new file introduced is scanned immediately. This method of protecting a system can be taxing depending on the role of the system and the footprint of the agent.

Signature-based anti-virus

The most common component of anti-virus solutions is the signature set used to detect known malware threats. In order to leverage the anti-virus to protect systems, the solution must have a known fingerprint of the malware to offer detection and mitigation of the threat. This fact alone is a significant shortcoming of the typical anti-virus solution and is the primary reason malware infections are extremely successful in today's threat landscape. There is also a lag time for anti-virus vendors to become aware of a new malware, reverse engineer, and provide a signature update to users. In some cases this is mere hours, and in other cases it is may be several days. While the signature is being developed, the malware has free reign on the user network. This design in anti-virus is most well suited for known, low-hanging fruit type malware threats.

Heuristic anti-virus

The behavioral detection method used by anti-virus is called heuristics. This method attempts to identify a malware threat based on what actions are taken by the malware, again using known behaviors for known malware types. The limitation to the behavioral analysis is that it has to still have some known fingerprint to determine what the malware threat is. Without a prior knowledge of the malware, heuristic analysis offers little advantage over the signature-based nature of anti-virus.

Implementation considerations

Anti-virus for the user endpoint may always be a requirement, but other more effective methods are fast becoming a replacement for anti-virus on server endpoints. Server endpoints are typically the systems that run the enterprise, and adding more software that is always running as a service is becoming less tolerable when performance is crucial. This becomes a challenge especially when security teams want to push another solution to protect the enterprise systems because it almost always requires another agent. When possible, strive to get more from what is already installed on the system, or look for methods that are forward-thinking such as application whitelisting to possibly reduce agents on server endpoints.

The overall effectiveness of anti-virus is reliant upon the research team of the vendor providing the software and how quickly they are able to update signatures and heuristics to detect the newest malware. Anti-virus vendors are unable to protect against the latest threat until they have a sample of the malware that can be reverse engineered and inoculated based on a unique characteristic found within the code. Any deviation from this unique characteristic will render the developed signature ineffective for the next variant. Fortunately, anti-virus vendors are quick to find variants and create a signature for protection. This reactive facet of the solution should be weighed carefully when selecting a solution. Not all anti-virus is equal nor should anti-virus be the only enterprise solution for malware detection and mitigation.

User account management

User account management is not often considered a security mechanism, but accounts on the system are some level of access that may be the door in for malicious activity. When a system administrator leaves an organization, their user account should be disabled and removed from all systems; failure to undertake this process is negligent. Another way to look at this is it is easier to use an account that is known to access a system versus finding another method to exploit the system. Priority review of system accounts should be in accordance to the system classification and other security policies as applicable.

User roles and permissions

An area of constant challenge is properly defining system users and roles to perform required tasks. This is less of an issue for server systems, but a significant issue for end user systems. In order to install software and perform some system functions, the operating system may require elevated privileges. Instead of leveraging a software management system to install requested software, users are given permissions temporarily in order to perform the installation. There are two issues with this scenario. First, software needed to perform a business function should be owned and maintained by the organization allowing for version control, patching, and proper licensing. Second, the organization's IT standards should have rules in regards to non-business software installed on business assets. In fact, one of the biggest drivers for BYOD initiatives is this very subject, *software*. However, these legitimate and non-standard install requests force the IT support teams to provide elevated access on systems. These elevated privileges then get used to inadvertently install malware as it requires these elevated privileges most times to install and cause havoc.

Organizations should have a method to provide the software being requested or only temporarily provide the elevated privileges. The norm is that these temporary privilege elevations remain and are not temporary at all. In haste, sometimes users are just added as system administrators as this is commonly the easiest path to resolving the incident ticket and will make the user happy.

When these accounts become rogue, meaning the user is no longer with the organization or due to incorrect permissions they were able to create more accounts, the organization becomes vulnerable to account misuse, unauthorized access, and malicious activity. The process to gain elevated privileges should require additional scrutiny and only in accordance to the security architecture and policies to protect the organization's data and assets. If these requests become the norm versus the exception, perhaps the organization should re-evaluate its position on enterprise software. If the software cannot be purchased, maintained, and installed by IT, then it should not be on enterprise systems. This is the case where one issue creates a more critical issue of regular business users having permissions that only the internal IT support staff should have. Because of this, the same IT support teams are tasked with responding to increased malware in the enterprise and supporting non-enterprise applications.

User account auditing

In order to ensure that there are no rogue accounts on systems, the enterprise should perform user account auditing across all systems on a regular basis. Once all accounts are discovered, they should be referenced to understand their purpose; if rogue accounts are found they should be disabled. Also, maintaining a termination list to reference for accounts that should have been disabled or deleted at the time of termination should be a formal process. Without auditing the environment for rogue accounts or accounts that were supposed to be temporary, there will be an increased risk of misuse and unauthorized access. If the accounts were used to install software or for a non-interactive process, chances are that the accounts have elevated privileges leaving the system and data vulnerable.

There are tools to aid in this discovery and these should be a part of the overall system and user management processes within the organization. The tools should be run, at a minimum, quarterly to coincide with the most generally accepted password expiration standards.

Policy enforcement

To this point, we have covered several technologies to protect enterprise systems, and the final component is process related, which is policy enforcement. We covered security standards and policies in *Chapter 3, Security As a Process* prior to any protection topics being presented. This is because in order to have a position on how to protect systems in the enterprise, the trust models need to be built and required policies written as a guide to what methods to employ. The benefit of having policies is that there is a communicated enterprise-wide statement on how the enterprise expects employees to use assets and consequences to actions contrary to policy statements are also made explicit.

There is a standard set of policies typical to all enterprises across industries such as acceptable use and technology use. Regardless of the controls implemented to protect the system, there will be administrators and other users with elevated privileges and this access must be controlled and monitored. In addition to this aspect of system operations, the system may be vulnerable to threats from the network. Users who violate policies by scanning or attacking an enterprise system should be handled in accordance to the policies written. Enforcement may come in the form of an implemented tool, but it may also come from the monitoring of user activity on systems. Organizations must determine the method of policy enforcement, but ultimately the success of policy enforcement will determine the overall security posture of the enterprise.

Summary

In this chapter, we covered multiple tools that can be implemented to secure systems in the enterprise. We discussed implementation considerations and value that each tool type and method provides the enterprise. Additionally, we covered how to implement the presented tools in a manner that minimizes challenges and increases value. Tools alone are not the only method to properly secure enterprise systems; behaviors must be identified and controlled through policy. Enforcing IT security policies is a process and may include tools to a degree but will be most complied with when enforcement is observed. It is challenging to protect systems from every possible threat. This chapter focused on leveraging the trust models developed to determine the best balance of security and risk when implementing a system protection strategy. Protecting systems in the enterprise is process and technology working in unison with the oversight of a skilled IT team to apply action. The next chapter covers the subsequent security architecture layer, which is securing enterprise data.

6

Securing Enterprise Data

Securing enterprise data can be a daunting task without knowing where the data is stored, processed, and how it is transmitted. Developing and enforcing a data classification model is a foundational component to securing enterprise data. This chapter will focus on the steps required to develop functional data classification and how to protect high-value data in the enterprise. Data discovery and protection tool types, placement, and implementation challenges for each will be presented. The emphasis is balancing the proper amount of protection and risk tolerance for access to enterprise data.

This chapter covers the following:

- Data identification and discovery
- Classifying enterprise data
- Data loss prevention methods and techniques
- Data protection methods and techniques such as encryption, hashing, and access controls

Data classification

Data classification is a process where enterprise data is identified across the enterprise and it is given a classification that requires specific handling methods when interacting with the classified data. It is important that during the classification exercise data owners are assigned, enterprise criticality scored, and supporting processes developed to ensure confidentiality, availability, and integrity. The ultimate goal of the data classification exercise is to discover all enterprise data and protect or destroy it based on its importance and impact potential. Impact potential is of importance when considering the impact of enterprise data compromise, loss, and legal limits for data retention.

Identifying enterprise data

A common perception is that all enterprise data is both stored in a database or network system and the presence of such data stores is known. The reality is with the changes to the network edge presented in *Chapter 1, Enterprise Security Overview* and *Chapter 2, Security Architectures*, this is commonly not the case, as data resides in many unknown and unprotected locations.

To begin the process of identifying enterprise data, a simple exercise of understanding the types of data the enterprise uses to function as a business is a good start. Once this has been documented the next step will be to understand the locations in which the data resides, both inside the network and elsewhere. These steps will form the basis for a detailed data classification model and ultimately serve as input to data handling policies, standards, and guidelines. The classification must be easy to understand and allow for simple identification of the data types within the classification model to ensure the process is followed and enterprise data is handled in a secure manner.

Data types

There are many data types that may exist in order for the business to operationally function. Depending on the industry, the data may consist of patented and trademarked intellectual property, regulated data, or other categories of data that must be identified, accounted for, and protected in accordance with internal policies and external regulatory bodies, laws, and mandates.

A careful examination of the data types present in the enterprise will lead to required controls that must be implemented in technology and process, and these must be auditable. Each enterprise, regardless of the previously mentioned data types, will have some level of employee personal data (human resources), network diagrams, application architecture diagrams, and more data types that may not seem to be critical to the business, but certainly have a risk associated with their compromise or loss. It is not always cut and dry what data has the most significance until all business processes are known. Business processes should lead to all enterprise data types that are interacted with directly or indirectly through the various processes.

Typical data types include:

- Employee human resources data
- Company private data (business plans, acquisition strategies, brands, and so on)
- Company confidential data (locations, network diagrams, and so on)
- Company public data (product releases, press releases)

- Consumer data (PII, credit cards, and so on)
- Medical data (HIPAA regulated)

Data locations

Data can be located in multiple places both internal and external to the enterprise network, including in employer-owned and employee-owned assets. This fact was presented in earlier chapters as a primary reason for the blurring of the enterprise network perimeter. The enterprise network edge has previously been emphasized as the primary data boundary because typically enterprise data would reside only within the network boundary defined by firewalls and other network equipment. Additionally, all enterprise data was intended to only reside on enterprise-owned assets. Because there has been a shift over time, due to data sharing requirements and convenience, data can reside literally anywhere.

An example is an employee making a decision to work on a task at home and uploading enterprise data to an online storage service or e-mailing the data to a personal e-mail account. It is understood that the employee is trying to be efficient and accomplish more work, but this simple act results in enterprise data residing on systems and in applications not owned or controlled by the enterprise.

Without technologies implemented to prevent this behavior and well-communicated policies, data locations will continue to be disparate and expose enterprise data to unnecessary and unexpected risk.

Typical data locations include:

- Network shares
- Document repositories
- File transfer systems
- Business partner and third-party systems
- Employer and employee laptops/desktops
- Employee-owned tablets/cell phones
- Employee/employer-owned portable storage (for example, USB drives)
- Online storage services
- Personal e-mail services
- Databases
- Backup media
- Replaced/failed system drives

Many of these data locations were presented in previous chapters and only represent the most common locations used by business users. Each enterprise should go through the exercise of identifying all the data locations within their network including approved and unapproved devices and services.

Third-party storage of enterprise data may require additional verbiage in business partner contracts, permitting the enterprise to require enforcement of protection mechanisms of enterprise data transmitted, processed, and stored by business partners and third parties. It is recommended that the enterprise perform a business partner risk assessment that would include data handling.

The discovered data locations will have more impact on the required data protection mechanisms than classification itself. Many of the data locations listed previously may not have a direct method to protect the data, so other methods will be required to ensure proper protection. This can be mapped directly to the classification model and may involve building new capabilities to enforce protection, preventing the underlying technology gaps from allowing unprotected interaction with the data.

The following diagram depicts the typical data interaction types of transmission, storage, and processing with pertinent data locations:

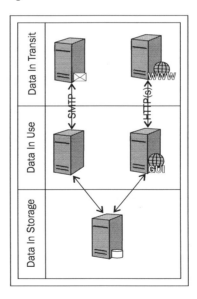

An example of a data interaction that may require additional protection methods is e-mail. **Simple Mail Transfer Protocol (SMTP)** — the protocol used for sending e-mail — is one example of an insecure method to transmit data, which requires additional protection for transmitting sensitive data. A tool that can provide encryption for e-mail is one option to provide protection over this medium. Additionally, the enterprise can make the decision to not allow e-mailing data that requires protection per a data classification policy. This method could be deemed as the protection mechanism, as long as it can be enforced.

Each one of these uses of data will have a unique set of challenges to provide the protection dictated by the classification model. A reasonable path to resolution is to first identify all data types and locations, gain an understanding of the technologies in use such as database types, and then determine the methods available for protection. Care must be taken to understand the total cost of ownership of any new feature or solution decided upon to provide the protection.

Reducing locations where protected data resides can reduce the complexity of implementing controls and reduce risk to the enterprise. After data is located it may be assessed that there are duplicate stores of data or that the data is no longer needed and can be removed from enterprise assets. This is a sound practice as it is a common method to reduce scope for compliance standards such as the **Payment Card Industry Data Security Standard (PCI DSS)**.

Automating discovery

Locating data can be a very involved and manual process without the use of tools specifically designed to "discover" data matching the unique criteria in an automated manner. As presented in the previous section there are multiple locations where data may reside, both in enterprise controlled and uncontrolled locations. Because data can be stored, processed, and transmitted, finding a tool that can detect pertinent data in these categories of use is essential to finding not only known data and processes, but unknown data types and processes that need to be understood, classified properly, and have associated controls implemented.

Discovering enterprise data within the controlled assets of the enterprise is much easier to accomplish than data discovery involving employee assets in an approved or unapproved implementation as observed in **bring your own device (BYOD)** scenarios. Detection at the network layer will be feasible but applying a mechanism to discover data residing on an employee or third-party asset becomes a challenge of privacy versus privilege to use the non-enterprise asset for business. To alleviate the concern in this scenario it may be wise to enforce a strict policy not allowing the use of non-enterprise assets to transmit, store, or process enterprise data. Another approach may be to leverage virtualization and allow access through secured virtual hosts. This allows interaction with enterprise assets and data through a strictly controlled environment and not directly by the non-enterprise employee asset.

Assign data owners

The process of assigning data owners is essential and must be completed for classification efforts to be successful. Assigning data owners brings accountability and can take a lot of guesswork out of data discovery. If it is possible to assign data owners prior to data discovery, it may save time; it is common for data to be discovered first and then hunt for the data owner.

It will be imperative to get input from the data owners on the data their processes encompass and to understand what it is, who uses it, how is it used, and where it is located. Knowing these characteristics of the data will help classify it and ensure the correct protection mechanisms are implemented. Data owners may have to involve other teams to understand how the data is stored and transmitted. For example, if the data is stored in a database, the owner may need to contact the database administrator to gain understanding of how the data is stored, permissions on the database, and what protection is implemented.

The data owners will have a vested interest in the proper protection of the data for which they are responsible within the enterprise. For new business processes and data requirements, classifying data and assigning owners at the design stage will significantly reduce the efforts to protect data and reduce associated risks introduced with the project. This early involvement will increase buy-in and may lead to a better way of doing business. In some cases, the various data owners do not communicate with each other and are unaware of how their data may be used by other teams. This exercise may bring these disconnects to light and the overall data classification purpose to the forefront of how all data is handled, allowing less IT security policing and more cooperation from data owners.

Assign data classification

Data classification is the act of assigning a label to identified data types that indicate required protection mechanisms, as driven by business risk and value. Data classification can be a simple chart or a complex solution that enforces data classification at its creation. Because data management has been mostly nonexistent, it may be difficult to implement a complex solution until other more simple processes are developed and implemented.

Once all data types have been identified, a simple table of the data types, along with the assigned classification and high-level protection, can be developed and communicated. Ideally, the table would have references to defined policies, standards, and procedures that provide a roadmap to proper use and protection of enterprise data. An example of a simple data classification model is shown as follows:

	Restricted confidential (Level 1)	**Confidential (Level 2)**	**Public (Level 3)**
Data type	Customer: • CC# • PII Employee: • SSN# • PII Company: • Merger Plans • New product	Customer: • PII Employee: • PII Company: • Internal documents	• Anything not in the previous sections. • Items considered to be available in the public domain.
Data protection	Data encryption, hashing, or tokenization	Restricted access permissions	None

After a classification model has been created, it has to be communicated and adopted by the entire enterprise, not just data owners and IT Security. It is good to have the data owners as the place where last checks occur and involve IT Security for guidance, but it is ultimately the responsibility of each person within the enterprise to protect enterprise data.

It is common for various departments within the enterprise to manage their own processes and interactions with third parties. In order to enforce data classification these various departments need to understand how their data is labeled in the classification model and at a minimum know where to go for help on how to implement protection mechanisms. It is understood that the marketing team or some other non-IT departments do not understand the nuts and bolts of data protection; the goal with the classification model is to cause enterprise users to think about the data they interact with and to question if they are handling it correctly. IT Security should always be accessible and their contact information readily available in the event their guidance is needed.

Typically, data classification fails due to lack of communication, users not understanding what data they are interacting with the data value to the enterprise, and the in ability to enforce. To get an understanding of how well data classification is understood, provide a survey to learn if user education is needed. If a process is not following the classification model, this is not a retaliatory opportunity but an educational opportunity. Proper communication of the data classification model and methods to ensure proper data handling will go a long way towards reducing the risk of data compromise and loss.

Data Loss Prevention

After completing the development of the data classification model and supporting processes including policies and standards a tool may need to be implemented to enforce data protection based upon the model. **Data Loss Prevention (DLP)** is an example of a tool that can enforce protection of data that has been classified by the enterprise. In the previous *Data locations* section several examples of data locations were presented to emphasize the complexity of data management and protection in the enterprise. DLP can help find data in these various locations, and in some cases enforce encryption, block insecure transmission, and block unauthorized copying and storing of data based upon data classification. There is significant benefit to having a solution with this capability, allowing automated protection within the enterprise, integration with existing solutions, and actionable reporting.

The primary purpose of DLP is to protect against the unauthorized exfiltration of enterprise data from the enterprise egress connections. Because this can be accomplished by several methods it is important to consider the capabilities of the DLP solution and how it can be integrated into the environment to provide the expected protection. The following sections will cover the implementation of DLP for the common data locations in the enterprise.

Data in storage

Data can be stored multiple ways in an enterprise network, commonly in network shares, databases, document repositories, online storage, and portable storage devices. Data may reside in these locations as part of a business process or simply for convenience of access by employees. When evaluating the storage locations in the environment, identifying the business case for the method should be the first step in deciding if this method will be approved in accordance to policies, standards, and the finalized data classification model. I will use the portable local storage method as an example exercise for evaluating the use of storage technologies and the risk introduced by their use. Based on the *Acceptable use policies* and *Data handling policies* sections in *Chapter 3, Security As a Process*, a series of questions needs to be answered to determine how to properly assess the use of the technology in question.

For example, consider a local portable storage device used by employees:

- Is the use of this storage type permitted?
    - If no, then how can this be enforced?
    - If yes, does the use of the type of technology affect the security posture of enterprise data?
- Can enterprise data reside on this storage type?
    - If so, how does this affect the security posture of enterprise data?
- What type of data may reside on the technology?
- Who will control the technology?
- What protection mechanisms must be implemented to protect data?
- How will the protection mechanism be implemented and managed?

More or fewer questions can be asked, to reach a decision on the use of portable storage technologies. Some technologies will require more input than others, as well as a complete understanding of the interacting business processes. It may be decided that only certain storage technologies are permitted for storing enterprise data of certain types with low risk to the enterprise in the event of data loss.

A DLP strategy can be developed to ensure all data locations are accounted for including employer-owned systems such as employee laptops. Most DLP solutions have the ability to scan data stores and also provide an agent that can be deployed on end systems to monitor and prevent unauthorized actions for classified enterprise data. The locations where data will reside as part of a standard process can be scanned for the specific data types that have been identified in the enterprise data discovery phase. If a discovery scan was initiated to identify data in locations, it can be used in an ongoing scheduled scan to continuously monitor the data stores for data that should or should not reside in the data location.

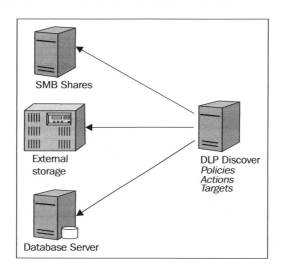

In order to provide protection for the discovered data, either an automated function within the DLP solution can be used to move the data to a secure location, or implement other methods to restrict access as the data is discovered. Another method that can be employed is to simply report on the discovery findings, and investigate the business reason for the data residing in the location. In order to employ automated protection methods for data in storage it is imperative that the effects of such actions are completely understood to minimize impact to critical business processes. A majority of enterprise cases will be a manual process of investigating the reason for the data residing in the location and working toward moving the process and data to a secured method. This method is least impactful and is recommended for enterprises with new DLP implementations.

In cases where the data location is an employee laptop, it may be acceptable to take more aggressive steps to protect the data resident on the system—including deletion. As more portable storage devices are becoming commonplace on the enterprise network without authorization, deploying an agent to employer-owned assets may be the best method to enforce data loss prevention at the end point, in essence never allowing the system to store the data on any local drive including portable attached storage. This solution does not solve the employee-owned assets problem, which introduces several complexities including privacy, management, supported platforms, and risk. Refer to the *BYOD initiatives* section in *Chapter 2, Security Architectures* for more information on approaching this trending topic.

A method to reduce DLP complexities is to identify systems that may be multipurpose data stores, such as file servers, and may have more lax permissions versus a tightly controlled and specialized database server. There is value in scanning database servers such as identifying a misconfigured database storing unencrypted data.

 Data discovery scanning should be prioritized based on risk and communicated to owners prior to scanning to ensure buy-in and accountability for remediation.

Data in use

Data in use is data that is actively processed within an application, process, memory or other location temporarily for the duration of a function or transaction. Examples of data in use are point-of-sale systems, call center systems, web applications, employer end systems, and servers. These are systems and applications that are in some way interacting with enterprise data, but not storing long term, only long enough to perform a function or transaction.

Data in use is the unique facet of DLP that is a little more complex than dealing with data in storage or data in transit. In use implies that there is an application or function involved to read, add, remove, and modify data. Even though using data is a business function, if required, there may be reason to ensure that the data is not handled in an unauthorized manner that could lead to loss. Data in use can be monitored by an agent installed on the end system to permit only certain uses of the data and deny actions such as storing the data locally or sending the data via e-mail or other communication method.

Typically, the DLP agent that resides on the end system will be inserted low in the TCP/IP stack to ensure it can detect data before any encryption can be applied such as SSL (HTTPS) that would allow circumvention of network-based security mechanisms. Due to this behavior, implementation on employee-owned devices introduces privacy issues because any personal transactions such as online banking, medical record lookup, and so on may be detected and details of the transaction stored in the DLP database for review.

This scenario must be carefully evaluated when considering a BYOD deployment for employees with access to classified data. This is not an issue for employer-owned assets covered by well written security policies informing employees there is little expectation of privacy when using enterprise assets for personal use. Most policies indicate no personal use of enterprise assets is permitted, but in reality it is not generally enforced, with some probability of private data being detected and stored within the DLP solution. There should be a process for removing this data, if not needed for an investigation, to ensure some level of privacy for employees.

Several benefits can be derived from using an Endpoint DLP solution for preventing data exfiltration including limiting where data can be stored, how it can be transmitted, and what applications can be used to interact with the data. Preventing the saving of classified data to attached storage devices or removable media such as CD/DVD can prevent large amounts of data loss for otherwise undetectable methods of exfiltration.

No network monitoring device will detect if thousands of medical records are saved to a local machine and moved to a USB storage device, but Endpoint DLP can detect and prevent this action. Another benefit of the solution is preventing USB-attached storage at all, not just when coupled with a classified data type. Many other security threats are introduced to environments through these small portable devices with high capacities for storage. Implementing an Endpoint DLP solution will add an additional layer to the overall DLP strategy where data is directly interacted with in the most vulnerable state.

Data in transit

Data in transit is data that is being moved from one system to another, either locally or remotely, such as file transfer systems, e-mail, and web applications. The focus of DLP for data in transit is specifically data leaving the enterprise through egress connections. It is expected that insecure transmission of sensitive data occurs within the network boundary due to the perception of the secure internal network and many industry standards allowing for unencrypted, clear text transmission of data. However, it is recommended that all data including credentials be transmitted only using secure methods. A simple reason for this practice is to ensure protection regardless of network architecture and design changes.

It is common to have many communication methods available in the enterprise for day-to-day business including e-mail, file transfer, web portals, instant messaging, and conferencing services that include voice, video, and instant messaging. With these business conveniences come additional methods to transmit data out of the enterprise, many times encrypted and therefore invisible to network-based security technologies. Various DLP solutions have accounted for this fact and provide solutions capable of intercepting and decrypting communications to look for classified data. There are commonly solutions for HTTP/HTTPS, FTP, SMTP, IM interception, and inspection.

The following diagram depicts an example Network DLP solution implemented for e-mail, web, and general network traffic interception, inspection, and mitigation:

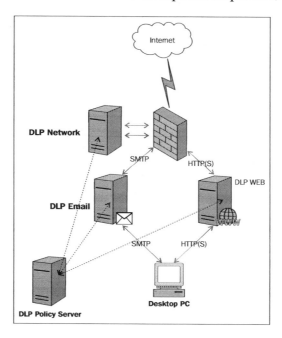

The DLP solution for data in transit is typically deployed at the network egress connections and is configured to look for specific protocols and inspect data based on configured policies. For specialized implementations there are solutions that provide e-mail and web gateway technologies that can act as complete web proxy and mail forwarder implementations in addition to DLP.

In these scenarios the traffic leaving the network via one of these communication methods is sent to the DLP appliance, decrypted if configured, and inspected. Once inspection is complete actions will be taken as per the policy configuration. Typical DLP actions may include block, permit, and encrypt detected data. Generally, this is configurable per data type, source/destination pairs, senders, recipients, and so on. The level of customization depends on the DLP solution. Flexibility of the DLP solution should be evaluated prior to purchase and implementation.

 Developing use cases is of utmost importance when selecting a solution to protect enterprise data and has to be managed and integrated into the operational functions of the business.

There can be several business processes identified that transmit classified data via insecure methods and can be managed using the DLP solution to report current state, transitional states, and provide accountability for future instances. It is advisable to communicate intentions of the DLP solution prior to sending a report to a business unit asking them why they are doing something that violates policy or the classification standard. Of the three DLP implementation areas, in transit tends to get the most attention because it provides confirmed instances of data leaving the enterprise network. Because there is typically less trust associated with external entities and networks than internal violations, priority will probably be focused here and some level of risk analysis performed to determine the best course of action for long-term remediation. In fact, most proof of concept implementations start with a network implementation of DLP to identify data in transit leaving the network.

Network-based DLP is one of the easiest methods to determine what data types are leaving the network and in what manner, secure or insecure. It also has the least amount of effort associated with the implementation, because no agent software is needed for the basic network monitoring solutions. There is more work with the e-mail and web-specific solutions, but these should be carefully considered for implementation and be understood as to how they would integrate with existing technologies. The e-mail and web solutions can typically perform URL filtering, and SPAM protection, which may already be implemented in another solution. This can complicate the overall implementation; collaboration with other teams is essential when considering these two technologies.

A decision may need to be made in regards to what function each security appliance will perform. For instance, if the **next generation firewall (NGFW)** can support URL filtering with user mapping, the decision needs to be made as to whether the NGFW feature will be used or if all web filtering and DLP functions specific to web traffic will be a feature that DLP will provide.

Because this technology has far reaching capabilities into most teams' areas of responsibility in an enterprise, it must be well communicated especially to network related teams if separated from information security. A little collaboration up front will go a long way to finding the right fit for DLP in the organization and alleviate unnecessary tension where internal lines are drawn but DLP blurs the lines of roles and responsibilities.

Having implemented Network DLP, E-mail DLP, Web DLP, and Endpoint DLP most data loss scenarios will be detected and can be prevented with a high rate of success. As with any security technology, the enterprise adoption and maturation of processes will determine the overall success and value-add. A phased approach and consistent communication with the involved teams will ease the transition into the use of another security technology that will take time to manage and remediate findings. If this can be presented as a service of IT Security there may be additional gains of internal trust and cooperation because there is immediate partnership in the resolution to secure enterprise data.

DLP implementation

In the previous sections, the common methods of discovering data and protecting data from exfiltration were covered. The challenge with this toolset is deciding what methods to employ, in what phases, and how to digest the output from the tool. Implementation itself may not be much of a challenge but operationalizing the solution and delivering value on the investment may pose more of a challenge.

The best method to implementing any solution in the enterprise is to first understand the problem to be solved, and then determine the course of action. This is probably truer with a solution like DLP than most. Because DLP will span multiple teams within the enterprise and have several technologies involved, collaboratively coming to an agreement on how to proceed with a DLP implementation is critical to the success of the program. The following sections will cover the DLP solutions presented, approaches to successfully implementing them, overcoming challenges, and getting value from a DLP implementation.

DLP Network

DLP Network is the simplest solution to implement in an enterprise environment because fewer IT teams need to be involved for implementation. It is also the quickest method to determine what data is leaving the network in an insecure manner, therefore identifying bad business practices or malicious behavior can be done with little effort and some cross-functional coordination. Because the network component of DLP must be able to see all traffic at the network edge, the network team will need to be involved. A challenge here may be the use of SPAN ports, if there is no other aggregation technology in use. SPAN ports can be a challenge on switches because many times there is a limit to how many can be configured and it can be taxing on the switch backplane where all data must traverse for the switch to move data.

[It is highly recommended to have an aggregation strategy and supporting technology implemented not only for DLP but also for other network monitoring tools.]

The size of the network egress connections will also have an effect on the size of the network implementation. Some DLP solutions are appliance based, whereas others run on standalone server hardware, but both must be sized properly for the amount of data that will be inspected. If too much data is sent to the system and the network interfaces are overrun, some data will be lost.

Having a good understanding of protocols in use at the network edge is valuable information that can be used to limit the types of data the DLP solution has to inspect. This can increase performance and reduce unnecessary inspection of protocols that are unable to be inspected, such as SSL, without a decryption capability and other protocols not in use.

If the plan is to provide actionable data to other teams within the enterprise, knowing what teams own enterprise processes will be important in order to provide feedback and options for remediation, where there is a security issue introducing risk to the enterprise. It is good practice to communicate intentions of any introduced technology, if others will be held responsible for data it provides. Simply providing a team with a report from a tool they have never seen and demanding they fix what is detected does not foster the collaborative environment needed for DLP to be successful. This is a fact for all facets of the overall DLP solution.

DLP E-mail and Web

In the enterprise the two most used technologies are probably e-mail and the Internet. Introducing a new method to access either technology may be met with more apprehension than the basic network portion of DLP. In order for the e-mail or web solution to be effective they must be inline, or otherwise configured to receive e-mail or web communication, inspect, and be able to take action. This is not a passive implementation and can affect traffic leaving the network via these two methods. Planning the implementation and working with the teams responsible for the surrounding technologies, like existing Internet proxy servers and e-mail forwarders, will ensure proper placement of DLP and an agreed upon implementation. Consider the use cases for implementing DLP E-mail and Web carefully before designing the solution and developing policies.

Overall, there are few options for the designs of both technologies because they must be able to take action on the traffic; so understanding the design requirements along with the existing implementation of like technologies will highlight the areas of most significant change in the way the current solutions are working. As mentioned in the *Data in transit* section previously, the issue of overlapping technologies was presented as one challenge that may be difficult to overcome, especially if there is significant investment in an existing and overlapping technology, or a highly sought after feature purchased to only be scrapped in lieu of the DLP solution. Generally, this type of challenge will be contained within IT and can be resolved without engaging the business, as these are transport type technologies that will remain unnoticed until there is a policy violation or service impacting failure.

The primary purpose of the DLP E-mail and Web solutions is to take the necessary actions to protect enterprise data from insecure transport and exfiltration through e-mail and web over these communication methods. Taking action in this scenario will involve either direct or indirect user interaction and therefore must be communicated to the users explaining how the DLP implementation changes the use of e-mail and web within the enterprise. DLP E-mail solutions will also affect those business partners that receive encrypted e-mails with instructions on how to retrieve the protected e-mail. A thorough review of business processes that will be affected is recommended to ensure nothing is impeded from functioning and impactful to the business. A phased approach can be leveraged, either using DLP Network or using the e-mail and web solutions in a permit, but alert mode, allowing identification of insecure business practices that can be remediated in collaboration with the business process owner, without impactful mitigation actions.

The most significant relationship that requires buy-in and collaboration will be the messaging and network teams because both DLP technologies will change how they operate these services for the organization. Early communication and involvement of these two teams will ensure a design that meets the security requirements and integrates well with the existing infrastructure. Also, having the expertise of these teams available for implementation, troubleshooting, and long-term operational support is invaluable.

DLP Discover

Another DLP solution that requires significant forethought and interaction with other enterprise teams is the DLP Discover solution. DLP Discover is the tool that can scan network shares, document repositories, databases, and other data at rest. In order to access this data, an account with permissions will need to be configured, to allow the scans to open the data stores and inspect for policy matches. Having an understanding of the use cases involving data at rest and knowing where the data resides should be a significant portion of the planning for a Discover implementation. Before making a decision on what product is purchased to meet the requirement to scan data at rest, ensure the primary data locations are supported by the solution to realize the intended value-add.

Some products perform specific functions of DLP discovery better than others. It is recommended to test each product in the real environment to gauge the effectiveness of each solution in the environment where they will be used. Once Discover has been run in the environment, carefully review the results to identify strengths and weaknesses of the product. Look to see if the product detected the known data types that should be detected; if it did not, look for possible misconfiguration and test other products on the same data set to look for differing results.

Because the DLP Discover solution is looking for data at rest and scanning hosts to enumerate policy matches, it may be advisable to run scans during off hours as the solution may increase the I/O on the system being scanned and impact performance.

There can be permission errors that will impede the success of the scan; testing by initiating a limited scan can help identify simple issues that will otherwise derail the scan. If there are file auditing controls in place, the DLP solution may trigger alerts based on file access operations, therefore, teams that perform monitoring functions need to be aware of the Discover host and scans so time is not wasted trying to hunt down an issue that does not exist.

As mentioned before, this tool can also be used to find data when it is unknown what data is at rest in the various data locations. In this scenario, communication and collaboration with system administrators is very important in order to get accounts set up and information on the data locations such as share names, URLs for web-based document repositories, and so on. It can be a great exercise to evangelize the DLP product in the environment that can provide useful feedback and knowledge about the environment that would otherwise take a significant amount of time to discover. A strategy can then be developed to protect the discovered data by running scans on a regular basis to ensure data stores do not become adulterated with classified data, putting the enterprise at risk.

Once DLP discovery has been configured and set up in the environment, it is a good validator of a properly implemented data protection program. Discovery of classified enterprise data can hone in on educational issues, bad business practices, and erroneous storage of data that would normally go undetected.

DLP Endpoint

The last presented component of DLP to consider is the closest to the end user where the human interaction is the highest and, in theory, where the greatest risk is introduced to enterprise data – DLP Endpoint. DLP Endpoint is an agent-based technology that must be installed on every end point. Unlike the other technologies that are more process and design focused, Endpoint is a numbers game. In a typical enterprise, there will be more end point systems than any other hardware combined. This requires a significant implementation of agents that have to be installed, managed, and the output operationalized for meaningful and actionable reporting.

Installing the agents in a common enterprise setting is not too difficult as most enterprises have software management tools to install applications remotely on end point systems. The agent will still need to be packaged and tested on the various supported operating systems. Once installed the agent will check in with the policy server and this must be carefully monitored to make sure there are no communication issues and that the intended coverage is in place for DLP Endpoint. Agent status will change depending on the state of the system (on, off, or disconnected from the network), but the total number of hosts should match the number of agents deployed.

Because the number of hosts will be more than with other types of DLP solutions, incidents may be exponentially more, and careful planning of enabled policies will help with deciding the best approach to the end point solution. For the end point solution a specific goal can be the most affective, such as configuring blocking actions for classified data and attached local portable storage versus alerting on the presence of the data on the end point. As mentioned previously, the agent will install itself low in the TCP/IP stack, therefore any access to HTTPS websites like online banking, online shopping, and other personal sites will trigger the DLP solution and create and incident. If the goal is to make sure employer data is not transmitted from the host, then pre-classifying data or setting a threshold on the number of records may be the best option for detecting a possible exfiltration issue versus an employee making an online purchase.

There will be a lot of output even when the most basic of policies is set. It will be very important for the DLP operations team to quickly address false positives, tune the policies, and focus on what will make the most impact in protecting enterprise data from compromise and loss. If there are patterns in the output, then creating customized reporting to capture the pattern will be important to capture trends and focus on real issues.

The last and most important statement on DLP solutions is that it will take some time to find the norm in the environment, even if it is bad. The intelligence that can be gathered from this powerful tool can highlight security awareness issues, bad business practices, and illegal or malicious activity. At times it will all look the same, but the trained eye will know how the business functions and will be able to decipher good from bad. It is recommended to implement DLP in the monitor mode first, while these patterns are learned, to reduce the potential impact to the enterprise.

Encryption and hashing

Encryption and hashing technologies are different and will be explained to avoid confusion, as detailed analysis of both and how they fit into the data protection strategy of the enterprise, is covered in this section. Both encryption and hashing are typically what is thought of when data protection is discussed whether in storage, transit, or in use by applications. Usually, the immediate afterthought is, this is going to complicate business processes or break something important. The teams who have the most work to do, the developers and application teams, generally will have the most heartburn over potential changes to application code, batch jobs, and processes that make the business run. Encryption and hashing are both very important to the overall security posture of the enterprise and must be an integral component of the enterprise security architecture.

Encryption and hashing explained

There are several forms of both encryption and hashing that have various uses depending on many variables. Both have their strengths and weaknesses, complications in implementation, and overall protection capabilities. There are two distinguishing characteristics between encryption and hashing. First, the process that creates the final representation of the data, and second, the method by which the original data is retrieved. It is these characteristics that will be the deciding factor on which is used for specific data protection scenarios. Let's take a more detailed look at both and see some viable uses for each. Note that this is not meant to serve as a de facto reference on encryption and hashing, but provides enough information as to how encryption and hashing can be used in the enterprise as part of the overall security architecture.

Encryption

Encryption is the method of mathematically generating a cipher text version of clear text data to render it unrecognizable. This method is based on really big numbers called prime numbers to limit the possibility of creating the same cipher text for different data and to make it as mathematically difficult as possible to derive the clear text from the known cipher text. With this stated, all standard encryption algorithms are public and can be reviewed, the algorithm is essentially the source code that shows the interworking of the encryption method. This is done to ensure the validity of the encryption algorithm, ultimately guaranteeing the users of the encryption technique that their data is protected.

There are two general types of encryption – symmetric and asymmetric. Both types of encryption require keys to perform the encrypt and decrypt functions. It is this factor in encryption that causes some security standards to consider encrypted data as having the same value as the data itself. This means if an enterprise loses encrypted data, it is the same as losing the data without it being encrypted. This is, due to encryption being a two-way algorithm. For instance, data encrypted using a symmetric key can also be decrypted with the same key. Essentially, having the key is all that is needed to transform the cipher text back to clear text, thus running the function again, the clear text can be transformed back to cipher text. This is possible because the key is mathematically related and the unique factor added to the algorithm at the time of encryption to ensure the cipher text is unique. Because the math in cryptography is extremely advanced, the subject in this chapter will remain at the level of basic operation. Coverage of asymmetric encryption is covered later in this chapter and functions differently than the previous example.

The factors that make one encryption stronger than another at a high level are the key length, rounds of encryption, and salting. Rounds refer to how many times the data is run through the encryption algorithm to generate the cipher text, and salting is the process of adding random bits, a password, or passphrase to the encryption process to increase the strength of the cipher text. There are several well-known encryption algorithms including, but not limited, to:

- AES-128 (Advanced Encryption Standard, 128-bit)
- AES-192 (Advanced Encryption Standard, 192-bit)
- AES-256 (Advanced Encryption Standard, 256-bit)
- RC4 (Ron's Code 4, named after Ron Rivest)
- DES (Data Encryption Standard, 56-bit)
- 3DES (Triple DES, 160-bit)

There are many more available options for encryption that should be considered. For example, some are faster, which may be a consideration when the system using the encryption does not have a lot of processing power.

AES-128 is the recommended version to use due to a collision issue in AES-256 that results in identical cipher text for differing clear text data. An overall encryption recommendation cannot be made, as there are several factors that must be considered when selecting an algorithm for implementation.

Given next is an example of an encrypted file, text.txt, that I encrypted using OpenSSL AES-256 symmetric encryption. OpenSSL is a tool found natively on Linux and Mac OS X systems and can be installed on Windows.

The original file content is shown in the following screenshot:

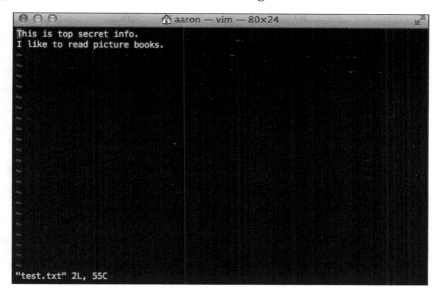

The encrypted file content is shown in the following screenshot:

It is easy to see that the second picture is not readable text; it certainly does not have the clear text words from the previous screenshot. I can now decrypt this file using the same encryption algorithm, (AES-256), to view the content.

The decrypted file content can be seen in the following screenshot:

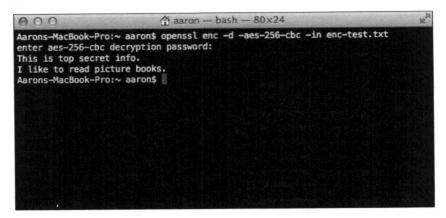

This last example illustrates the two-way function of encryption. The key used to encrypt the original data can be used to retrieve the original text from the encrypted data.

Asymmetric encryption is different than symmetric methods because the master key (private key) is never shared; it remains with one party in the encryption process. The best example of this in use is SSL certificates used for online security. When a purchase is made online at a website using SSL (browser will show padlock), the user's browser will establish an encrypted connection to the web server. All data encrypted is done so using the server's public certificate and key.

The public certificate and key pair is just that, public, everyone has access to it. The public certificate/key pair can only perform one side of the encryption process—encryption. It is not possible to use the public certificate and key to decrypt. Only the private certificate and key can decrypt data encrypted with the related public/key pair. In order for this to work there are a few things that have to happen. First, a private key and certificate must be generated, then from these items a public certificate and key can be generated. This is the process of creating the mathematical relationship between the public and private certificates and keys used. The primary benefit of this method is that the private components only have to be in one place. As with symmetric encryption all parties must have the secret key.

Another form of this type of encryption is **Gnu Privacy Guard** (**GPG**). This is an open source implementation of the now commercial PGP asymmetric key encryption solution. To understand how this works, see the following example:

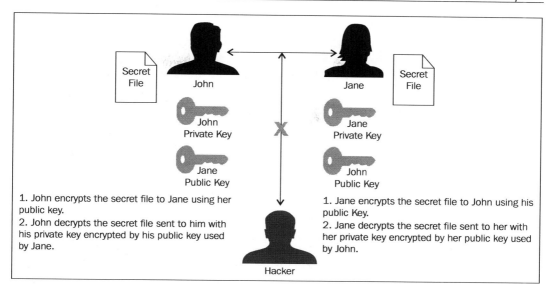

1. John encrypts the secret file to Jane using her public key.
2. John decrypts the secret file sent to him with his private key encrypted by his public key used by Jane.

1. Jane encrypts the secret file to John using his public Key.
2. Jane decrypts the secret file sent to her with her private key encrypted by her public key used by John.

Each type of encryption has its use and must be considered when making a decision on how to encrypt data and communications within the enterprise. Another consideration is key management, due to the importance of securing the private keys a process should be developed to ensure the proper creation, deletion, and rotation of keys used in the enterprise.

Encrypting data at rest

Data at rest that meets the encryption requirements of the data classification model may reside in several of the previously discussed data locations and they need protection. This may come in the form of encryption and can happen at the location of storage, prior to storage, or during the process of storing. Each of these methods requires discovery into interacting business processes and use of the data to ensure the processes and applications can support the method used.

Another aspect to encrypting data at rest is online versus offline encryption. Typically online encryption is in effect while data is accessible and offline is in effect when data is not directly accessible such as on backup tapes, turned off systems, and so on. Another example of offline encryption is a whole disk encryption, once the operating system is booted and the volume is decrypted for use; technically the data is no longer encrypted and can be accessed in an unauthorized manner until the next boot.

Database encryption

Before I present database encryption, I want to communicate that most approaches to data protection will only protect the data from unauthorized access and physical theft of system hardware. I stress unauthorized because if a web application is exploited, the access will be authorized and simply misused. If the exploit was against the database, this may not be the case. But this should not be an Internet accessible service, and database encryption in this case should be sufficient to protect the stored data.

Data stored in databases can be encrypted via two methods. The first method utilizes the built-in encryption capabilities of the database itself to protect the stored data. This can be beneficial when attempting to make encryption invisible to the applications and processes that are accessing the data. All permissions, views, and protection are managed within the database. One caveat can be the implementation of the database on the underlying system. If not configured properly the system administrators can circumvent the database encryption. The second option, which is much broader in spectrum, is encrypting at the application and process layer. All data is encrypted before it is stored in the database. This method may make sense in environments where the database is not in the control of the enterprise or in a shared environment where a pivoted attack could cause a compromise of enterprise data. Some challenges with this method include building the encryption capability into the applications and managing the encryption keys that have to be used. Management and protection of the encryption keys becomes multiplied in complexity, as only one application has to be compromised to get the key. For smaller encryption domains with little to no complexity, this method may be the most cost-effective solution, especially if all the applications are homegrown, as in-house experts can make the necessary modifications to add encryption. More detailed approaches to database security are explained in the following sections.

The need for database encryption

Typically, database encryption is a requirement of security standards that introduces significant complexity into the overall applications and processes that must access the data. This can provide little increase of security when the data at rest is live. The definition of live—the database is up and the trusted applications and processes are accessing the database, the misuse of these factors in our trust model will not be mitigated by encryption.

The primary concern of database encryption is to protect the data from prying eyes, a person, application, or process that is not trusted per the trust model to access the data. An example may be a system administrator; their access to the system should not taint access to the data in the database due to the elevated system privileges. This, in practice, would be strict adherence to the trust model, thus the reason for its existence.

Methods of database encryption

It is a good practice to apply encryption when the system is not in the physical control of the enterprise, for database backup procedures, to apply strict data access controls, and to meet compliance requirements. The methods to encrypt the database data are numerous, and each has its benefits and drawbacks.

There is no right or wrong way to encrypt data as long as the encryption or hashing uses a standard method that has been independently reviewed, and does not have any known weaknesses in the algorithm. Selecting a solution should go beyond the marketing slides of the vendor and involves research and proof of concept testing. The method and complexity used by the applications and processes that must interact with the encrypted database will drive the correct implementation with possibly some modification to the applications and processes.

Application encryption

Application encryption, in this case, is simply stating that the encryption of the data occurs in the application not the database. The significant difference here is that the data arrives as already encrypted in the database. A challenge with data protection, especially in environments where the network equipment is not owned by the enterprise, is snooping, else a simple misconfiguration of network equipment leads to the exposure of sensitive enterprise data. A method often employed is securing the communications between systems and passing the data clearly over a secure channel.

This can be rather complex, and if the secure channel has an issue and for some reason does not provide a truly secure communication path, then the data gets exposed and can be without any indications from the application or systems involved in the communication. Regardless if the secure channel can be created, encryption of the data can be enforced at the application. This has performance benefits and reduces the complexity of the overall system. A consideration is application level encryption that will require all processes and applications to have a method to decrypt and encrypt the data that was initially encrypted at the application. Typically, this is accomplished using a shared private key, a bit of an oxymoron, but this is where we have arrived at the moment with encrypting keys. Another method leverages public/private key encryption, much like the previously mentioned authentication mechanism. A key change in the environment would be significant, potentially shutting down the application for the duration of the key rotation, also requiring testing time.

The primary benefits for using this method are:

- Database performance gains for not using encryption at the database tier
- The data is always encrypted in the databases (no DB admin or SYS admin visibility)

- Each application that must use the data in some fashion is responsible for encrypting the data
- Data encryption is implemented end to end regardless of communication channel security

Selective database encryption

Selective database encryption refers to encrypting only portions of the database; typically selected columns that contain sensitive data. This method is often employed not only to reduce the overall load on the database server for encryption, but also to make it easier for the DB admins to ensure the data inserted into the database is correct. This method of encryption is controlled at the user, process, and application level. With this configuration role assignment will control database table and columns view permissions.

The downside of this type of implementation is that the DB admin has full control over the database encryption, if the individual decides to see the data in an unauthorized method; it is a simple change the DB admin can make without peer review. With this scenario, monitoring and detection of the unauthorized change would be the only real protection from this unauthorized access. Additionally, SYS admins can have access to the data in the database simply due to having "root" access to the system. They may not be able to see the encrypted columns, but access to all clear data is feasible if the database is not configured to mitigate this vulnerability.

There are requirements for certain industries and datatypes to have a regular key rotation after a given period of time, to reduce the risk of data exposure through key compromise. It is a general principle that the longer an encryption key exists the more likely it will exposed; remember that the key is supposed to be secret, so exposure is bad. When a column or a series of selective columns is encrypted versus the entire database, time to rotate a key is greatly reduced, which affects production down time.

ID	Name	Phone	Email	Credit Card	Social Security
1	Nate U.	614-555-1212	nateu@*****.org	4************1234	***-**-****
2	Toby P.	614-555-1213	tobyp@*****.net	4************1235	***-**-****
3	Steve R.	614-555-1214	stever@*****.edu	5************1236	***-**-****
4	Todd B.	614-555-1215	toddb@*****.com	3************1237	***-**-****
5	Jason S.	614-555-1216	jasons@*****.net	4************1238	***-**-****

Example of database column encryption

Applications, processes, and users with access to the database will only be able to see what their permissions allow, including the ability to view encrypted columns. Usually, the view of encrypted columns will be asterisk for character replacement to allow recognizable field data without compromise on privacy and confidentiality. The column-level encryption will authorize an authenticated session to insert, delete, and change data accordingly.

In most cases, the application and processes accessing the database will not have access to decrypt the entire column data but just enough data to make a determination. An example of this is logging into the website of an online retailer and changing the credit card number on file. The user will see maybe the last four digits of the card number and other information, such as the expiration date, to identify the correct payment method. The viewing of only the last four digits of the credit card number is an example of partial column decryption controlled by view permissions in the database for the web applications.

Complete database encryption

Encrypting all data in a database is an example of complete database encryption, resulting in all tables being encrypted regardless of their sensitivity. This method is vulnerable to the rogue DB admin, but should thwart the snooping SYS admin. Data encrypted in this manner is also safe from database backup snooping and data loss. Not all data stored in a database is protected by law, mandate, or regulatory compliance, and requires encryption. But, not all data should be made public.

Encrypting the entire database may be the method chosen to ensure that no data is visible without the correct authorization to decrypt data, essentially a specialized view to see the encrypted data. This method will protect the data in the database from unauthorized access and reduce it's exposure in the event a backup of the data is lost or stolen. The method implemented must make sense from data protection and risk analysis perspectives.

Tokenization

Another method is to "tokenize" sensitive data for use in applications and storage in the database. **Tokenization** is a method that assigns a value to a segment of data, so that the initial sensitive data value no longer exists. All processes, systems, and applications are able to process the token value as they would process the sensitive data, however, this method ensures that the token has no real value to anyone or anything outside of the process.

A common use for tokenization is in the retail industry for the replacement of credit card data within the network and assets. Because tokenization is not encryption or hashing, there is no mathematical relationship or known reversal method known outside of the tokenization system; recovery of the initial sensitive data is nearly impossible. This allows retailers to escape the prescriptive security controls required for systems, processes, and applications that typically interact with credit card data. This method also makes it more difficult for sensitive data exposure and compromise. There may be customization required to implement tokenization, but it is an option gaining momentum.

File share encryption

Every enterprise has servers that store data for use in processes, applications, and for general use by users. As with databases, many operating systems offer native encryption, generally offline encryption, and can be accessed by system administrators, which may be considered as unauthorized access and a security violation.

There are technologies available that will encrypt data as it is being written to the file system. This same technology can apply permissions above the underlying operating system enforcing least privilege and ensuring only the necessary processes, applications, and users have permissions to access data. The method of encryption within the application is also a viable solution to ensure that only the necessary processes and applications have permissions to interact with the data.

Encrypting data in use

Data in use is data that is being accessed, created, modified, or deleted, typically by automated processes or human beings. An example could be fraud investigators leveraging stored credit card and transaction information for an investigation. In this scenario, access to the data is necessary but should not be visible to prying eyes on the network. This can be accomplished by ensuring commercial software provides secure communication and that views can be created to ensure that only the fields needed are viewable.

The enterprise will need to understand the complexities of data access for business processes and applications to decide what methods of encryption to implements across data access technologies.

Encrypting data in transit

Data may need to be transmitted internally and externally to the enterprise in a secure manner to support a business function. Although not all data has to be encrypted for a business reason (laws, mandates, compliance), it is good practice to only use secure transport methods to transfer data. Typical protocols used for secure transmission include SSL, SFTP, FTP-S, and SSH, in addition to proprietary solutions. You should carefully evaluate the solution to ensure the encryption methods are sound and meet the requirements of the enterprise. If the transport cannot be secured, then the data itself must be encrypted, however, this does not mitigate unauthorized access to the encrypted data. The data may not be decrypted, but with insecure transmissions, not only is the payload accessible, but credentials are also passed in clear text, which could lead to further compromise.

A technology that is fast becoming a solution for secure transfer is web based and allows any user or organization with an Internet connection and browser the ability to securely upload and download sensitive data using a web interface to send encrypted e-mail notifications. The recipient receives an e-mail notification that there is a file waiting for them to download. The user authenticates and accesses the data uploaded. Each organization will need to assess the data transfer requirements of the business and build the correct solutions to ensure proper data protection while in transit.

Tokenization

A relatively newer solution for removing sensitive data from business processes, applications, and user interaction is tokenization. This method is commonly presented as a solution to reduce PCI DSS scope and reduce business risk associated with storing credit card numbers. Tokenization is the process of generating a representation of data, called a token, and inserting the token into the processes where the original data would be used. A database is used to map the original data to the token value, allowing for both values to be retrieved if needed, and to maintain a real value for the token.

An example is when credit card numbers are inserted at point of sale and then sent on for authorization. Once authorization occurs there are only a few reasons the credit card would need to be maintained beyond the transaction. Since these reasons don't really require the credit card number itself, a unique value like a token can be used to allow business intelligence, fraud investigations, and card tracking to continue while removing this sensitive data from the systems involved in transaction processing.

There is no real standard for tokens but one method to consider is format preserving, meaning the output token would look like, in this example, a credit card number to all processes, applications, and users, reducing complexity in rewriting applications for new formats and confusion for humans that have to read the output format. Tokenization, as with all data protection methods, has to be evaluated to determine if it is the correct fit for the enterprise use cases.

Data masking

Another method that can be used to render data unusable but recognizable is data masking. This method is commonly used in processes where there is human interaction. An example would be looking at your stored credit card information at an online retailer. Typically, your credit number will be masked (series of asterisks) except for the last four digits, so you can identify the card stored while not divulging the full number. This is done so that if your account is compromised, the number is not there to be stolen and used for fraudulent purchases. A similar method can be achieved in database views and specialized encryption solutions to enforce the least privilege and access only on a need-to-know basis.

This solution has pros and cons that should be considered prior to selection as a method to protect sensitive data. Masking as used on a database implementation is simply a view presented with the original data intact and viewable by database administrators. While the solution does provide some protection, it is not at the same level as tokenization, encryption, or hashing. A pro to this solution is the relative ease of implementation. Since the actual data is not manipulated the challenges introduced by the other methods are not present. Since there is no encryption or hashing involved, there is no additional processing power required, application changes, or key management required.

Using masking should only be considered for viewing restrictions in systems and log output and it is not truly a data protection method.

Authorization

Authorization, granting permissions based on who or what the authorized is, is a very important part of the enterprise data protection and security program. Each one of the previous sections on data security relies on proper authorization to underlying operating systems, applications, and the data. This facet of data security highlights the defense in depth mantra of information security. Regardless of the technologies implemented for encryption, tokenization, and masking, a developed process for authorization including access provisioning, account removal, level of access, and auditing will not only ensure that the data remains secure, but provides a defensible data security strategy that can aide in reducing risk and cost associated with external auditing engagements.

Developing supporting processes

Once the enterprise has decided that data classification must occur and action must be taken to prevent misuse and loss of data, there must be processes in place to ensure actions can be taken to enforce and assign accountability for data protection in accordance with enterprise policies and standards. It is good to have a technology that can help the organization, but if it is not operationalized properly it will become a burden and not provide the intended value, therefore undermining security initiatives for secure data storage, transmission, and use. Because data is at the center of the enterprise whether accessed by automated processes, applications, or humans, any changes to secure data must be a collaborative evaluation and implementation as the nature of enterprise data protection is a cross-functional implementation and may require significant resources to implement. All supporting processes need to be identified and developed (if nonexistent) to ensure a successful data protection component in enterprise security architecture.

Summary

Securing data in the enterprise can pose a very challenging set of obstacles, further complicated by external requirements to do so. There are many methods and approaches to securing data at rest, in transit, and in use involving various types of technologies. The use of DLP, encryption, tokenization, data masking, and authorization are proven methods of securing data in the various states in which it may exist.

This chapter presented real-world scenarios and caveats for each technology that should be taken into consideration before any solution, or set of solutions, are selected and implemented. Topics covered thus far have been focused on all aspects of securing data through process, network security, system security, and lastly, data security. The next chapters will present securing data access through wireless networks; the human aspect of security, and developing supported enterprise security architecture.

7
Wireless Network Security

This chapter will build on the foundations set in previous chapters with a focus on wireless network implementation. The convenience of wireless networking is a benefit used by most enterprise users to increase productivity and gain mobility. The ability to connect to the network over wireless signals poses security challenges and can be the source of network compromise if not implemented correctly. Threats to wireless network security continue to increase; it is imperative to consider the current methods of wireless exploitation and plan for future vulnerability discovery. To ensure minimal risk introduction through wireless network implementation, configuration considerations must be assessed and the wired network protected from inevitable wireless network attacks. Additional resources for implementing secure wireless networks are provided in *Appendix C, Security Tools List*.

This chapter will cover:

- Securing wireless networks
- Wireless network authentication
- Wireless network encryption
- Wireless client security
- Network segmentation
- Wireless intrusion prevention

Security and wireless networks

The nature of wireless networks extending access to the internal network beyond the physical boundaries of the enterprise introduces complexities in properly securing access. In the standard internal network implementation, physical access is required to cable into the network in order to gain access to enterprise resources; to date this has been the method of ensuring trust for hosts connecting. Though this is not well-evaluated logic, the same rationale has been generally applied to wireless networks. Because wireless networks allow a level of anonymity for connecting hosts, a degree of trust must be established for connecting hosts and the infrastructure providing the wireless access.

In order to provide security through obscurity, methods such as hidden SSIDs and MAC address filtering have been employed to keep the wireless network invisible to eavesdroppers and more difficult to connect to for an unknown host. Unfortunately, these methods fail due to the very nature of how wireless works. When a host is configured for a wireless network it will send a beacon frame out looking for an access point serving the network. This design eases the connectivity process for users, but can allow an attacker to learn of a network that is cloaked by not broadcasting the SSID. Additionally, simple wireless network traffic sniffing can provide the information needed to circumvent MAC address filters by observing connected hosts for their MAC addresses. The MAC address of a valid host can be spoofed with little effort rendering the filtering ineffective. Knowing the SSID and having a valid MAC address does not necessarily gain an attacker access to the wireless network, but it does provide information that can be used to launch an attack. The attack can be directly against the wireless network or generation of a fake access point to harvest credentials from unsuspecting wireless clients. Either scenario is not ideal for an enterprise responsible for protecting internal resources. Before implementing a wireless network, it is important to determine the best method to reduce risk by implementing authentication and encryption methods that secure the wireless network regardless of whether the network is advertised and client MAC addresses are visible. Methods to secure wireless networks involve a layered approach that addresses each tier of wireless network communications. Not only is the security configuration of utmost importance, but so is the physical protection of the wireless infrastructure, much like any other network devices that provide physical connectivity to the enterprise network.

Securing wireless networks

Items to consider when implementing a secured wireless implementation include:

- Client and access point authentication
- Wireless network encryption

A quick note on SSID cloaking and MAC filtering

It was once thought that simply hiding or **cloaking** the presence of the wireless network was sufficient to thwart attackers. And adding MAC address filtering to limit host access was considered a valid method to "authenticate" hosts. Both of these methods have proven to be ineffective to secure a wireless network implementation. Cloaking or attempting to hide an SSID is easily undermined by the inherent nature of wireless network communication design. When a host has already connected to a hidden network, the next time the wireless card is enabled, the hosts will automatically send a beacon frame with the SSID in an attempt to find an access point serving the network. This traffic is sent in the clear and can be sniffed out of the airwaves. Once the network SSID is broadcast freely into the airwaves, it is no longer hidden or secret. Think of hidden SSID as camouflage. Camouflage is not meant to make the camouflaged thing invisible, but harder to see at first glance. The SSID may not be apparent at first, but a little patience and it will appear and be available for attack.

As for MAC address filtering, a similar behavior is exhibited by the wireless network. To recall, a **MAC address** is the unique burned-in hardware address of the network interfaces on a network device. Because this value is unique, using MAC address filtering in theory would allow limited access to the wireless network based on this unique address. Due to the broadcast nature of wireless networking, with a little time sniffing the airwaves, available SSIDs can be learned in addition to successfully connected hosts. With easily accessible tools to spoof MAC addresses and send a deauthentication frame, an attacker can gain access to the wireless network as the valid hosts. In this type of implementation, host authentication is achieved solely by the use of the unique MAC address. The access point has no other method to validate the connecting hosts; with a matching MAC address on the allow list, access is granted.

Due to these limitations and easy circumvention both of these methods are ineffective for securing a wireless network implementation. The following sections provide detailed methods for securing wireless networks using more advanced authentication and encryption configuration.

Wireless authentication

An important part of configuring a secure wireless network is authentication. **Authentication** is the method to prove a user or system is who or what they say they are. In the case of user access to the wireless network, the user has to provide either a valid key, or username password pair (credentials) to gain access to the network. There are primarily two methods of authentication: **shared key** and **802.1X**. Shared key authentication is typical for home user wireless networks, but enterprise wireless networks commonly use some form of 802.1X authentication leveraging a user directory, certificates, two-factor authentication, or some variation of technologies. In some cases, the enterprise may have to leverage a shared key authentication method because of limitations of devices using the wireless network or due to the lack of 802.1X capabilities. Commonly shared key implementations are called personal and 802.1X implementations are called enterprise. Both will be covered to explain the differences, advantages, and caveats of implementing each method.

Using shared key

The shared key method of authenticating to a wireless network is the simplest method from a configuration perspective, however, long-term support of the solution and security are significant areas of concern for a large-scale enterprise implementation. Implementation is very simple with a shared key configuration; devices only need the SSID and the correct shared key to connect. This is the extent of the configuration and authentication process. The secret key is typically stored locally on devices for ease of connecting to the wireless network. The key storage method varies by implementation and should be understood by the security team to determine if additional controls should be implemented to protect the key. In the case of Microsoft Windows, the key is hashed several times using the SSID and key combination and stored in the registry. This process ensures the key is stored securely, mitigating easy compromise. To authenticate with the access point, the device does not actually send the key over the air, instead a hash representation is sent. If the value matches, the access point knows the key is correct and completes the authentication process. Security issues with this type of implementation are explained in the next section. Shared key authentication should be cautiously used in the enterprise or used in very limited and low-risk portions of the network.

Caveats of shared key implementation

There are several caveats to using a shared key authentication configuration in an enterprise network. Because the key may be a static value on a device or in storage, it can be extracted and cracked offline or brute forced online, as this method does not prevent this attack via account lock out. Also, the key must be shared in order for every device to connect to the network; this philosophically is an issue with secret keys (not really secret if everyone knows it) and mandates a regular rotation of keys to remain more secure. Anytime a shared key has to be rotated, every device must be reconfigured with the new key. Depending on the size of the enterprise, this can be a significant amount of work and impacts the enterprise. The wireless secret should be managed through a formal key management program enforcing key rotation at a minimum when a user with knowledge of the key moves positions or leaves the company, becomes compromised, or has reached the end of the accepted crypto period (length of time a key may be in use).

Using IEEE 802.1X

The **Institute of Electrical and Electronics Engineers (IEEE)** standard for authenticating to a wireless network is 802.1X. This standard is commonly known as the enterprise authentication method in wireless deployments, an example is WPA2-Enterprise. The 802.1X standard relies on several components to provide security including client software (for example, Microsoft's Wireless Zero Configuration) known as the supplicant, authenticator (in this scenario an access point), and an authentication server such as Active Directory for user authentication. For this type of wireless authentication, users do not need a secret pre-shared key, only the correct client configuration and valid credentials managed by the authentication server. Benefits to this authentication method include no key management and directory storage of user credentials enforcing wireless security policy. Examples of security that can be added include account lockout after a number of consecutive login failures, minimum password length and strength, and centralized account management. With the additional security features and no secret key to protect from compromise, this is the only method that should be considered for enterprise wireless networking implementation.

Some wireless solutions allow the enterprise to offer "guest" wireless access to non-employees for access to the Internet or limited internal network access. In this scenario, a local credential store for time limited access to the wireless network would make sense especially if the requesting user is truly a guest. Adding an account to the central credential store would be more involved and potentially introduce security risks to the enterprise. Leveraging the wireless solution itself for authentication is hybrid in the fact that neither a shared key nor a central user directory is used for authentication; it is native to the wireless solution. Minimal to no risk should be introduced with the guest wireless access because it should have no access to the production wireless or wired networks unless in a limited manner with security controls implemented to enforce restricted access.

Another method of authentication using 802.1X is user-based certificates and two-factor authentication schemes. Both require user credentials (username and password) in addition to having a valid certificate or token, essentially providing two-factor authentication, something you have and something you know. User certificates have traditionally been accepted as a second factor of authentication to add to user credentials serving as a two-factor method. The benefit of these methods is that a portion of the user's credentials can be revoked or changed without affecting everything. For instance, the user's password can be changed but the certificate does not have to be revoked. If the certificate is compromised, it can be revoked and the user never has to change their password. The added security is one portion of the authentication method can be compromised and access will not be permitted without the other authentication component. It can be argued that a certificate is a questionable component of two-factor authentication, but it has one of the characteristics that are required of the 'something you have, something you know, and/or something you are', while in this case the password is 'something you know'.

Caveats of 802.1X implementation

Implementing 802.1X does require other services that may not be implemented in a small enterprise but are common in the medium and large enterprise such as a user directory, certificate authority servers, token-based technologies, and other two-factor solutions. Using 802.1X for wireless authentication is considered the enterprise solution and offers several enhancements over the pre-shared key personal authentication configurations, but there are complexities that may not allow an implementation to use this method. Some devices cannot be configured to use an enterprise configuration for wireless and have been purposely limited due to processing power associated with encryption algorithms offered on enterprise implementations. Because users will use their primary network credentials to authenticate, a misconfigured host can lockout a user's account. While this does not seem like a real issue, it should be accounted for from an operations perspective so the help desk can resolve the issue quickly.

The enterprise will need to create procedures for using the chosen 802.1X authentication method and account management such as user account provisioning and revocation. If the authentication method is certificate based, the length of validity must be determined, and a process for renewal should be in place to ensure service to users is not impacted. Because two-factor solutions provide additional authentication capabilities, some in rather unique ways, there may be specialized operational requirements for administration, use, and maintenance. The skill required for each must be understood to ensure the proper skill set is in-house to operate as an enterprise class service to users. An improper implementation and configuration of the user directory can minimize such an implementation to simply an authentication mechanism, not necessarily a secure authentication mechanism. Proper security should be configured within the chosen 802.1X method. Examples include password complexity, minimum password length requirements, securing certificate server and store, and proper system protection for each component to ensure accounts are not compromised in another fashion and the wireless used as a second stage in a network compromise.

Wireless encryption

This section will cover the protection mechanisms available with the existing wireless standards and implementations. Some implementations should be avoided and others are highly recommended. The protection of wireless transmissions is of utmost importance because the data is literally flying through the airwaves with no physical boundaries such as those available in a wired network implementation. Knowing what implementations to avoid, and what configurations provide the most security are covered in the following sections.

Each of the wireless standards such as WEP, WPA1, and WPA2 have supported encryption protocols that can be used to secure the wireless setup communications along with payload containing user data. WEP was the first solution and since has been broken, and the use of the more secure WPA1 and WPA2 are recommended. There are new methods of breaking these wireless protocols being developed, so before settling on a method it is important to understand the weaknesses along with the strengths that can be leveraged natively or require other methods to secure.

 The standard in wireless security today is WPA2. There are two versions of WPA2 that can be used depending on the environment. Home users can leverage WPA2-PSK (sometimes called personal) and enterprise users should use WPA2-Enterprise.

WEP and WPA1 will be covered more for a brief historical purpose but to also communicate that WEP must absolutely be abandoned, and WPA1 has weaknesses that should lead to the abandonment of its use in the home and enterprise.

WEP

Wired Equivalent Privacy (WEP) was the first method of implementing security for wireless networks. The encryption used is RC4 and supports 40-bit and 104-bit key lengths. The issue with WEP was the method by which data is sent back and forth with the wireless access point; it is a predictable algorithm with repeatable output that with enough management packets captured, the pre-shared key could be learned. Easy to find and use tools such as the Aircrack-ng suite make this task trivial and therefore WEP should never be used on any wireless network.

WPA

The next generation of security for wireless networks came in **Wi-Fi Protected Access (WPA)**. With WPA, the **Temporal Key Integrity Protocol (TKIP)** was introduced to provide an additional level of security per packet. In this implementation, each packet has a uniquely generated encryption key versus the static key used with WEP. The primary benefit being that if somehow a key was compromised, it is only good for the one packet and subsequent packets would use a new unique key and will require each packet key to be compromised in order to compromise an entire conversation. In addition to this enhancement, an improved integrity method was implemented to mitigate replay attacks that were easy to accomplish with the CRC method used in WEP. Unfortunately, there are vulnerabilities present in WPA too that allow the cracking of WPA when using pre-shared keys. The weakness is a legacy from WEP and is present in TKIP implementations.

WPA2

When implemented correctly, in enterprise mode with no pre-shared key, WPA2 is the most secure and recommended wireless encryption solution. With the introduction of AES-CCMP for authentication and encryption, there is no real comparison to WEP or WPA from a security perspective. Though more system resources are required when implementing AES, the benefit is that there are no known attacks outside of a weak PSK if present. At the time of writing, the only known vulnerability with WPA2 is when it is implemented using a PSK allowing brute-force attacks to gain access to the wireless network.

Wireless network implementation

In this section, we will begin to tie all the components together that ensure a successfully secured wireless network implementation. The previous sections introduced terminology, provided history, and set the stage for the recommendations presented in this section. We will discuss the recommended configuration for an enterprise wireless implementation including wireless signal leakage, client configuration, encryption, authentication, using certificates, and other security considerations.

Wireless signal considerations

An important element of wireless network implementation is signal strength and limiting signal leakage. The wireless signal must be strong enough to provide the coverage necessary to be useful. However, it's range must also be limited to ensure the wireless signal is not reachable too far from the physical boundaries of the enterprise. There are many reasons to attempt striking the balance of signal strength and limiting the range. These include security, availability, and courtesy for close-by businesses. This section will cover considerations for wireless signal configuration.

Implementation of the wireless network should include a spectrum analysis to not only ensure proper coverage, but to ensure the network does not extend too far beyond the physical boundaries of the enterprise buildings. There will be some level of leakage but it should be minimized for security and interference, as both can have undesirable effects on the wireless network implementation. When the wireless signal leaks too far from the intended area(s) it becomes more susceptible to attacks, as the network becomes known easier from farther distances and this distance factor is a benefit for attackers who do not need to be in close proximity to the enterprise to attack the wireless network. This reduces the likelihood of apprehension and overall risk for attacking the network. Interference is another side effect of too much leakage, though this is more of an issue if other wireless networks are operating in the same airspace and on the same channels. It is advisable to limit wireless network overlap and leakage for increased security and performance.

Wireless network range can be affected by the type of antennas used to provide the necessary coverage and will be influenced by the environment in which the network is being broadcast. The two most common antenna types are directional and omni-directional, both have their use and can be used together to gain the best coverage and limit signal leakage. An example is a wireless network broadcast in an environment with a glass front building. Omni-directional antennas may be used deeper in the building and directional antennas used near the glass front broadcasting inward to provide strong coverage internally while limiting the signal through the glass front.

An assessment of how the wireless network will be used should be conducted to best determine what types of antennas to use and placement within the enterprise. Generally speaking, directional antennas will be able to cover greater distances, while omni-directional antennas are great for localized saturation of wireless signals. Another example of when a directional antenna would be preferred is building-to-building signal transmission. Two buildings with direct line of sight can use directional antennas to extend the network using wireless. This method also limits signal leakage, only allowing network connectivity for direct line of sight antennas. There are tools to calculate antenna range, but it is recommended to leverage a wireless specialist for the specific implementation. If you are familiar with antenna theory, then a tool such as the following calculator can be used provided by RadioLabs, Inc.:

```
http://www.radiolabs.com/stations/wifi_calc.html
```

End system configuration

With operating system vendors eager to provide ease of use, the wireless card can be configured to auto connect to familiar SSIDs. This feature is convenient, however, when operating systems are configured in this manner wireless connections are established based only on the SSID, not a valid access point. Configuring the enterprise end systems to force a manual connection and authentication to an access point will ensure hosts are not connecting automatically to rogue access points that are possibly malicious without any human intervention.

Another consideration when implementing a wireless network in an existing wired network is dual-homed connectivity. A host with dual-homed connectivity can simultaneously connect to both the wired and wireless networks potentially introducing risk to assets within the wired network infrastructure from the extended access feasible with wireless. Unfortunately, this configuration is permitted by default on most systems and operating systems. Additional configuration is required to limit dual-homed network functionality and force only one live connection type at a time. For example, on Windows-based systems there are a few options such as third-party software, registry edits, and group policies. Of these options, group policy is recommended because the configuration can be centrally managed ensuring consistency across systems and reduced operational overhead.

Dual-homed network configurations introduce the possibility that a compromise of the wireless network connection could impact the attached wired network. This feature and capability should be disabled. A configuration allowing dual-homed connectivity is a significant security issue especially if other controls are not configured such as mutual AP and client authentication, and network segmentation (firewalls, not access control lists).

Wireless encryption and authentication recommendations

The three security implementations for wireless networks, WEP, WPA, and WPA2, have been briefly covered to provide an overview. This book is not meant to be a comprehensive resource on the subject but provides recommendations for securely implementing wireless networks within the enterprise with strong encryption and authentication mechanisms. When these two components are implemented correctly, the threat of man-in-the-middle attacks are mitigated, and both the wireless clients and access points are mutually authenticated ensuring valid clients and wireless network are connecting. Additionally, leveraging the best encryption methods protects all data traversing the wireless network including the initial setup of communications. This was the weakness in WEP, hence the stern position on avoiding its use.

Encryption

Remember, encryption is the protection method for not only data traversing the wireless network, but also wireless management communications. To date, the best option for encryption on a wireless network is WPA2 with **Advanced Encryption Standard (AES)** and **Counter Cipher Mode Protocol (CCMP)** – WPA2-AES/CCMP. All other currently available encryption methods have been proven to have weaknesses that put any enterprise using them at risk of compromise over wireless.

Authentication

The purpose of authentication is for a person or device to prove who or what they are by using a method such as credentials, certificates, or unique system-specific configuration files. This section provides recommendations based on currently available methods that ensure the most secure wireless authentication implementation to date.

The following are a few authentication mechanisms:

- 802.1X
- Client-side certificates
- EAP-TLS
- Unique system check

WPA2 and 802.1X have been covered, but the additional authentication mechanisms listed require coverage because they require more planning and process to effectively implement. These methods are generally not implemented due to the additional configuration required, but are ultimately the only methods to properly secure a wireless network from common and easy to exploit attacks.

Implementing these technologies together provides the most secure environment. There are dependencies on one or more to work and therefore planning on how to implement is critical for successful implementation. If all methods are implemented, then Public Key Infrastructure (PKI) is a requirement for this type of implementation. If non-existent in the enterprise, this service will need to be designed and implemented securely prior to configuring wireless in this manner. Additionally, some type of authentication system must be implemented such as RADIUS, LDAP, or Active Directory to authenticate users to the wireless network. The authentication of a user can, among other things, determine what VLAN they are assigned to and which resources are accessible via wireless.

Client-side certificates

The purpose of client-side certificates is to enforce mutual authentication of the client and access point on the wireless network. The certificates must match in the standard way of a public and private certificate so that any impersonation of the client and access point is not feasible. The most common attack on clients is a fake AP type attack where a bogus AP is configured to look legitimate and the client will attempt to authenticate to the fake AP versus the legitimate AP. The outcome being that the attacker running the fake AP can steal credentials as users try to authenticate to the wireless network. In environments with 802.1X, this would compromise the user's network credentials and can be used to authenticate to other hosts on the network. For the typical user their credentials may not have much value, but system and database administrators are high-value targets. The genius of this attack is that it typically goes unnoticed and as the attacker will use valid credentials on other systems, no red flags will be raised as the compromise enters further into the network.

When using certificates for authentication, access to the wireless network will not be feasible without a valid certificate, therefore, even with credential compromise, access to the wired infrastructure will become more difficult removing the attack surface from the wireless network. This requires the attacker to find another method to gain network access. Loss of credentials is serious nonetheless; enforcing mutual authentication mitigates this threat. In this scenario, the certificates provide a pre-authentication service; certificates must be validated prior to any authentication or access to the network.

EAP-TLS

Extensible Authentication Protocol-Transport Layer Security (EAP-TLS) provides a secure tunnel for authentication, further mitigating the man-in-the-middle attacks against the authentication mechanism, that is RADIUS. Using certificates, a secure tunnel is created for authentication to RADIUS or other authentication services mitigating credential harvesting over the wireless network. Even if credentials are compromised through another method, authentication will be impossible without the client-side certificate.

Unique system check

A method becoming more commonly used to validate enterprise wireless clients is a unique system check that looks for a specific registry entry or service on the authenticating host to ensure it is what it says it is, an enterprise asset. This method is commonly used for VPN access and is now becoming a method for post-authentication checking of the validity and integrity of the system. If these checks fail, then the system is not granted access to the wireless network. Granted these checks can be spoofed, but these checks in additional to the other methods create a significant challenge for attackers. The challenge of accessing the wireless network should deter the most common attacks.

Wireless segmentation

Implementing a wireless network within the enterprise can provide a high degree of mobility for enterprise users allowing access to enterprise assets no matter where they are located on the campus. The access to critical infrastructure should be properly segmented to ensure the security of the assets from unauthorized access that may be successful via a weak wireless security implementation. In environments with a securely implemented wireless infrastructure, it is recommended to also segment the networks with an intelligent firewall to detect and mitigate attacks over the wireless network. Some compliance standards such as the Payment Card Industry Data Security Standard (PCI DSS) mandate a segmentation of the wireless network when any portion of the wireless network connects to the cardholder data environment. It is a good practice to keep the critical enterprise assets segmented not only from the wireless network, but also from the general user population.

Segmentation is more than connecting the access points to a different switch or configuring in a VLAN. The services used by the wireless network for authentication, DNS, and other network services should be segmented in a manner that will not allow circumvention of security controls or compromise of credentials on wireless network to allow direct access to critical assets including credential stores. Segmentation can most easily be accomplished using a firewall with strict policy adherence to ensure changes to the firewall rules do not reduce the effectiveness of the segmentation.

Wireless network integration

The primary purposes of wireless networks in the enterprise are generally two-fold. First, provide employee access to enterprise assets anywhere on the premises and second, provide guest wireless access for non-employees such as vendors and contractors to access the Internet and VPN services of their respective employers. These two primary use cases warrant considerable planning and control to ensure there is no cross-over of the two domains.

Wireless networks are meant to extend network access beyond what is typically not physically feasible or inexpensive enough to provide wired infrastructure. When enterprise users access the wireless network, access to enterprise systems, applications, and Internet are expected, but to provide the access requires integration into the existing wired network. User authentication, IP addressing using DHCP, e-mail, web, and other network services must be able to get the information from somewhere in order to provide the level of access required to get an IP address and be able to authenticate users to network resources. This dependency on network services may be an issue if shared with critical enterprise assets without the proper security implemented, such as network segmentation and possibly stand-alone solutions, as mentioned previously.

Wireless network intrusion prevention

An important part of security monitoring for a wireless network implementation is a wireless intrusion prevention system. A wireless network should be treated as any other network type, each susceptible to attack and intrusion. What makes wireless networks unique is their boundaries are not limited by a physical boundary and the wireless specific protocols that must be used. Attacks to a wireless infrastructure are unique to the implemented protocols and require a system that can detect and mitigate these unique attacks. Wireless authentication and encryption are the primary attack vectors, but the wireless network infrastructure is a target as well.

It is common to have rogue access points in the airspace of the enterprise wireless deployment, but being able to determine the intent of the rogue access point is the purpose of a wireless intrusion prevention system. To be clear, a **rogue access point** generically is an access point in the same airspace as the enterprise wireless network though not a part of the enterprise implementation. Additionally, a true rogue AP is connected somewhere on the wired network of the enterprise. Simply detecting another access point in the range of the wireless network does not necessarily make the access point a rogue access point. Being connected to the wired network, impersonating a legitimate access point in an attempt to harvest credentials, and being used to launch other attacks against the wireless deployment are characteristics that further define a rogue access point.

A wireless intrusion prevention system can not only detect attacks over the air, but can also determine if the rogue access point is connected to the wired network. Several wireless vendors have the capability built into their solution allowing for a standard AP to act as an intrusion detection device leveraging the management system to apply signal analysis for attacks. The solution should also be able to identify all access points within the wireless implementation and detect when an AP has been physically altered, replaced, or is simply not a valid member of the wireless network.

If the enterprise has a wireless implementation, a wireless intrusion prevention system should be implemented to protect the network as the wired network is protected. PCI DSS, which focuses on cardholder data environments, has worthwhile guidance for general security practices for properly securing the wireless environment. Detected attacks must be alerted and security staff should be monitoring alerts to ensure a quick response to possible wireless network intrusions.

Summary

Wireless networks are as common as wired networks in today's enterprise environments providing access to internal assets from anywhere on campus. With this convenience come additional attack vectors to enterprise assets and data that must be planned for and proper security mechanisms implemented for mitigation. Implementing secure encryption and authentication methods can provide a wireless network to enterprise users that meet their needs and ensure the security of enterprise assets. It is important that a layered approach of security is implemented to address the attacks common to wireless networks including having an intrusion prevention mechanism to detect and mitigate common and advanced attacks. Supporting processes for alert management is essential not only to wireless security, but also to the overall security of the enterprise. Next, we will discuss the human element of enterprise security. With all the technology in place to secure the enterprise, a simple action by a user can undermine the effectiveness of implemented controls. The next chapter will cover methods to address the risk introduced by us, the *humans*.

8
The Human Element of Security

The human element is the least secure and least controlled aspect of enterprise security. Because of the inherent vulnerability of human trust, we are prone to the tactics of social engineering. Social engineering: the primary method of convincing humans to give up sensitive data or click on a malicious link takes many forms. Common communication methods such as e-mail, social networking, and even the telephone are used to trick humans for malicious purposes. This chapter will focus on the human element of security and provide methods to protect against well-executed social engineering attacks. The importance of effective security awareness training will be presented, along with methods for securely using business networking sites, and methods to detect social engineering through e-mail, social media, and the telephone. Often, the threat to enterprise data comes from the associates who maintain the systems that transmit, process, and store data. User monitoring and physical security will complete the chapter on the human element of security.

This chapter will cover the following topics:

- Methods of social engineering
- Mitigation techniques for social engineering
- Detecting malicious e-mails
- Securely using business networking sites
- Effective security awareness training

Social engineering

The easiest thing to exploit in any enterprise is the people working in the enterprise. The reason is because we, as human beings, are naturally trusting and want to think that there are, in general, no ill intentions when another human being interacts with us. This is the very weakness that makes us humans susceptible to **social engineering**; the act of getting an individual to take an action or provide information for the purposes of unauthorized access or to gain private information. There are many methods used to social engineer an individual: e-mail, phone, social media, and in-person interaction. This adds to the complexity of thwarting such attacks because they are not always perpetrated in the same manner, and can be of high quality to ensure the bait is taken. What makes these attacks successful is their believability; the communication is in a context that makes the proposed scenario a possibility and not beyond imagination. Sometimes the e-mail phishing source will leverage a technique that we have been tuned to take a certain action every time with a mindless click of a mouse button. An example of this would be the Java pop up asking if we want to trust the source of the Java application and run whatever application it is that "requires" Java. The following pop up is actually created using the **Social-Engineer Toolkit (SET)**, not a legitimate Java application:

This "fake" Java pop up is indeed a Java pop up. Unfortunately, when it is trusted and the **Run** button is clicked, the hacker gains unauthorized access to the system. The setup is the all too familiar Java pop up; we are trained to click yes, to accept the risk, so we can see what it is we want to see, but while it seems benign, clicking yes allows an exploit to be run on the system. Though a closer examination of the pop up and the actions leading to the pop up should arouse suspicion as to why there is a pop up and whether the Java application is something that should be trusted, is the source trusted? In this case, the answer to the previous questions would be no.

The following screenshot is what the hacker saw in the scenario we just discussed: a connection to the victim, a fully patched Windows XP SP3 system.

```
[*] Connection received from: 192.168.1.191

*** Pick the number of the shell you want ***

1: 192.168.1.191:WINDOWS
2: 192.168.1.191:WINDOWS

set>
```

There are well-known social engineers such as Kevin Mitnick who pioneered the art of hacking the human, called social engineering. There are now well written open source tools to launch social engineering attacks such as SET, written and maintained by Dave Kennedy. Tools such as the SET can be used in training and in penetration testing to validate security awareness training efforts.

Social engineering is an important part of the enterprise security landscape and is the most successful attack vector next to SQL injection in poorly written web applications. If an enterprise is not focused on or aware of the threats social engineering poses, easily mitigated attacks will continue to be successful, many of which are not detectable by the most commonly used anti-virus and other endpoint protection methods. Mitigation is rather simple once end users understand what is a legitimate interaction versus a social engineering attempt; do not open, click, run, accept the request, or give away information. This may seem a daunting task but from an implementation perspective, this is the easiest- and lowest-cost solution to stopping most desktop malware. Complexity is introduced because retraining our trusting minds to first question and prove the intent before action is a learned response only mastered by repetition. Perhaps because the brain is the most complex computer, reasoning becomes the most effective method of mitigation; but we continue to fail the test in this area.

The diverse and convincing methods of social engineering are a contributing factor to the continued success of gaining unauthorized access to networks, systems, and sensitive data. Unsolicited e-mails and phone calls continue to be a method used by social engineers to install malicious software and convince users to provide credentials, and other information that aides in further exploitation of the target enterprise. The extremely skilled social engineer will leverage in-person techniques to gain physical access to the information that is desired.

The following is a simple diagram from
`http://faculty.nps.edu/ncrowe/oldstudents/laribeethesis.htm`
that shows the difference between the traditional hacker path versus the
social engineer:

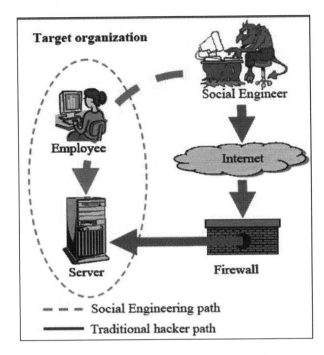

The next sections will cover these methods in more detail and provide methods to
mitigate these techniques by applying sound security principles.

Electronic communication methods

The methods of electronic phishing are becoming more complex as we become more
educated on the simpler methods used successfully in the past. E-mail is the most
common and the primary method of phishing as it reduces the risk to the social
engineer and can be perpetrated completely online. As social media—such as Twitter
and Facebook—has infiltrated the enterprise, using these communication methods
has become a significant threat vector for malicious software infections such as
botnets, Trojans, and viruses. It is important to be aware of the methods employed
by social engineers in order to determine the best strategy to mitigate the threats
each of them poses.

Spam e-mail

The most common method of social engineering continues to be e-mail as there has been little security built into the Internet e-mail system to thwart this malicious behavior. Even with solutions like Sender Policy Framework (SPF) designed to mitigate spam, spam continues. More can be learned about this solution at `http://en.wikipedia.org/wiki/Sender_Policy_Framework`. Anyone can send an e-mail to another person for free with complete anonymity. There are also several free e-mail services available on the Internet and e-mail addresses are easily customizable to look however the sender wants it to look. Additionally, e-mail addresses are easy to spoof making the e-mail look like it is coming from a legitimate source. Some methods used by attackers include the target enterprise's e-mail system that is configured in an insecure manner allowing the malicious e-mail sender to send extremely convincing e-mails to enterprise employees.

One example of a continuously successful type of spam looks as though it comes from a legitimate banking institution requesting payment information or other personal information in order to take over the account or steal the information directly. It is easy to spot a spam e-mail when the bank is incorrect, but when the institution is correct, it becomes increasingly more difficult to determine if the e-mail is legitimate by simply reading the e-mail and observing the sender and recipient e-mail addresses.

Identifying a spam e-mail is difficult and really should not be the responsibility of the end receiver to be an expert in identifying it; but when the controls in place fail or do not exist, the only method to avoid e-mail-based fraud is the knowledge the end user has to make the right decision. Long gone are the days of poorly written e-mails riddled with spelling and grammar errors that were easy indicators that the e-mail was fraudulent. A spam e-mail today is very well written with legitimate graphics, many times dynamically downloaded from the real entity to add to the bait, enticing the end user to click on the link given in the e-mail that will lead to fraud, theft, and installation of malware for further exploitation or annoyance. The crafty spammer understands spam analysis methods so spam is especially crafted to bypass analysis-based blocking. This requires more end-user diligence and more authenticity checks to detect and block unwanted e-mails. Unfortunately, this is a very complex and ever changing process that allows unsolicited e-mails to reach enterprise recipients; it merely reduces the number of e-mails that make it to the end user's e-mail inbox. Some cloud-based services and locally installed solutions provide a user-managed quarantine to allow flagged messages to be reviewed by the end user to determine if the e-mail is valid and authentic. If so, the e-mail can be removed from quarantine. While this is a good method to reduce false positives, it does rely on the ability of the end user to make the right decision.

Key indicators of a spam e-mail

The following are a few key indicators of a spam e-mail:

- There may be promised financial gain by taking action.

- The e-mail is unsolicited: the end user did not request or initiate the communication.

- The e-mail requests personal information such as account, SSN, and credit card numbers.

- The e-mail contains phrases such as, Urgent Action Required, validation of account by providing username and password are required to ensure the account is not suspended and shutdown. It may also ask for financial information.

- Sometimes, the e-mail may contain a link to perform the action requested. For example, an HTML e-mail will show the alias but hovering over the link will indicate the real URL. Also, viewing the HTML source of the e-mail will show the real URL.

In case an e-mail is received that seems like there may be a real issue with an online account, verification request, or some random message online, the best option is to manually browse to the known legitimate URL and check the validity of the request, removing any potential redirection through the link in the e-mail. Some of the most damning security breaches of the largest security companies were perpetrated through specially crafted e-mails to the targeted recipient. Understanding the methods used in a spam e-mail will provide a good starting point for detection/ mitigation technologies and employee education. The next screenshot is a spam e-mail I received at my Gmail account. Let's analyze the e-mail for some of the indicators I mentioned previously. I will also point out a few characteristics of the e-mail by analyzing the e-mail header.

"PLEASE DO NOT IGNORE"   Spam x

MS TINA ███████ <test@█du.ru>   Jan 7 (2 days ago)
to undisclosed recipients

⚠ Why is this message in Spam? It contains content that's typically used in spam messages. Learn more

Dearest Attention,

I have been waiting for the response of my last email to you till date, i have not heard from you again, so i decided to email and remind you again. I am Ms Tina ███████ and i have been suffering from ovarian cancer disease and the doctor says that i have just few weeks to live. I am from (Trondheim) Norway but based in Africa since eight years ago as a business woman dealing with gold exportation.

Now that i am about to end the race like this, without any family members and no child. I have 8 Million US DOLLARS in a bank in Africa which i instructed the bank to give to St Andrews Missionary Home in Africa. My mind is not at rest because i am writing this letter now through the help of my computer beside my sick bed. I also have 4Million US Dollars in another finance firm and i instructed the them to transfer the money to the person i have directed to them, that they should release the funds to him/her, but you will assure me that you will take 20% of the money and give 80% to the orphanages home in your country for my heart to rest when i must have died. I got your email address through my search for a reliable person and trustworthy person from your country's directory.

I MADE THIS DECISION AFTER LISTING TO THE NEWS LINE ABOUT 100 YEARS OLD WOMAN WHO SECRETLY DONATE HER FORTUNE UPON HER DEATH, YOU CAN CHECK BELOW FOR DETAILS.

http://www.myfoxspokane.com/dpps/news/dpgoh-woman-donates-secret-millions-upon-her-death-fc-20100305_6410207

http://www.youtube.com/watch?v=O8o-e-iLsUM

As soon as i hear from you, i will give you instructions and the finance firm information so that the funds will be released to you immediately. I did not mention the name of the finance firm here for security purpose as i don't know how many people that have access to your email. Once i am assured that you are the rightful owner, i will give the information as stated earlier.

Yours fairly friend,
Tina ███████

N:B-PLEASE KINDLY RESPOND TO MY PRIVATE EMAIL ADDRESS FOR CONFIDENTIAL REASONS(tinaf███@gmail.com)

The most noticeable indicators are the subject line, in our case, **"PLEASE DO NOT IGNORE"**. This emphasizes the importance of the e-mail to the receiver, and will tempt us to open and read the e-mail. The next indicator is the large sum of money — $4 million — of which the e-mail recipient will receive 20 percent if they engage with the sender. These are two of the primary indicators listed previously. Let's further analyze this e-mail to look for other inconsistencies.

Notice the sender address ends in `.ru`, though the sender indicates to send replies to a Gmail-based account at the bottom of the e-mail. This seems odd, doesn't it? Now let's look at the e-mail header. The e-mail header provides more technical details on where the e-mail originated from and how it was routed to the end recipient.

```
Delivered-To: xxxxxxxx@gmail.com
...Omitted...
Return-Path: <test@xxxdu.ru>
Received: from xxxx.xxxdu.ru (mx.xxxdu.ru. [8x.25x.xx7.xx5])
      by mx.google.com with ESMTPS id c3si797402728bz.68.2013.01.07.16.50.22
      (version=TLSv1/SSLv3 cipher=OTHER);
      Mon, 07 Jan 2013 16:50:25 -0800 (PST)
Received-SPF: pass (google.com: best guess record for domain of test@xxxdu.ru designates 8x.25x.xx7.x5 as permitted sender) client-ip=8x.25x.xx7.xx5;
Authentication-Results: mx.google.com; spf=pass (google.com: best guess record for domain of test@xxxdu.ru designates 8x.25x.xx7.xx5 as permitted sender) smtp.mail=test@xxxdu.ru
...Omitted...
Reply-To: <xxxiskeytxxx@gmail.com>
From: "MS TINA xxxISKEY"<test@xxxdu.ru>
Subject: "PLEASE DO NOT IGNORE"
...Omitted...
```

I have bolded the information of importance for this spam e-mail, as shown in the previous screenshot. First, the return path indicates yet another e-mail address—test@xxxdu.ru. I have purposely obfuscated information with x's. This is the e-mail address of the sender as seen in the **From** field. Looking at the **Reply-To** field, we can see another e-mail indicating a different Gmail address. Essentially, there are three e-mail accounts referenced or used in this communication, further complicating the discovery of the "real" sender.

Next, let's look at the **Received-SPF** field. It states that the e-mail passes the SPF check. Knowing that the e-mail is spam, the SPF pass indicates the ineffectiveness of this authenticity check and leaves the recipient vulnerable to malicious e-mails. This is a clear indication that the source host is a spam solution and the sending e-mail was not spoofed. For the record, Gmail did indicate that this e-mail was spam, but what if it was delivered to another e-mail account. Would it have made it to the inbox leaving the receiver to decide if the e-mail is legitimate?

Mitigating spam and e-mail threats

There are several e-mail solutions available for detecting and blocking spam—both in the cloud and locally—at the enterprise level. Leveraging these types of solutions would be a tier of protection and should be deployed with other security configurations to reduce the likelihood of spam making it to the inbox of enterprise users. The following is a list of other options to reduce the impact of a received spam:

- Set e-mail client to text only, disabling HTML e-mails
- Turn off auto preview of received e-mails
- Right-click on HTML-based e-mails and review the source code for their link information

- Read the e-mail header and look for inconsistencies similar to what we saw in our example

- Send the e-mail to the enterprise spam reporting e-mail address for security review

As with all facets of security, education on the subject is a must for an effective security program that reduces the threat of technologies used by the enterprise.

Social media

We have adopted social media as one of the best marketing tools to date and almost every industry and enterprise is leveraging the available technology. It is an easy way to reach a large number of potential clients and partners; but with any social medium, it can be used for malicious purposes too. When instant messaging was the most popular method to chat with friends, strangers, and peers, it was common to get unsolicited messages with a link and an enticing message to encourage the recipient to click on the link. Now, we get unsolicited followers (Twitter) who can view all communication sent to the public forum and send unsolicited messages in response to a key word used in the communication.

The idea of social media is great because the sender does not need to know everyone who receives the message and can allow marketing to a much larger crowd than the immediately known circle of influence. Additionally, some of the new forms of social media allow followers to resend the communication to their followers, furthering the reach of the initial communication.

The initial intent of the technologies in this space was for the home user, not the enterprise. Thus many of the typically required security controls for enterprise implementation are non-existent or poorly implemented. With the lack of enterprise focus and widespread use, the enterprise security teams struggle to protect the enterprise, as employees willingly use the technology without understanding the threats that are present. This is not as much an issue at a personal residence but can pose a significant threat to the enterprise.

The tactics used today leverage the common outbound permitted traffic of the enterprise, sending a link to a malicious site through the social media tool allowed from inside the enterprise network. Securing the communications is not the default for many of the tools in use, so credentials, and other information sent over this medium are readily available for eavesdropping. If social media technology is to be used by the enterprise, it is a must that the security team is involved to ensure the proper controls are in place and guidelines are developed for the proper enterprise usage of the technology. Neglecting to take this approach will lead to compromise and leakage of personal and enterprise sensitive data.

Mitigating social media threats

When leveraging social media technologies, it is difficult to protect the access once it is permitted. There are solutions available that can be implemented as a proxy to analyze the communications and block defined data from being transmitted over the communication medium. The most effective method is educating users of the technology about what to look for in communications that may be an attempt to social engineer employees and use diligence when using the technology. A formal set of guidelines for enterprise usage of such technologies should be developed, in addition to security policies that should include approved use of social media on behalf of the enterprise.

There are several online resources for the development of social media policy. An Internet-based wizard driven tool such as PolicyTool (http://socialmedia.policytool.net/) may be a good start. However, the enterprise legal team should complete a careful review of the license agreement. This tool is an example and is not endorsed by the author.

In-person methods

Occasionally, to get the information or access desired, a social engineer will need to meet the target in person to perpetrate the scam. It may be that the desired systems are not Internet accessible such as a credit card reader, ATM, point of sale, or other critical systems intentionally inaccessible for security purposes. The social engineer will find a target with access to the system or device, and through coercion convince the user to infect their system that has access and leverage that exploitation to gain access to the intended target of value. There is speculation and substantial proof that Stuxnet (a recently discovered malware used against Iran) was perpetrated by providing infected USB media to contractors with access to internally protected nuclear facilities. The USBs were inserted into the contractor machines. Once on-site, the malware activated and attacked the internal systems causing significant damage to the nuclear systems. Somehow the contractors were convinced to plug the "trusted" USB drives into their laptops, more than likely through social engineering.

In order to gain access to a system or other information in a physical capacity, the social engineer will need to have a convincing story and play the part well. They are imposters and will be whoever they need to be to achieve the desired outcome. A great cartoon representation of the social engineer imposter comes from http://redwing.hutman.net/~mreed/warriorshtm/impostor.htm.

Just like this cartoon, it is a matter of picking the right mask to convince the target:

An example would be a computer repair technician coming on-site to fix a computer problem providing physical access to install software, modify hardware, or simply steal the desired system. This is one method used to install card skimmers in retail locations at point of sale, ATMs, and gas station pumps. The successful social engineer will gain as much information about the target as possible to be convincing, including choice of clothing, badges, paperwork, and so on to avoid suspicion and accomplish the goal.

Mitigating in-person social engineering

In order to mitigate the in-person social engineering attacks, the enterprise must develop stringent physical access protocols to enterprise systems and restricted areas. The methods used can vary, but should include some combination of the following:

- Official identification (badges)
- Validated authorization
- Some form of secret, which may be a word or code, only given to assigned and dispatched persons to perform the on-site function

In addition to the initial validation of the on-site visit, basic physical security practices should be followed. For example, requiring a person to observe the technician at all times and requiring bag checks, and so on to stop or identify physical theft of systems. The social engineer may also use the information to develop the perfect exploit for the exact version of platform implemented or software installed.

Phone methods

An old but very effective method of social engineering is by phone. It has been a tactic for a long time since phones are available to more people and have been around longer than the Internet. It was the first anonymous method of contacting a target thus minimizing the risk of getting caught or leaving a trail for prosecution. This is still true today and social engineers are leveraging advances in technology to take this method further. Using tools that allow desktop sharing and remote control, attackers convince users that their computer has an issue; and to fix it, they must allow the attacker to remote access into the system to correct the issue. Once remote access is gained, the social engineer will install malicious software while the user watches, thinking that it is a program to fix the reported issue. This method has been on the rise in the last few years because it ensures the attack is successful with no waiting on a click of a malicious URL sent via e-mail.

In less sophisticated scenarios, the social engineer calls with a convincing story and persuades the end user to provide personal and business information, credentials, or whatever the social engineer is seeking to obtain. The most challenging component of detecting this method is anyone can be anybody on the phone. Through a little research, the social engineer can impersonate a high-level executive. The fear of letting down an executive alone will lead most end users to divulge information, even if warned to never provide that information to anyone over the phone.

Mitigating phone methods

As with all social engineering threats, it is the decision of the employee at the moment in time that matters the most. Preparing users for these types of encounters and knowing how to handle a pushy social engineer will be the most effective in mitigating this type of attack. Users can be prepared by providing them with the tactics used to get information from them such as the type of information being requested, the scenario in which they are being engineered, and teaching methods of questioning the social engineer. An effective method is to ask the engineer more detailed information about what they are asking, such as instead of providing your social security number to them, ask them what number they have on file or what are the last four digits of the number on file. Seek to get more information from the individual and, if necessary, ask for a callback number and involve the security team to determine the legitimacy of the contact. Additionally, if the internal number is not published, this can be an indication of a random call in hopes that the social engineer would get an answer. Asking how they obtained the number or other questions that may throw the engineer into a defensive position may end the conversation, because the target is not considered a soft target. In any circumstance, *never* provide confidential information to anyone on the phone.

Business networking sites

As resumes may be making their official exit and the business networking sites provide the history and experience information hiring managers are looking for, a lot of specific information is made freely available to the public.

The following are a few example business networking sites:

- LinkedIn (`http://www.linkedin.com`)
- Plaxo (`http://www.plaxo.com`)
- Ziggs (`http://www.ziggs.com`)
- XING (`http://www.xing.com`)

Everyone from the lowest to the highest ranks in corporations builds comprehensive online profiles for business partners and potential employers to learn about them. This information may include work history, education, specialties, and current project information; all of which can be used to social engineer the individual.

The use of these sites is a significant business advantage due to the dynamic nature and features available to reach out and network with others in the same field or find job candidates. These sites usually have a feature that allows individuals to be e-mailed by those interested in doing business with others and can provide e-mail addresses, phone numbers, and other methods of contact or Internet presences maintained by the individual. These other accounts can also provide more information to build a successful social engineering attack.

The communication methods available within these sites provide a similar attack surface to e-mail and instant messaging. Under the guise of legitimate business interest, an engineer can send a malicious e-mail with a link to something that on the surface makes sense, but it leads to a compromised server that will install malicious software on the victim's system. For the normal user with limited access, this may not be as big of an issue versus if this is the CEO or a database administrator with access to very sensitive communications or data.

Mitigating business networking site attacks

It is important to be aware that anything posted on the Internet is accessible to the public and caution should be practiced anytime this forum is used to communicate. There will be instances of unsolicited communication through the sites used for legitimate business purposes. All communication should be treated as untrusted unless from a known trusted source. All links should be examined before being clicked and careful examination of the context of the communication can provide an insight to the true nature of the communication. If the recipient does not know the sender, the communication should initially be considered unsolicited spam with a lower priority for replying or reading.

Job posting sites

Job posting sites are a necessity and used by job seekers and employers to find available positions and candidates. Typically, career seekers upload their resume and create a profile highlighting their skills and capabilities for potential employers. To make sure that job candidates see the latest available positions, employers upload significant details about open positions to attract the right talent. Without this information, career moves and finding talent would be very challenging. Some level of detail must be provided by both parties to make sure the candidate and employer are a good fit.

While both parties are providing details in order to attract the other, the provided information can be too telling and allows a path for successful social engineering of both parties. The information provided by employers seeking candidates can include detailed information about systems, applications, and operating systems deployed. Information provided by the candidate not only includes job-related skills but personal information that anyone who pays for access to the site can use to reach the candidate.

A skilled social engineer will scour job postings to get as much detail as possible on the enterprise based on posted open positions, experience, and skill requirements. Usually the employer will provide information on type of systems, versions of software, and deployed solutions. The following is an example from a real posting on http://www.monster.com:

Database Administrator

- Working knowledge and experience with LAN-based network operating systems, preferably MS Windows 2000, XP, Windows 7 Enterprise, Server 2000, 2003, 2008, and Active Directory
- Microsoft SQL 2005, 2008; Oracle experience a plus

This information is a great starting point for the social engineer to impersonate as an MS associate addressing a license issue, an interested DBA asking more detailed questions, or a recruiter seeking more information on software versions to make sure they have it correct for potential candidates. Do you see how quickly a social engineer can develop a plausible storyline to gain credentials and other sensitive enterprise information?

Job seekers must also beware of unsolicited "recruiter" calls asking for more information such as social security number to get the process started with an "interested" employer. Sometimes, the interaction is less malicious and simply an effort to get a commission-based position filled; so a call is received about a skill set you don't have but you are told of a proposition about a great opportunity to make a lot of money. These are all methods of abusing and misusing information posted to job seeker-related sites. The next section will provide techniques for protecting the enterprise from social engineering attacks based on information posted in job openings.

Mitigating job posting-based attacks

It is certainly a fine line between just enough information and too much information for posting in job openings. Employers should be cautious about the details provided on job posting sites that would give too much insight on the inner workings of the enterprise. Avoiding furnishing specific software versions and operating systems to reduce the fingerprinting information for the attacker is ideal. It is common for a social engineer to use the information for a job posting site to call the target and get them to provide enough details to allow the engineer to develop an exploit specific to the target's version of software. Job postings should be generic and specify just enough information to get candidates with the right skills; the more detailed information can be presented during the interview process and skill-based aptitude tests. It is good practice to have HR, legal, and information security involved in public communications, including job postings especially in the areas involving IT.

Security awareness training

Educating the employees of an organization about general security practices and specific enterprise policies is the purpose of security awareness training. In essence, the security department attempts to reduce security incidents in the environment by presenting basic security principles in the hopes that the end user will not take an action that can cause the enterprise risk through data loss or downtime. The effectiveness of such a training has continued to be scrutinized. However, it is a requirement for standards such as the PCI DSS and is, in general, a good practice.

In order for security awareness training to be effective, it must be tailored to the organization and the various teams that will receive the training. Not all individuals or teams will have the same knowledge of technology and security, so a one size fits all approach will not have the intended effects on the security of the organization. There are components that are generic enough that they should be included in all the presentations of the material such as general and acceptable use of common technologies in the enterprise, data protection, and password management.

Providing users with easy to understand and follow guidelines is the key to material retention and proper action when a scenario is realized. Once the material has been presented, a series of exercises should be given to test the users' knowledge on security in the enterprise as it pertains to their common and unique circumstances. An administrative assistant will have different scenarios than a database administrator, though each must know how to react to prevent a security incident such as handling a phishing e-mail. Once the material has been created and presented to associates, it is imperative to maintain education to ensure coverage of the latest threats and methods at least semiannually. Testing of the associate population on a quarterly or semiannual basis will give the security team ample data to determine what works and what needs to be improved in the training material. Additionally, testing can provide data that is indicative of certain behaviors that may require more attention in training materials.

There are several ways to keep the enterprise population aware of current threats and keep security awareness topics fresh in their minds. The ultimate goal of security awareness training is that the automatic user action taken would be the correct action whether it is not clicking on a malicious URL, inserting a USB found on the ground into their computer, or refusing to provide credentials to a stranger on the phone. In the sections we are about to see, computer-based training, instructor-led training, and other awareness training methods will be covered providing information and guidance for each method.

Security awareness training is an excellent way to provide a face to IT security and foster an environment of cooperation and collaboration that will positively impact security in the enterprise. It is also important to note that the more effective security awareness training is, the more associates will increase their overall secure computing knowledge that can be leveraged at the office and at home. It is more likely that the user's home computer will be subjected to more threats than in the office, whether a target or part of a wide cast net. Computer use is typically more risky at home due to lack of controls, and so it is important to educate users to exercise caution whenever using technology, no matter where it is being used.

Training materials

There are several free and paid for training materials, and options for security awareness training. Though official training may only occur once or twice a year, to increase effectiveness there should be multiple methods employed more regularly to educate and keep the concepts fresh in the enterprise associates' mind. This can be done in the form of regular newsletters, posters, and office pinups. Providing an easily accessible interface to IT security is also a requirement for effective enterprise security. Materials should always have a method of contacting IT security. Providing a friendly interface will increase cooperation across the enterprise reducing security incidents because proactive action will be taken. Depending on the budget allocated for such efforts, training can be as simple or elaborate as needed; it must be effective and measurable. All materials used in security awareness training must be demographically aware, ensuring the education is tailored to the right audience(s). The following table shows the possible pros and cons with each of the covered training methods:

Training method	Pros	Cons
Computer-based training	Very cost effective and users can take them at their own pace. This solution is the simplest to implement and provides flexibility for user location and time to access the training.	Cost of productivity loss unless users are willing to train on their own time.
Instructor-led (classroom)	Promotes interaction and allows questions to be asked and answered in a positive environment.	Can be difficult to get all the users together in a class. Additional cost for productivity loss.
Newsletters (on-going)	Regular updates, can address current trends. Also great for recent incident lessons learned. May also be coupled with associate surveys to measure retention of concepts.	May be difficult to keep readers' attention and ensure the publication is read. Regular e-mails may become annoying to users.

Computer-based training

In order to reach a large number of enterprise users, **computer-based training** (CBT) may be the best option. It is common for large enterprises to employ this method for multiple reasons:

- The large numbers of users that must participate in the training reduces the cost associated with lost productivity and facilities.

- Delivering the material in this format allows for each user to go through the training at their own pace over the time period given to complete the material. Everyone learns at a different rate and this medium allows each user to move at their own pace without impacting others going over the same material.

- The electronic format of the material can be accessed at anytime—maybe even from home—allowing users to be in a comfortable environment conducive for their learning or to simply go back over previously viewed material to ensure retention of the material.

In general, this method is popular because it can drastically reduce the cost of security awareness training and allows for central management of changes whether in sections of material or the whole learning package. Typically, there are quizzes along the way and a test at the end of the training; this can all be centrally managed with a CBT course greatly reducing the effort of training facilitation and material maintenance.

 When deciding the depth of topic coverage that will be presented to users, consider the broad knowledge base to ensure maximum effectiveness. Because CBT methods are impersonal, there is no ability for users to ask questions in a real-time interactive way.

The primary benefits of CBT training are:

- No written materials needed
- No requirement for instructors
- Training can be completed on employee's time

Classroom training

It can be argued that some subject matter is better taught in person with human-to-human interaction. The effectiveness of one method over another is dependent on several factors. Classroom training allows working through realistic scenarios and in-class participation leads to questions (maybe with character twists) that can be added to truly test retention of concepts. These factors may influence the determination to select a delivery method.

Classroom training does, however, require a lot more planning and cost to facilitate versus CBT and this is exponentially based on the number of associates that must be trained.

Methods to reduce cost may include:

- Offering the training at several locations simultaneously, effectively reducing the overall time required for training
- Facilitating a co-sponsored training offering with other local enterprises to share the cost and foster local collaboration

Instructor-led training can provide added benefits not available to an associate leveraging a CBT course to learn material such as simple question-and-answer sessions or getting more clarity on a training topic. This method may also yield more measurable results for a wider range of skill sets because a good instructor will be able to gauge the retention of the students while teaching and adjust accordingly to ensure the student gets what they are supposed to get from the training. Other methods of training do not have this characteristic and may be less effective at a holistic approach of teaching security awareness; basics are best suited for other methods.

Associate surveys

A method to measure how well IT security is keeping the enterprise population educated and aware of enterprise security is through the use of associate surveys at random intervals. There does not need to be a regular occurrence of surveys, however, regular newsletters can provide a constant reminder of good security practices. Without a consistent security message being presented to users, the security awareness program may continue to be a mindless and unfortunate annoyance to the enterprise users measurable improvement in security. Though the survey would be less about opinions and more like a quiz, it is a light touch interactive method to get vital information on how the enterprise population has retained security principles and thinks about security and the training methods used by IT security.

Surveys can be extremely effective because they can be submitted anonymously, allowing the associates to be honest and provide constructive criticism, without the fear of retaliatory actions. Associates may also find this a great way to share their thoughts on a topic without having others offering opinions such as in a classroom setting. Requesting inputs from associates on a quarterly basis is enough to get the data needed without overwhelming them, and allows IT security the time to gather the results and make adjustments where necessary. If beneficial, the associates can be provided with a method of contact for situations when something may need additional clarification, or IT security seeks more information in order to resolve an issue and develop in an area of weakness.

Common knowledge

Areas of common knowledge are generic security issues that can be understood and that relate to every associate, such as policies or securing a commonly used technology such as e-mail. There are security topics that each enterprise associate should be aware of and must understand that are not role specific or based on individual expertise. A quick look at the list of policies in the employee handbook should provide these topics; if this does not exist, please see *Chapter 3, Security As a Process* to learn what standard policies should exist. Implemented enterprise security policies should be the basis of the security awareness training for all associates to ensure everyone is operating from the same set of expectations and understands how their role affects the security of the enterprise. The common knowledge sections of the training should be globally relevant and able to be grasped by all associates regardless of any specific role in the organization. This training can also include activities recently observed in the news such as new hacking cases, or other scams that the associates may become a target of while working or at home. A majority of security incidents are a result of users bringing unsafe home computing habits to the workplace. The security of the enterprise is the responsibility of every associate, not only the IT security team.

Specialized material

In addition to the common knowledge material developed around enterprise security policies and expected behaviors, there is a need for specialized material that is role specific. Each department has unique roles within the enterprise and will access, use, and create various types of data of varying levels of sensitivity. For instance, an administrative assistant will not necessarily need to know the best way to handle credit card numbers in a database, but a DBA will need to know this.

As trust models are developed and roles more accurately defined, the correct training material will become more apparent. Some roles can be grouped together based on the data types and processes shared amongst the defined roles to simplify the effort by reducing the number of specialized training packages that need to be developed. By specializing materials per the unique roles in the organization, the more complex facets of data security can be presented to limited users. This will increase the effectiveness for these specialized groups while not alienating general users in roles that do not have access to sensitive data or processes. Therefore, in theory, their actions would less likely cause significant loss or compromise.

Effective training

For training to be more than mundane and have the intended effect on enterprise security, it must be intentional in nature and not a checkbox exercise. There have been several studies over the years on the topic of effective training that focus on the methods by which humans learn best. The methods commonly used by all successful training packages leverage several forms of information dissemination and recollection techniques to ensure retention for individual learning types.

In general, there should be a combination of:

- Visual presentation
- Guided and free participation
- Note taking
- Material review

Effective tools should be leveraged such as posters and office area materials that will jog the users' memory on a topic from training and impact how the users behave. The NTL Institute (http://www.ntl.org) developed "The Learning Pyramid" explaining passive and active methods of learning. The following diagram is a depiction from the *Centre for Teaching Excellence Blog* (http://cte-blog.uwaterloo.ca/):

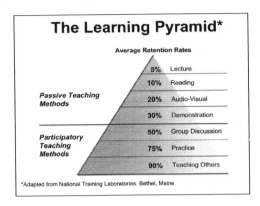

The Learning Pyramid*

Average Retention Rates

5%	Lecture
10%	Reading
20%	Audio-Visual
30%	Demonstration
50%	Group Discussion
75%	Practice
90%	Teaching Others

Passive Teaching Methods

Participatory Teaching Methods

*Adapted from National Training Laboratories. Bethel, Maine

Well-developed training material is the difference between an effective security awareness program and a failure that only meets a compliance requirement. A method to ensure the selected training methods and materials are suitable for their intended purpose is to select users that represent the intended audiences and trial run the training, get feedback, and test for retention. Early planning and focused development of the training program will yield higher success rates in retention and a measurable positive impact on enterprise security.

Continued education and checks

As with anything taught and learned, regular digestion of the material maintains retention and forces new habits. As stated earlier, security awareness training is an on-going process and cannot only be used as an annual or semiannual exercise. Formal training may be provided at these intervals; but as new methods are used to exploit the human aspect of technology, continued training via newsletters, posters, e-mails, and other mediums must be a part of the program to reach optimal effectiveness.

A good exercise for the security team is to run random security awareness checks using tools such as the SET written by Dave Kennedy, or commercial solutions such as PhishMe (http://www.phishme.com) to test user responses to simulated social engineering scenarios.

Actions must be repeated several times before they become a habit; this is the intention of security awareness training programs. It is important to note that all data gathered during these checks is to be non-retributory, as the reason for the check is to validate the effectiveness of training, not to hold persons responsible. It is negligible to punish employees when not properly trained on how to handle security-related issues. Consistent training and communication on security and expectations must take precedence; future infractions can be weighed for actions to be taken.

Access denied – enforcing least privilege

The strength of any system is only as strong as the weakest link; in the case of technology, *humans* are the weakest link. We are in the information sharing age where data is everywhere, available, and systems can be accessed all over the network and Internet; but this comes with a cost. Access to data and systems can lead to unintended consequences especially if the access is not necessary. This is common for the enterprise data center. All data center assets are available over the network. Though application access may be limited, this does not stop all threats to the data accessed through the applications or that which resides in databases and network shares located in the data center. The need for accessibility has overridden the integrity and security of enterprise data leaving it vulnerable to whatever or whoever finds a way onto the network.

In our trust model paradigm, a careful examination of the present processes, applications, and users that need access to enterprise data must drive our definition of roles, trust, and protection mechanisms required to secure interaction with the data. Because this is not the normal process used to develop data access controls, enforcement of least privilege is many times non-existent. If the access being requested does not adhere to defined access policies, then it should be denied until the requesting access is properly designed and configured to reduce the weakening of the data security posture.

Initiatives such as **Bring Your Own Device (BYOD)** highlight the need to fiercely restrict general and direct access to data to only those which have the correct trust. Virtualization is a technology that is an excellent example and method of achieving this level of access control. It will not matter what device is on the network if the only devices that can touch the data are enterprise owned, secured, and monitored. Hosts that are compromised will not have direct access to assets of value—ideally no enterprise assets— and limited only to their own segmented switch port that provides IP addressing and access to a virtual environment.

Other implementations include truly segmented networks such as those the US government uses with network access control configurations that limit or deny access to sensitive networks and high-value assets.

Until this paradigm is accepted in the enterprise, there will be continued malware outbreaks, system and data breaches, and loss at the hands of the humans who use the network and access enterprise data. It is not a right to have access; it is a privilege, and privileges should be given only when certain conditions are met, as defined by the enterprise trust models. It should be acceptable and common to deny access to critical data and systems when access requires a weakening of security; "temporary" access should not be considered. Significant investment is made in security and senior-level support is needed to ensure new solutions and enterprise initiatives are purchased and developed with security as a key component. If this does not occur, it is best to prepare for data loss and compromise.

The next sections cover the unique roles that system, application, and database administrators play in the enterprise. These roles have elevated access privileges to sensitive network areas and high-value assets. With this access, there is great responsibility and a greater need to enforce least privilege while operating in a multi-tenant situation. The first section provides an overview of administrator-level access with the subsequent sections covering the system, application, and database administrator in detail.

Administrator access

The role of an **administrator**, by definitions is the individual or team that is officially responsible for the system, application, or process of which the responsibility is given. This is a significant responsibility and possesses authority and access to the entity in its entirety. Because of this overwhelming ability to see all and do all, the access should be monitored and implemented in a fashion to reduce the unnecessary compromise of all components within the technical sphere of control of administrators. Therefore it is further necessary to segregate where possible and define territories of control, access, and ultimately, responsibility.

Systems in any enterprise will require an administrator account or group to properly maintain the operating system and installed software. True ownership of a system can be rather convoluted in the common enterprise where one team owns the hardware and OS and another team owns the application(s) and related data. To further complicate the matter, in instances when the system is a security system, administrator access becomes a significant matter to address.

Administrator access is based on the role of the administrator (system, data, or application) and must be implemented in a manner that enforces separation of duties by limiting access to view and modify the other components that may be resident on a single system. In addition, to control access to other components within the context of the role, least privilege should be the guiding principle for access provisioning. To ensure continued security of administrator credentials, the password should be changed at least every 45 days or when an administrator group member leaves the enterprise or changes roles.

System administrator

A necessary role within the enterprise is the **system administrator**; usually a team within IT that is responsible for all system hardware and operating systems implemented. The role may also include software management on servers and end user systems within the organization. The system administrator is the most privileged account on any system (root for *nix-based systems); but for simplicity, system administrator will be used in this text. This elevated access allows potential access to data that resides on the system that is beyond the scope of the administrator role and must be limited to enforce separation of duties and confidentiality of the data. The system administrator must not have access to anything other than the OS and software packages where an agreement exists between the system administrator and the application owner.

System monitoring must be in place to ensure the defined roles are enforced especially when there is no technical capability to do so. All system administrator access should be logged, reviewed, and corrective action taken if necessary. A method to ensure individuals are accountable is to assign unique login credentials for each system administrator. Tasks that are general in nature such as automated patching may use a service account that does not permit interactive login.

As presented earlier, specialized security awareness training should be developed for this unique role within the enterprise to communicate the acceptable and expected behaviors of the system administrator. Because this role typically has elevated privileges across the enterprise, training on targeted social engineering for system administrators is advisable as they are prime targets for a malicious hacker to exploit for expedient data access.

Data administrator

Data administrators or **data custodians** are ultimately responsible for the data in the enterprise for a given application or process. The availability, confidentiality, and integrity of the data must be controlled and maintained by the data administrators and *only* the data administrators. All access to the data and how it is used must be through a formal process and must not be a result of inherited access, nor residual access due to a lacking access removal process. The data administrator must be able to speak to any modifications, deletions, or other interactions with the data they are responsible for maintaining.

In most cases, the data administrator role is the responsibility of the database team because most data in storage for applications and processing resides in some form of database. Though it may be more difficult for a system administrator to gain access to data, the database team has direct access on an almost constant basis. The daily tasks of the database team consist of building databases, testing, and maintenance activities all of which should be monitored, logged, and peer reviewed.

Also, much like the system administrator, the database administrator is a prime target for malicious hackers to more easily gain access to enterprise data. It is much easier to social engineer a database administrator than to penetrate a well-secured network. Special security awareness training should be written and communicated to this highly important team. Some of the largest breaches have been phishing attacks targeted specifically at the team who has the most access to enterprise data: the database team.

Application administrator

The role of **application administrator** is to define and manage roles within the application, application maintenance, and application user provisioning. The administrator may or may not need access to view, modify, or delete the data accessed by the application and will be a case by case implementation. Typically, the application is the interface to the data residing in the database, process, or application, and therefore role assignment is critical to the overall security of the resident data. The application administrator must manage any and all access to data through the application by placing users into the correct roles based on the requirement for access. Leveraging the defined trust models and mapping users to available roles will ensure consistent implementation across applications.

This role may have more or limited access to enterprise data depending on the configuration of the application and how it interacts with data. Being a step back from the data store (database), there is technically a limit to the interaction with data and many times it will be the application accessing the data, not a user or administrator of the application. It is a good practice to log all application access and actions to ensure this assumption remains true. Though it can also be assumed the application administrator will have the most application access: changes to the configuration of the application, added users, and permission changes should be logged, monitored, and reviewed for legitimacy.

Although the application administrator is not the most privileged user with access to enterprise data, there is enough interaction to ensure this interaction is acceptable. Developing specialized security awareness training for this team can reinforce the need to ensure least privilege, and as needed access to data interacted with by the application. Again, this team is a prime target for malicious hackers and will many times be exploited to gain credentials, access to data, and other systems to attack. Keeping this team aware of this potential will hopefully keep them sharp on account review and other application behaviors indicative of compromise.

Physical security

The last component of the human element of security we will cover is physical security. It can be stated with a high degree of confidence that the most important facet of security is *physical security*; there is no security if access to systems is not limited or controlled. Another way to look at this is, if the system can be physically removed from the data center with nothing to prevent the action, then network access controls provide no benefit; therefore all other security is irrelevant.
A scenario covered in the *Social engineering* section was the attacker attempting physical access to enterprise systems in order to gain access to enterprise data. This section will briefly cover the need for physical security controls, primarily the human interaction control.

In order for enterprise associates to protect the enterprise from well-trained social engineers who show up in person, they must know what to look for in behaviors and know how to react according to policy and training. This can only occur if the scenarios are practiced and rehearsed continuously. In my opinion, this is one of the areas that require the most time and attention, especially for retailers, and organizations with several remote locations.

Each of the controls implemented must be working together much like network-based security controls. An example may be where a suspicious individual enters the corporate office. A compelling story is told that requests access to computer systems for an unscheduled repair, however, the paperwork seems legitimate and the person looks like they could really work for the company they claim to. Is this person supposed to be in this location? Well, truthfully it could be hard to determine if all controls were monitored individually and the whole picture missing. In this scenario, let's say the individual possessed no identification; maybe it was left at home or lost. How else can the associates determine if this person should really be on-site and accessing enterprise computer systems? Scenarios should be used to educate associates on the many methods to enforce controls, while being OK with turning the suspicious person away.

Common physical access controls include:

- Company-issued badges (employee and visitor)
- Cameras (hidden and plain sight)
- Guards (stationary and mobile)

Requiring a company badge and a chaperone for visitors reduces fraudulent access attempts when these controls are effectively implemented and monitored. Access to data centers must require authorization from a higher-level individual than the person requesting access as this additional scrutiny not only increases security, but may also enforce formal change control processes. Constant monitoring with cameras not only aids in post-event investigation, but if used properly can help identify suspicious behaviors of would-be attackers. The presence of guards is more of a mental message to would-be attackers that someone is watching and may take forceful action to stop you.

The physical aspects of security should be an integral component of the security awareness training program to ensure threats are identified and stopped before entering the physical enterprise perimeter.

Summary

There are several security concerns for the enterprise many of which can be directly influenced by the users, owners, and administrators of data and systems. Training employees on how to properly use enterprise data and use secure computing behaviors is a significant and important role for IT security. The enterprise must take ownership of its data and operate from the perspective that the data is supreme and all access must be authorized. It is also important that IT security builds a program where users know how to reach out to security for help and guidance; security cannot be a shadow organization that everyone fears the very existence of. Security should be a business enabler, for example, by taking steps to provide secure access to Internet-based solutions when requested. This chapter covered the human element of security and focused on social engineering, security awareness training, and methods to secure the enterprise, starting with the associates. In order to change enterprise security, it must be communicated that it's everyone's job to make the enterprise secure, not just the security team.

The next chapter continues with security monitoring, which was presented briefly in this chapter, as a method to detect malicious behaviors of privileged users in the context of being a victim to social engineering.

9
Security Monitoring

This chapter will guide the reader through the process of developing an enterprise monitoring strategy based on importance as determined by analyzing defined trust models. Examination of the critical data in the enterprise will help determine what should be monitored, who should monitored, and to what extent. Once a monitoring strategy has been developed and implemented, managing the data from disparate systems will be discussed using a Security Information and Event Management (SIEM) solution for event management, correlation, and alerting.

This chapter will cover the following topics:

- Monitoring based on trust models and network boundaries
- Privileged user monitoring
- Network security monitoring
- System monitoring
- Advanced monitoring tools

Monitoring strategies

An enterprise that has matured into a security conscious organization with controlled data access and secured infrastructure driven by well-defined trust models will need to establish methods of monitoring assets and users. Traditional methods of monitoring are primarily driven by network boundaries defined logically and physically where networks of differing trust levels connect to each other. This paradigm of security trust levels is based more on control rather than data access, focusing the security monitoring only at these network boundaries. Unfortunately, the internal network is left insufficiently monitored for the most part regardless of who or what is accessing enterprise infrastructure.

In order to know what is happening on systems, the network, and who is accessing data, new monitoring strategies must be employed to detect and mitigate malicious and unintended behaviors.

A comprehensive monitoring approach may be overwhelming depending on the size of the network: servers, end user systems, applications, network equipment, and security mechanisms. There is the possibility of collecting too much data and essentially rendering the monitoring tools useless and ineffective. A systematic approach to developing the monitoring strategy is the key to implementing a usable and effective solution or set of solutions; solutions that provide the necessary data and intelligence to differentiate expected traffic patterns from abnormal patterns indicating a security incident is underway. The enterprise must agree on who and what is to be monitored and to what extent. A great place to start this analysis is the previously defined trust models that are built around data access and required security mechanisms.

While it is, and should remain a common practice to implement security monitoring at the network boundaries, there must be a method of validation for common threats typically observed at these control points. There is an expectation of detection and mitigation of attacks at the network boundaries via tools such as intrusion prevention and firewalls, but attacks that continue to be undetected to the intended target by these technologies must still be detected and/or mitigated at the host, application, or operating system. Not only is it necessary to have monitoring tools implemented, but also expertise is required to interpret the output and identify patterns in the output either manually or by an automated capability.

In the most likely implementation, security monitoring will be designed based on trust models, network boundaries, and network segments (unique environments within network boundaries). There are valid reasons to implement monitoring in this fashion as previously discussed. Applying new security architectures to existing environments will require transition phases and some "best practice" configurations will always remain. Firewalls, intrusion prevention, and web application firewalls may always reside at the network perimeters—both internal and external—as a first layer of defense mitigating the more common threats. Moving to a data-centric model for security is the necessary progression in order to maintain protection for data in the ever-changing physical environments. A combination of enterprise controlled environments and those not owned or controlled by the enterprise will be required.

Monitoring based on trust models

Trust models are the basis for the security architecture presented in this book and the recommended foundation for enterprise security monitoring. Data-centric security and monitoring is the most effective, as it is specific to the data present and is as transient as the data itself. A matrix of data type trust models and required monitoring can be developed and re-used for each implementation of subsequent, same data types. This will ensure consistency no matter where the data resides, and is the best fit for enterprises leveraging cloud services and BYOD initiatives to reduce cost and increase the availability and resilience of critical systems, applications, and services.

Data criticality as defined by the enterprise trust models should be the primary dictator of the complexity of security monitoring required. This does not imply that no monitoring will exist for less critical data; but monitoring may be significantly more intricate with alerting and automated incident generation for critical data versus, for instance, a simple log entry at the application layer for non-critical business data. This is an oversimplified example, but there should be an exercise to determine required security monitoring for the defined data types that are input to the enterprise trust models.

The following table is an example of how the matrix may look for generic data sets with varying levels of criticality. It is important to note that risk may not play a significant role in developing security monitoring requirements; the criticality label implies risk.

Data set 1	Credit card numbers, SSN
Criticality	High
Required security monitoring	Data, Operating system, Application, Network, User

While this table is a simple example, the details of how to monitor will be built out by the overall monitoring program and the selected methods to monitor at each tier of data access. The purpose of this exercise is to fully develop a data-centric security monitoring requirements matrix. The following sections are the monitoring points within the trust model that warrant further discussion and strategies to effectively monitor throughout the layers of the defined trust models.

Data monitoring

Data, which is the center of our trust model, is the most valuable asset of the enterprise and where protection and monitoring should have the most focus. Access, modifications, additions, and deletions must be carefully controlled and monitored to detect intended and unintended actions taken on enterprise data. Tools such as file integrity monitoring can be leveraged to track all interactions with data in both structured (databases) and unstructured (documents, spreadsheets, and so on) formats.

A simple example of file integrity monitoring can be seen using the MD5 tool natively in Linux and Mac OS X. This tool performs a hash calculation on the file and provides an output. As long as this file is not changed, the MD5 output will remain unchanged. In the event that the file is modified, this MD5 hash will change. This is the principle used in file integrity monitoring solutions.

In the following screenshot, a secret file (`secretfile`) has been created with the text **This is a secret file.** inserted:

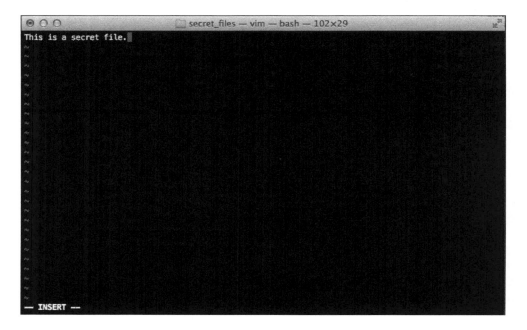

In the following lines, an MD5 hash is calculated for `secretfile` using the md5 command:

```
Macbook-pro$ md5 secretfile
MD5 (secretfile) = 273cf6c54c2bdba56416942fbb5ec224
```

Now, the text in the file will be altered slightly and another MD5 hash performed:

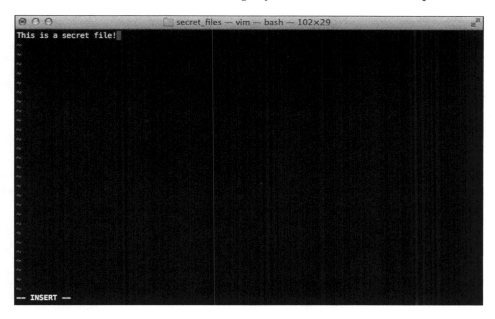

```
Macbook-pro$ md5 secretfile
MD5 (secretfile) = f18c89748147fea87d3d8c7a4e0f4c93
```

A quick comparison of the before and after MD5 hashes indicates the file has been modified in some way from the original version.

- Initial file MD5: 273cf6c54c2bdba56416942fbb5ec224
- Modified file MD5: f18c89748147fea87d3d8c7a4e0f4c93

Monitoring can also occur within systems where the data resides natively such as using database monitoring tools provided with the solution in addition to or disparately from third-party solutions. It is cautioned to rely solely on native tools that can be controlled by owners of the systems and may be a liability to the monitoring strategy.

The benefit of using a separate solution controlled by a third party within the enterprise such as IT security is the reduction in collusion and enforced separation of duties. Auditors of monitoring solutions will look for this to be the case to ensure that, for example, members of the database team are not in collusion with each other and making unapproved changes to data or inappropriately accessing the data residing on systems in their control.

Mature data monitoring solutions have the capability of not only detecting access and modification of data, but also determining by whom, allowing for a full audit trail of data activities. A process to analyze the data output from monitoring will need to be developed and tweaked as needed to maximize the benefit and adoption of the technology within the enterprise. Some solutions offer the option to auto-accept detected changes for the most common and insignificant changes. This is beneficial as the change is still captured but no human investigation is required unless there is a system incident.

 Data output from such tools can be significant and seem overwhelming. In order to minimize the amount of data, start with critical application directories and system files. The ability to decipher tools' output may be a collaboration between system administrators, application administrators, and IT security. As with any type of detection tool, fine-tuning is required to reduce the false positives and to capture the most significant and actionable data.

The primary attributes of data to monitor are:

- Timestamp (date and time).
- Who or what interacted with the data. This is captured by file metadata and other methods depending on the solution capabilities. Limit the integrity checks to the most significant files.
- What actions were taken on the data.
- Approval status for detected actions. It is recommended to have integration between change control systems and the file integrity monitoring solution for mapping of detected changes to approved changes.

These attributes should be captured within the solution; it is implied that any new detected actions will be considered unapproved until reviewed at which time the approval status can be updated accordingly unless automated. Essentially, the same fields are required for all technologies providing forensic data on detected events, and in common with intrusion prevention, firewalls, and logging. The data captured by such tools is a portion of the required information to form a complete picture of a security incident. It is essential to have the ability to reconstruct all activities involving data interaction for a complete data protection and monitoring program.

Process monitoring

Enterprise processes are the reason for data creation, collection, and manipulation and many times actions occur in an automated fashion; the success and failure of these processes can be of significant impact to the enterprise. It is imperative to have complete and thorough monitoring of data processes for early detection of intended actions and anomalies that may be indicative of failure or malicious intent. On the other side of this is the monitoring of successful process runs and anomalies with successful access, indicative of malicious intent or erroneous process implementation and configuration.

All processes identified during the building of the trust models will need to be assessed for their level of criticality, based on type of data affected by the process and business criticality of the output of the process. Process monitoring, because it may be automated, will have different monitoring points than that of human-based data interaction. The trust level assigned to the process may determine the level and granularity of required monitoring.

Attributes of process monitoring are as follows:

- Timestamp (date and time)
- Process name
- Account the process runs on
- Success/failure

The exact attributes of a process to monitor are as unique as the process. The attributes that we presented are the recommended minimum attributes to monitor. There may also be a secondary process that validates data postprocessing and this may require more detailed monitoring attributes. Because automation is a significant portion of data processing, it is important to monitor access to the process itself and any configuration changes made to the process that may be indicative of planned, erroneous, or malicious changes. If the process is script based, a file integrity monitoring (FIM) solution can be used to monitor the script for changes; if it is job based, the monitoring may need to be configured on the system running the job and may be similar to application monitoring concept and configuration. The primary purpose of process monitoring is to ensure it is running as intended by data verification and there is no unintended modification to it, its function, and its intended output.

Application monitoring

Application monitoring can be multifaceted depending on the environment the application resides in and access to varying data with varying levels of criticality. Each application in the enterprise will need to be defined per enterprise trust models and analyzed for unique attributes that need to be considered for monitoring. If the application has the capability to service authenticated and unauthenticated users, the monitoring strategy may differ depending on the authentication status of the application user. This is an attribute of applications in the e-commerce environments where the casual browsing client is not authenticated, but a customer with an account may login and have access to additional portions of the site with more application functions available.

An application needs to be monitored much like a process and supporting process scripts. An application serves as the interface between data and people so its functioning status is important to ensure critical business functions persist and customers and business users have the required access. In addition to the attributes monitored for processes, application availability must be monitored to meet service-level agreements and to reduce negative impact to the business. Application monitoring should be implemented for all business-critical applications. The extent of application monitoring will be determined by criticality and access level to sensitive data.

Attributes of application monitoring are as follows:

- Timestamp (data and time)
- Application name
- User authenticated/user unauthenticated
- Application up/down status

  This can be achieved via multiple methods including application calls, application and system logs, and service TCP/UDP port checks. It is advisable to leverage a monitoring method that will provide the most accurate status. An example is a basic website. To ensure it is up, a simple probe of TCP port 80 could work; but what if the application was broken but the port was still listening? In this scenario, an HTTP GET of the website's main page would produce a better status than the simple port probe.

User monitoring

The example in the previous section describing a web application that supports unauthenticated and authenticated users will require monitoring of both, but the authenticated user will have access to more application functions. Additional monitoring of the authenticated user is required as they will have access to more data and data input functions of the application.

User monitoring is a requirement across all aspects of the trust models because users will interact with data, processes, and applications by various methods and an audit trail must exist for all actions. In the case of a web application, only the authenticated user has a name and other information; the browsing user is just an IP address and maybe a user-agent type in the logs. For internal applications with access to data, authentication is almost always going to be required; if it is not, then the application should be rewritten to enforce authentication to establish a reliable forensic audit trail.

User monitoring extends beyond applications to the network, systems, and data. All access in the just discussed scenarios must not only be monitored for audit trail purposes, but also for behaviors indicative of malicious intent, misuse, and erroneous configuration. Erroneous configuration may be the use of user credentials in scripts and other automation that is not generally a recommended behavior. In the case of detected user credentials in scripts, an alternative method such as public/private keys or a service account should be used for authentication. Data loss prevention tools can help detect this type of misconfiguration, both locally and as the credentials are passed over the network. This will also protect the user in the event that the credentials are compromised.

Attributes of user monitoring are as follows:

- Timestamp (data and time)
- User ID
- Actions
- Source and destination IP addresses
- Login and access attempt's success/failure

User monitoring at the network, system, and operating system level will produce unique pieces of data that when correlated create a complete picture of user actions. It is imperative to leverage user authentication where possible to ensure only authorized individuals are accessing enterprise assets.

Monitoring authenticated access can also detect possible credential misuse by an authorized individual or unauthorized use of credentials. Authentication provides non-repudiation for actions taken by a user and is a powerful and necessary protection for the enterprise in the event that malicious actions result in employee termination. Monitoring of user actions can also lead to discovering application configuration and design errors when actions detected are unintended and result in a success status from the application, but may lead to elevated privileges or erroneous access to sensitive data.

Without monitoring user actions, the enterprise will not truly know what user actions are being taken against its networks, systems, applications, processes, and data.

Monitoring based on network boundary

Security monitoring at the network boundary is a basic defense in depth tactic to mitigate the most common threats observed from low to high security network segments. The most common boundary is the enterprise Internet edge, and the best example of a low to high security network segmentation that should have monitoring in place for enterprise protection from the uncontrolled Internet. There are other network boundaries that may require monitoring such as business partner, subsidiary, virtual private network (VPN), and service provider connections. Each of these network boundaries connects a network uncontrolled by the enterprise to the enterprise network, and therefore the trust level is not as high as that of the internal trusted network. Because threats often come from other external networks, monitoring at these connections can provide valuable information about the security of the connecting network and allow the enterprise to implement the proper security mechanisms to protect enterprise assets and data.

Depending on the connecting network and the associated risks, the level of monitoring can be more or less complex. In the case of employee VPN from employer-owned devices that only allows connections with enterprise assets, the monitoring may be less than the business partner VPN, where the trust is less due to reduced or non-existent control over connecting networks and devices. In the case of BYOD, the VPN connection (if permitted) must be monitored as any other untrusted connection.

However there may be internal network boundaries wholly owned and controlled by the enterprise that, depending on the connecting segments, will require different monitoring approaches. Examples of internal boundaries are the boundary from the DMZ to the internal network and the internal network to a secure internal segment. Each of these may be treated as trusted, or the DMZ to internal may be treated as an external network and have monitoring like the Internet edge.

In order to ensure consistency, it is ideal to create labels for the boundary types defined by the enterprise and assign monitoring requirements accordingly. The following table is an example of assigning network boundary types a label and defining required security monitoring:

Network boundary type	DMZ
Trust level	Low
Required security monitoring	Network, Operating system, Application

In this previous example, the only variable being analyzed for trust is the network boundary and it is not user specific. Monitoring of users, applications, and operating systems should be implemented in scenarios especially when the user is simply known by IP address. Monitoring and mitigation may only occur using the network layer information of the transaction.

Monitoring based on network segment

There are some network segments that have a higher value based on criticality to the business. These segments may require additional monitoring not only to adhere to regulatory compliance or other requirements, but also to ensure that the administrators, owners, and IT security are aware of what is happening in a particular segment of the network.

Each segment of the network should be assessed for value (typically determined by the assets located on the segment) to the business in order to determine the risk of negative impact to the segment, and thus the business. In order to identify segments of high value, use the discovered information from the trust model building exercises. This will primarily end up being a list of systems that may reside on various segments in the network both insecure and secured. There may be a decision to move a system or set of data to a protected segment during this analysis, in order to reduce the complexity of monitoring required for the identified segments. If providing a secured segment is not a priority, then developing a flexible monitoring strategy regardless of physical or logical location of the data and systems should become the focus; and this method of monitoring by segment should be abandoned.

All segments that are well defined should be labeled with a criticality level of low to critical. Required monitoring for each segment can be decided by using the scale of criticality. Building a matrix for monitoring will provide the standard for each segment providing a repeatable and consistent methodology.

The following table is a sample of what a matrix may look like for this type of exercise:

Segment name	Criticality	Required monitoring
Segment_1	Low	Network, Operating system
Segment_2	Medium	Network, Operating system, Application
Segment_3	High	Network, Operating system, Application, User
Segment_4	Critical	Network, Operating system, Application, User, Data

Segments should be documented according to their purpose such as HR, PCI, e-mail, and so on, with all indications of naming, controls, and monitoring self-explanatory. It is advisable to leave publicly accessible segment information generic, but provide mapping in a protected manner to reduce confusion for internal IT. This method is only effective if the network has a clear demarcation of network segments where monitoring can be strategically located on the network and controlled. If the segments are not truly segmented, then data may be skewed with meaningless data from other segments. The following diagram is an example of an internally segmented network (Segment_4) for the purposes of PCI DSS scope reduction:

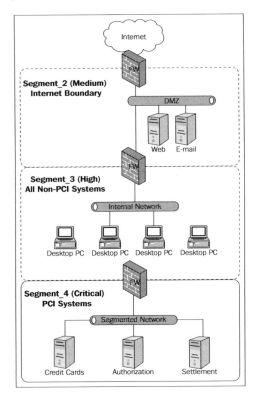

Privileged user access

Privileged users are a special faction of the user base in the enterprise with elevated access permissions to systems and data. This elevated access status above and beyond the standard user can be an excellent path of compromise for intentional and unintentional actions expected by the account with the permissions. If actions by this faction of users are not properly monitored, it can lead to significant loss to the enterprise. It has been a long time discussion in information security on how to properly monitor accounts with elevated privileges having access to sensitive data and critical processes.

There are generically three types of privileged users: power users, system administrators, and data administrators. It is possible to extrapolate additional account types but most commonly these are the overarching defined account types. Each has a specific purpose for interaction with the system, data, or both at a level that provides additional access above what a typical user would have. The access would typically be provisioned due to a legitimate business requirement; however, with the added access, additional monitoring must be implemented to assess role activity and ensure the proper controls are in place to ultimately reduce the risk associated with the access. Risk in this case can be criminal intent, accidental negative action, or malware-initiated activities.

All privileged user actions should be logged and reviewed. If the action is questionable or unknown for the user type, then review by application and data owners can be leveraged for the assessment. This review can aid in the determination of whether the action was intentional or due to system compromise. Up to this point in the monitoring section, several methods have been presented that will detect access and modification of critical data and system files. Either real-time or regular review of monitoring output is required for monitoring to be effective.

Privileged data access

The most difficult access to monitor is the privileged access to sensitive data. Because the role requires access to data, and sometimes, in non-traditional methods, it can be difficult to determine malicious intent and to confine data only to approved systems. When privileged users access data, it is typically in a direct fashion over secure communication channels, making it near impossible to know what specific data is being accessed and potentially transmitted to other systems not initially intended to securely store the sensitive data. Data access monitoring may help but if the access is intended as per the role and access permissions, this becomes a non-absolute method to monitor access and determine intent because access is granted. To help provide a better understanding of expected data access and actions, profiling "normal" behaviors can highlight the anomalies, behaviors outside the expected "norm".

It may become a requirement to protect the data in a fashion that access is monitored but certain actions not specifically required for the role are restricted and enforced by a technical solution. Arguably, this is the best practice—a simple least privilege enforcement—though many times this implementation is uncommon. In order to enforce this method, controls need to be implemented on the privileged user's system and access may need to be brokered by a security system to mitigate transmission of sensitive data to less secure systems.

Because this user type has, in essence, the keys to the kingdom, it is imperative that every action the privileged user executes is monitored for anomalies and other behaviors beyond the scope of the assigned role. This will require authentication mechanisms for each action that is specific to an individual and not a group of users. An area where this is an issue is with database administration and the use of additional elevated accounts within the database infrastructure. A series of monitoring logs including database activity must be carefully correlated to ensure an individual can be associated with specific actions. A regular audit of actions should be performed to ensure the actions are within the bounds of the role and any discrepancies accounted for and approved by management. There are several commercial tools available for privileged user monitoring but management of the solutions and review of the output must be a mature process with accountability for unapproved actions.

Privileged system access

System administrators may arguably be the holders of the keys to the kingdom with more access than the database team. In many cases, the database servers are implemented in a configuration that allows system administrators access to the data content while not actually being in a database administrator role. This is a flaw in implementation, but can be discovered and mitigated through a review of configuration. Apart from databases, all other data residing on systems in the enterprise is accessible by system administrators regardless of the owner of the system and sensitivity of the resident data. This level of access across the enterprise should be taken very seriously and monitored heavily as this is the most abused access in the enterprise. Leveraging system-level monitoring capabilities is a method to achieve auditing privileged user system access.

Another method is to leverage encryption technology that is able to provide access based on the authenticated user and rightful owner of the resident data on a system. It is understood that trust is a significant part of being an enterprise user, however, trust alone will not thwart human behaviors of curiosity and personal gain. These are all intentional actions so far; but what about the unintentional consequences of privileged system access by the standard enterprise user?

When the standard user has gained privileged-level access to their system, typically to install an application, the system is left vulnerable even to a simple user error in judgment in additional to intentional actions. It is a common occurrence in the enterprise to have users request local administrator permissions in order to install a software package, but this access if really needed should be temporary in nature. The primary cause for malicious software installation is the unintended consequence of a user action; but this has also led to some of the most notable hacking instances in recent history, one example being RSA. RSA, the makers of SecurID, were hacked using a spear-phishing technique, when the user opened the e-mailed attachment, malware was installed as the user which held elevated system privileges. Once installed, it allowed hackers to gain the information they needed to further exploit RSA systems and compromise the most critical data supporting the SecurID product.

In the previous example highlighting the dangers of elevated user accounts, a simple click to open an infected link caused serious damage to RSA. This is such a common occurrence that new security technologies are flourishing such as the FireEye Malware Analysis System, which is able to examine malware in real time from these attack methods and provide mitigation.

A process should be developed to revoke the access once the reason for elevation has be achieved, either in an automated fashion or through manual action. If possible, enforcing all application installs via software package delivery or by PC support will ensure users do not gain and maintain elevated system privileges. There are capabilities within Microsoft Windows such as Group Policy that can be used to temporarily elevate a user's system privileges, and then remove them after the requirement is fulfilled.

Monitoring the actions of users with elevated privileges even on end user workstations is advisable for a small scope of actions, so that remediation efforts can be managed. In any instance of privileged system access, monitoring and regular auditing is a must to reduce the likelihood of system compromise, misuse, and data loss through user actions.

Privileged application access

Most applications have roles defined such as user, power user, report user, administrator, and so on. The purpose is to limit the access various user types have to the data resident or accessible by the application and actions that can be taken within the application. Usually, the administrator is the only role with the ability to fully manage the application including adding other users, managing application settings, and full read, write, edit access to data. With the administrator role comes additional responsibility that should be assigned cautiously, monitored, and managed meticulously to reduce the impact of misuse, and unauthorized access through poorly managed accounts assigned by this role.

Because the privileged application role has the permissions to add accounts, this activity should be monitored and should follow a formal change process based upon the data resident in or accessible through the application. It is in general a best practice to enforce change management for all accounts added to a system or application, but the level of review may be limited based on the requested access and the criticality of the system and data.

Rogue application accounts can be detected through a regular audit process that should occur at least quarterly. This process should also be leveraged to remove old accounts that should no longer reside in the application. For example, terminated employees.

The best solution for account management is to use a centralized authentication, authorization, and accounting solution that allows for simplicity in account management across enterprise applications. The central system should enforce a policy of consistent password change requirements (not to exceed 90 days) to limit the window of compromise, though it should be mentioned that a shorter window should actually be implemented closer to 45 days. The longer a password is in use, the more likely it will become compromised; this is the primary reason for regular password changes. These are the most common and poorly implemented aspects of application security that put enterprise data at as much risk as the other components of enterprise security architecture.

During application installation there may be unique administrator-level installation accounts with default settings; these should be removed or configured to an acceptable security level prior to production deployment of the application. Any test accounts configured during setup or test of a role's access should be limited, and removed or disabled at the completion of testing. Any users that require the elevated privileges in the application must have a unique ID for proper security monitoring of account access. Use of any built-in administrator accounts should be restricted or disabled to ensure all administrator-level application access can be attributed to an individual. These accounts are easily overlooked and most times remain enabled with default passwords when implemented in production. This aspect of applications should be included in the quality assurance process and must include the IT security personnel for validation.

Consistent monitoring and auditing for activities associated with privileged accounts are the best methods for finding misconfigurations, erroneously elevated accounts, and to detect behaviors that may indicate account compromise, misuse, and malicious activity. The end result in a properly implemented application-privileged user security mechanism is more secure enterprise data.

Systems monitoring

An important aspect of security monitoring is the monitoring of enterprise systems. Systems are the foundational component of the enterprise network where data is stored, processed, and interacted with through applications. There are multiple methods to monitor systems, but the focus of this section is specific to security monitoring of the operating system and critical application files. This is typically accomplished through a combination of the standard security tools such as anti-virus, host-based intrusion detection, host firewall, FIM, and monitoring of operating system event logs.

In some cases, a honeypot-type technology is used to learn behaviors of network users and detect attacks against critical systems. Newer open source tools such as Artillery, by Dave Kennedy (`https://www.trustedsec.com/downloads/artillery/`), are able to perform all of these functions including active responses to detected attacks providing immediate system protection. This is one example of a tool that can be used to monitor enterprise systems for security events, possibly indicating a security incident. There are several options available for system monitoring; the primary methods will be presented in the next sections.

Operating system monitoring

There are three primary operating systems in use in the enterprise: Microsoft Windows, Linux, and Sun Solaris. Linux and Sun Solaris are more similar than Windows, and the approach to monitoring is similar as well. The primary difference being the use of DLLs and a registry in Windows while the other two operating systems use a complex set of files to run the operating system with all having a kernel at the center of the architecture.

When monitoring operating systems, these distinctions must be understood in order to implement the correct monitoring and provide output that is human readable and actionable. The most common method of operating system security monitoring is file activity/integrity monitoring. This is a solution that monitors access and modifications to critical operating system files and registry keys in the case of Windows.

When a change occurs, regardless if benign or malicious, it is recorded along with the forensic audit trail information to track the change to an individual or process responsible. Initially the use of FIM will produce a significant amount of data until tuned; as every change will be recorded, not all needs a response. Once tuned, the data can be invaluable in properly monitoring changes to the operating system and supporting files.

The following are the Windows files to monitor:

- Registry
- Dynamic-link libraries (DLLs)
- Configuration files
- Application files

The following are the Linux files to monitor:

- Configuration files
- Application files

Any detected changes should be investigated; and if there is a false positive or a constantly changing file, like a log file, it may be necessary to ignore these changes to reduce the amount of data to review. Additionally, all review must occur at a level above those able to make changes to enforce separation of duties and the risk of collusion. There are open source tools such as OSSEC (http://www.ossec.net/) and Tripwire for Linux (http://sourceforge.net/projects/tripwire/) that focus on FIM across the operating system and all other files resident on the system.

> The information security team should carefully review data output from FIM type tools and remove the common detected changes to reduce noise that system administrators will need to review. This step, sometimes called "forensically approved" changes, refers to changes that do not need to be reviewed, however, are saved in the system for forensic review at a later date if necessary. Taking the extra step to help the other teams with security monitoring will aid in embracing required security tools to protect enterprise systems.

Using FIM is an effective method to detect a security event on a system where files are added, deleted, or modified in response to malicious activities common to virus, Trojan, and exploit activity that will trigger an event in a properly configured FIM solution.

Where the solution has little value is *memory*; no files are manipulated in any way so the detection engine would not identify the threat. Solutions that address this issue are generically called application whitelisting solutions and control what has the permission to run based on a signature captured for legitimate applications. If the application that is attempting to run is not a known and trusted version of the application, it will be blocked from running. This method also detects and blocks instances where the executable of a legitimate program has been altered even in system memory.

There are several tools that can be used; and if outputted data is correlated in some manner, can provide a good indication on whether there may be a system issue. It is recommended to script common Linux tools such as ps, netstat, and tcpdump to see snapshots and real-time information on running processes and open network connections. Monitoring processes on Windows is just as easy with several tools such as perfmon, taskmgr, and netstat to monitor aspects of the operating system that may provide detail on security events affecting the system.

Commercial FIM solutions such as Tripwire (http://www.tripwire.com) support several operating systems, network devices, and security devices. This makes it a good candidate to evaluate for the enterprise environment. Using a combination of open source and commercial solutions may be the best option and has to be assessed for each unique environment. As with any security tool, it is important to have the supporting processes, policies, and standards in place to ensure effective use of the solutions and intended security as purposefully implemented.

In order to have an effective implementation, a phased approach may be the best to ease the impacted internal organizations into the process. Referencing the trust models developed with matrices of critical data and applications, a list of critical and sensitive systems can serve as the starting point for an overall enterprise implementation. Engaging the impacted organizations in decisions on solutions and the process to handle the output of such implementations can drive the correct solution selection and drive a more mature program. This is highlighted because in most enterprise environments there are a plethora of agents running on systems, and adding more without providing an initial value will make a FIM solution implementation all the more challenging. Several compliance bodies are mandating this type of solution is implemented and can be the catalyst to building a system security monitoring capability (if non-existent), adding a critical component to enterprise data security.

Host-based intrusion detection system

A **host-based intrusion detection system (HIDS)** is very similar to network-based intrusion detection, however, it is specific to the host or set of hosts where it is implemented. In a similar fashion of signature, anomaly, and behavioral analysis, HIDS performs the same function on network systems instead of the network layer. The benefit is more finely-tuned policies that minimize the noise of traditional network-based IDS where detection is for anything and everything that is protected by the IDS.

To make the point clear, IDS simply detects but *does not* mitigate. However, IDS can operate in an active response (send RST packets, and so on) making it essentially an IPS. For this section of the book, the term HIDS will be used referring the solutions with active response capabilities.

Having an HIDS solution implemented on enterprise systems provides unparalleled intelligence on what attacks and other network anomalies (malicious and benign) are being targeted at enterprise systems. It is sometimes difficult to determine if an attack detected at network IPS made it to the intended target; with HIDS, this is no longer unknown. If detected, it reached the intended target or set of targets. Most commonly used HIDS solutions perform more functions than intrusion detection. Often application whitelisting and FIM are features that can be leveraged bringing more value to the implementation by providing more security capabilities and reducing system overhead required for multiple agents.

There are some unique offerings in the area of host malware; intrusion detection that builds on trust is an integral theme of this book. The solution is able to leverage a number of sources and analyses to determine if the executable or file has benign or malicious intent and actions. The solution, Bit9 (`https://www.bit9.com/`), while not technically an HIDS, has a unique approach that has characteristics of HIDS, in addition to their special proprietary capabilities. While the intent of this book is not to dive too much into vendor specific attributes, there are a few solutions that are well known for their approach and warrant mention where the solution may be of interest for further investigation and evaluation.

When evaluating the implementation, an HIDS solution or any other host-based solution, it is important to consider management of the solution, level of provided support, and benefit to the overall security architecture, all of which helps to determine the total cost of ownership (TCO). There must be enough value and benefit that the TCO is acceptable. Because HIDS is an endpoint solution, management of the solution must be decided, both technically and organizationally. This issue remains a point of debate between security teams and system support staff. Commonly, IT security will be responsible for the policies implemented and configuration while the system support staff will maintain the software, including patches, and ensure it remains functioning.

As an industry, the move to HIDS has been a slow process, however, with emerging threats easily outwitting traditional methods of security, implementing HIDS-like solutions may be the only method of systems' security monitoring and protection effective enough to protect enterprise data.

Network security monitoring

The use of next-generation firewalls, data loss prevention, malware analysis, and intrusion prevention are the foundation of network security monitoring at the Internet edge and other network boundaries. As an integral component to defense in depth, these tools analyze all network traffic traversing the network and are typically positioned in areas of the most criticality. Each of these technologies has been covered in depth in the earlier chapters from the protection standpoint; this section will discuss leveraging the tools from a monitoring perspective.

In order to gain an understanding of what traffic is traversing the network and its intent, it is imperative to have a strategic implementation of these tools in a fashion that will provide the most valuable event data. This is particularly difficult as there is a significant amount of data that is analyzed, collected, and security events created. For each of these technologies, an evaluation of capabilities must be undertaken to determine the best configuration to reduce false positives, reduce impact to production traffic, and provide analysts with enough information to investigate potential threats and mitigate in an acceptable time frame.

Next-generation firewalls

The configuration of next-generation firewalls can be complex; and the temptation is to turn on every feature and log all the output. This may be necessary in some environments but must be carefully weighed as the more log data present, the more log data there will be to store and analyze. This can be costly in terms of storage and management and can reduce the effectiveness of the tool.

There are differing schools of thought on what firewall rules to log in order to ensure capturing of malicious traffic when permitted by a valid policy. An example is an HTTP-permitted access inbound to web servers; logging or not logging the data can be a detriment in either case. If the service is expecting connections, there will be a significant amount of log data, most of it legitimate. This, however, will require more log storage and more information for analysts to sift through for security events. If the traffic is not logged, then abuse of the permitted access can also go unnoticed. This is a primary reason for the design of next-generation firewalls that added additional analysis capabilities of traffic permitted and essentially will log and alert on anomalies only, reducing event data and more timely mitigation. By simply adding denial-of-service checks, intrusion prevention, and protocol analysis capabilities, the intelligence provided by next-generation firewalls proves more effective by detecting real threats and reducing the log data to be analyzed by analysts.

If the firewall infrastructure is unable to combine detection engine output to an incident, it may be prudent to limit the services enabled and leverage Security Information and Event Management (SIEM) to collect and analyze the data from multiple sources to get a single-pane view of seemingly disparate events to determine if in fact an incident is occurring or has occurred.

 Security Information and Event Management (SIEM) will be discussed later in this chapter.

Data loss prevention

Because data loss is a security event, it should be included in the overall security monitoring strategy of the enterprise. Though it is a very specifically built tool, the presence of sensitive data at an egress point of the network may be indicative of a security incident, not simply a bad business process. Regular analysis of incidents created within the **data loss prevention (DLP)** solution should be the role of IT security to look for potential behaviors of malicious intent through human- or malware-based exfiltration.

Care should be taken when handling the data collected by DLP as it usually consists of sensitive data that should not be viewable outside of the teams and individuals responsible for analysis and remediation. If it is possible to send generic events through an alerting mechanism, it may be a method to proactively alert security staff of an incident that warrants immediate attention. If the solution cannot send generic alerts with sensitive data removed, then manual analysis of events will need to persist allowing for confidentiality to remain intact.

The solution may be configured to decrypt traffic allowing for inspection of traffic that otherwise would exit the network without detection. If the enterprise has chosen to implement such a method, removing personal employee data from normal transactions such as online banking and purchasing should be a topic of discussion not only for privacy, but also to reduce incidents and alerts generated for benign network activity.

The enterprise should have other forms of data access monitoring, privileged user access monitoring, and system monitoring that, if configured properly, should yield similar results and can be combined with DLP output for validation. DLP is specifically designed for data loss and may not alert simply on misuse unless it is seen at an egress point of the network, including at the end user system. It is most typical for an alert to be generated in a DLP solution, then further investigation and analysis of the other monitoring components creates the complete scenario of data access, attempted misuse, and exfiltration.

A network DLP implementation is considered an edge technology such as a firewall and intrusion prevention providing only a small portion of the traffic analysis, if any, for analysts to correlate events. Therefore, this technology must be used with other technologies to be most effective in proactive detection and mitigation of data loss-related security events.

Malware detection and analysis

A technology gaining momentum as a must have security tool is malware detection and analysis at the edge using local- or cloud-based methods. The data output from such advanced tools is only as good as the analyst using the tools, requiring in-depth knowledge of malware analysis. These tools can however aid in environments with little malware analysis know-how by simply being able to detect, analyze, and provide actionable data on what the threat is and where it is on the network. Solutions offering these capabilities include commercial products by FireEye, RSA NetWitness, and Fidelis.

Security teams can then engage desktop and server support teams to take systems offline and remediate in a much faster time frame than attempting to manually find infected internal hosts. Because these tools are highly specialized, there is not much more information that can be gleaned from other security monitoring tools other than host-specific tools that may have detected the malware; but the reason these tools exist is the lack of traditional host solution's capability of detecting malware with no known signature. As with most security monitoring, the output from malware tools can provide details that infringe upon the confidentiality of those infected and must be handled in a manner to protect the privacy of those involved. Any correlation in security event data is helpful and should be the goal of using simple to advanced tools to provide comprehensive security monitoring of the enterprise infrastructure.

Intrusion prevention

Whether standalone or integrated within a next-generation firewall, intrusion prevention is still a very effective method to not only detect and mitigate threats, but also to provide valuable alerting capabilities for security analysts. Locating the **intrusion prevention system (IPS)** (outside the external firewall and inside the internal firewall for a basic DMZ) allows attack patterns to be easily detected and alerts sent to security staff for mitigation. **Distributed denial-of-service (DDoS)** protection is becoming a standard feature of traditional IPS and can alert security personnel of impending services' outages prior to occurrence; and, in most cases, can mitigate the threat by the simple nature of the predictability of incomplete and bogus service requests that are the basis of DDoS attacks.

Similar to other edge-focused technologies, IPS will only be capable of seeing single transactions between source and destination; what happens after the attack reaches a destination may or may not be detected by an IPS depending on the resulting callback traffic. IPS is also good at mitigating low-hanging fruit type attacks and can help conserve firewall sessions by being placed in front of the firewall; the downside is that if the IPS does not have a firewall itself; the amount of traffic will be significant and this must be considered before placing it outside an Internet edge firewall.

With the amount of data that could be alerted on, the security team must consider what requires immediate attention, as alerting would indicate urgency. Regardless of alerting, constant monitoring of IPS and security monitoring tools should occur to reduce security incident impact; this is the shortcoming of most teams as they are understaffed and have too many tools to effectively monitor. Careful analysis of IPS capabilities and alerting strategy will greatly increase the overall effectiveness of IPS.

Security Information and Event Management

SIEM or **Security Information and Event Management** has been mentioned a few times in the earlier sections and is gaining tremendous traction in security monitoring as the central intelligence of security operations. The primary benefit of SIEM is the ability to assimilate security and log data from disparate systems, analyze it all, and provide correlated output to security analysts.

Up to this point, disparate systems and their unique monitoring capabilities have been discussed, but those are all single intelligence, incomplete views of the complete flow of traffic as it traverses a network. A firewall, for instance, only inspects what is coming and going at the edge of the network, but has no cognizance of actions taken on a system for traffic permitted by policy. The SIEM solution (provided all logs are forwarded to it) will have a complete view of not only the permitted firewall traffic, if logged, but also what actions were taken on the target system; so a whole picture of a transaction is understood as data is collected at each point along the way.

At the center of SIEM is the correlation engine; this is the distinct component of the solution that ties all seemingly disparate events into an incident using proprietary algorithms and analysis of log data. This in conjunction with added features such as known botnet IP addresses, ability to import vulnerability data, and parse log data from several sources, positions the SIEM as the central single-pane view and authority on security events and incidents.

Not all SIEM solutions are created equal; evaluation of several solutions for the specific environment to be implemented is a wise approach as these solutions come at a price. Value must be driven from the solution, to warrant the expense. As with all solutions, there must be supporting processes in place for management, day-to-day operations, and remediation of incidents. A joint evaluation by all teams that will use the solution and will build the supporting infrastructure is recommended at the beginning of product evaluation. This will also help in the adoption of the new technology and responsibility required by such an implementation. There can and should be multiple roles configured in the solution to allow other teams outside of security to manage their logs, investigate incidents, and manage reporting.

Because the SIEM will receive data from multiple sources, the security team may manage security incidents; but it will take the collaboration and cooperation of other teams in the enterprise to have a successful and effective implementation. SIEM can be the central logging solution in the enterprise and most have the ability to also provide canned reporting for regulatory compliance and other security standards. The security team can provide the solution as a service and help the other teams with investigations and reporting, aiding in the cohesive environment for SIEM to thrive. It should be noted that the SIEM will only be as good as the data forwarded to it and those taking action on what it provides in the form of actionable security incidents.

Managing a SIEM can be a significant undertaking for the typical, undersized security team; and a managed solution may also be considered. There are **managed security service providers (MSSPs)** that offer complete management or co-management of enterprise SIEM solutions. A benefit to this type of implementation is that the heavy lifting is done by the MSSP, and only items that require action are sent via alerting mechanisms to the security staff and others required for remediation. This implementation type should be strongly considered if security operations are not performed well or are not a focus in the organization and benefit can be realized by focusing the security team on more pressing tasks such as architecture, engineering, and project engagement.

SIEM is a must have for the ever-evolving and complex nature of security operations. It is fast becoming a difficult task to set eyes on all the security technology being deployed to thwart the increasing threats to the enterprise. At a minimum, a centralized logging solution must be deployed with the ability to alert security personnel of malicious or anomalous traffic detected by deployed security technologies.

Predictive behavioral analysis

The last topic of this section is not a new topic, but one that is gaining more traction as human behavior lends itself to patterns that can be predictive of future action. Today, we rely on an analyst to recall if a certain behavior has occurred in the past with the same user or IP address, either by memory or review of previous incident data. This does not always occur, and predictive behaviors can be missed because no one is keeping track. Predictive behavioral analysis does not only apply to people, but can be something such as the Cyber Monday traffic patterns observed by online retailers. The first Cyber Monday was a shock, but analysis of traffic on the same day in previous years would have indicated a continued increase. Some online retailers had enough resources to handle the increase, others did not, and their online presences failed, costing them millions in revenue. This same analysis is used by denial-of-service solutions where the traffic is analyzed of a period of time and if certain behaviors such as incomplete conversations are observed, the source is penalized until the condition clears. If the condition does not clear and continues, the source is penalized to the point where communication is cut off to the target as the behavior has indicated that the source has malicious intent.

Being able to keep a running score of a user or IP address is at the heart of this method and can prove invaluable in stopping malicious action before it occurs, and therefore greatly reducing impact to the business. Financial institutions use this technique as a part of fraud detection; actions are closely monitored and known questionable actions raise red flags that can hone in on the monitoring and allow the financial institution to react almost immediately. Currently, the closest we have to this in readily available commercial security tools is active response to an already perpetrated action, not predictive mitigation. There are highly-specialized tools used for behavioral analysis that have been modified to work at the network layer to predict malicious behavior and take action. I think we will see a shift to this predictive technology provided it can help find the needle in the haystack of good and bad anomalous traffic.

Summary

Security monitoring is the success or failure of security in the enterprise. The latest breaches paint this picture clearly; each enterprise had security tools, but no one was watching. The most challenging and most significant role information security can play in an organization is keeping it safe from malicious attacks that threaten the data and sometimes the existence of the enterprise. This starts with sound security architecture, but is played out day-to-day in how well security operations are implemented through management and monitoring of security tools. In this chapter, we discussed approaches to security monitoring based on trust models, network boundaries, protected segments, and asset criticality. We then took a more detailed look at security monitoring of users, systems, applications, and the network. When this holistic approach is taken, a comprehensive enterprise monitoring program can be realized.

The next chapter will apply using security monitoring as an input to security incident management.

10

Managing Security Incidents

The focus of this chapter will be on presenting the idea of security incidents and response. First, we will define a security incident and then move on to developing the process of responding, including roles and procedures for remediation. Getting buy-in from other teams outside of security, including management, is key to the success and effectiveness of an incident response capability. The *Taking action* section will cover both internal response and leveraging of third parties when necessary. This chapter focuses on the basics of developing and implementing a security incident response capability in the enterprise. Incident response forms and process flow are included in *Appendix E, Security Incident Response Resources*.

This chapter covers the following:

- Understanding what defines an incident
- Developing security incident processes
- Building an incident response team
- Developing an incident response plan
- Taking action on security incidents

Defining a security incident

A security incident is as unique as the business type and all the components that make the business function. What may be considered an incident for an online retailer may not be of any significance to a healthcare provider. However, there are commonalities across all business types for events that indicate a security incident.

At the center of every enterprise is information technology; the systems, processes, applications, and data that provide the infrastructure and capability for the enterprise to facilitate the business that it conducts. It is expected that unauthorized access to a system by an online retailer or a healthcare provider would be mutually considered a security incident. It is also expected that because these are two distinct business types, there will be outlier events which, if detected, would trigger an incident response. Each enterprise will need to analyze its critical infrastructure and determine what would be considered an incident beyond the common incidents.

What makes a security incident is any action whether intentional, accidental, malicious, or negligence that causes a negative impact on, or loss to, enterprise data, systems, and applications. An exercise held with teams that are responsible for the various areas of the enterprise will identify what incidents are considered of what impact level to the enterprise and what actions would need to be taken. It is advisable to have this exercise led by the Disaster Recovery (DR) and Business Continuity (BC) teams as its output can be used as input for DR/BC planning. The security team can lead the mapping of the exercise output to technical response action.

For this capability to be effective it will require the collaboration and cooperation of the other teams much like enterprise security monitoring. It is likely that the same team members involved in security monitoring will be the team members defined as contacts for enterprise security incident response.

Common security incidents include:

- Unauthorized system access
- Website defacing
- Denial-of-service attack
- Malware outbreak (impact measured by the scope of infection)
- Password brute force attack
- Misuse as defined in security policies
- Sensitive data loss (accidental or malicious)
- Stolen computer equipment
- Unauthorized physical access to sensitive areas

This list is not comprehensive but it includes the most common events that trigger an enterprise incident response across industries. Thresholds for each will need to be determined allowing for the proper amount of attention and action required to remediate. For example, a virus found on a few systems may or may not warrant a full security incident response; it may only require the efforts of a few teams to remediate the issue and a lower-level incident ticket generated for historical purposes.

There would be a different response if the website of an online retailer was defaced. In this case, there is more impact to the business requiring more teams to not only remediate but potentially handle press, shareholders, the board, and others, because the incident has much higher visibility. It is easy to see that there are economies of scale because several attributes have to be assessed to determine the correct response for the individual enterprise.

Security event versus security incident

There can be confusion over what is a security event and what is a security incident, and how to know when detected or learned events become incidents. A **security event** is a component of an incident and when there are multiple correlated events, an incident is the result. However, in some cases the initially detected event can be the incident and be treated as such in response. An example would be a stolen laptop; it does not consist of a series of events that comprise the incident, the event itself is the incident. This involves a bit of semantics too, but for the purpose of this book, events will be treated as seemingly disparate entities and incidents, a culmination of events. An example of a security event is a triggered signature on an IPS. This may not require an immediate response, but several of the same or related events may indicate a larger issue and therefore would be labeled as an incident.

Typically, the security events far outnumber the incidents, in particular those that require a formal incident response. In the following graph, the number of events is fluctuating and is infinite over time while incidents occur at a much lower rate and are finite:

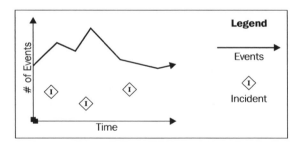

Developing supporting processes

Once the enterprise has determined that security incidents require a process or set of processes in order to respond properly, the security team must begin working with key teams to build the formal process. Because there will be a need for support from the various teams in the enterprise, it is important to involve them in the development of the incident response process. This will also enable the teams to build the necessary procedures to react to specific types of incidents.

The key concepts and knowledge transfer of a forensic approach to a response is important to ensure that legal action can be taken if warranted. As with security operations, it is equally important to have experts in various technologies provide input on the process and output procedures to reduce the impact of the incident response. There must also be a means to trigger the incident response process, ideally through an existing ticketing system. In order to ensure that the proper response is initiated, the ticket will need unique categories for security incidents, and severity levels to determine which incident contacts need to be alerted, and when to trigger other non-IT related responses such as HR, legal, and press release staff.

The next section covers building out the incident response process and highlights recommended supporting processes.

Security incident detection and determination

While on the surface most security incidents appear to be network-related, there are also security-related incidents such as physical access violations or social engineering where a packet is never sent over a network. SIEM, IPS, firewalls, and other network-based security tools will only detect and alert on network-based incidents, but other security incidents must be accounted for in the process and developed into the security incident response plan, the formalized output of building supporting processes. There are several threat surfaces for the enterprise and each should be identified and scenarios developed to determine how to detect an incident and the next steps. In some cases this will be reliant on deployed security monitoring tools, in other cases detection will rely on an employee to respond and alert the security team and other personnel of the event.

Physical security incidents

A physical security incident is much different from a network-based incident because it requires a human to detect the incident, such as a stolen laptop. There are some physical controls such as alarms and card scanners that log access attempts. These are typically handled by facilities' security and rarely is the IT security team alerted to these activities. IT security will normally only be involved in case some form of data was lost or stolen as a result of the lost or stolen asset. An example may be a stolen preconfigured network device that provides details on the internal network design. In the case of unauthorized access to restricted areas such as data centers, there may be a collaborative response with facilities security and IT security.

When no technology-based controls are in place, employees must be trained to identify incidents in their environment. They must also know what steps are required for the various types of physical security incidents they may encounter. Wherever controls have been implemented for physical security, there must be a coinciding reporting method for violations of the controls and/or policy to alert security staff of the incident to ensure prompt action.

Network-based security incidents

Security events detected at the network layer are almost too many to know which are of significant threat requiring immediate attention and which need to be ignored or simply monitored. With the help of correlation tools such as SIEM, identifying incidents can be easier through the automation of incident generation. There are methods and techniques used that will require manual review of security monitoring tools' output to look for anomalies such as packet analysis. It is common for something detected to be an anomaly that warrants investigation, however, it is never triggered as an incident in a SIEM. Whichever method is used to correlate events and generate an incident for investigation, an action will need to be defined in the incident response process and assigned severity and priority agreeable to all responding parties. It is advisable to have a security operations capability either within the security team or leveraging an existing network operations capability. The nature of network-based incidents requires constant monitoring and investigation. Some incidents will trigger the full incident response process, while others can be investigated and responded to within the security team or with smaller teams and do not warrant invoking the complete incident team.

Incident management

As with any enterprise process, the incident process needs to be managed to be effective and repeatable. An assessment of the existing enterprise incident management tools needs to be performed to ensure that the solution can be configured to handle security incidents separate from other forms of enterprise incidents. If there is no existing incident management tool, there may be a lag in responsiveness to critical security incidents and the overall response may be poorly executed.

It is important to have a unique incident management process within the incident tool to ensure that response severity, priority, and contacts are specific to security incidents. In most cases, the standard incident configuration is incorrect for security. Additionally, security incidents may include sensitive data that could implicate employees. Confidentiality is of utmost importance for security-related incidents requiring limiting of access to incident details to only the response team and key management members for proper, controlled dissemination of information.

Once the incident has been responded to and the incident closed, there should be a "lessons learned" session to determine how to mitigate the incident in the future, discuss improvements in response, and update procedural documentation if needed. It may also be required to adjust the severity, priority, and responding team members for the specific incident type to ensure the most effective response to future incidents reducing the overall impact to the enterprise. This is depicted in this diagram:

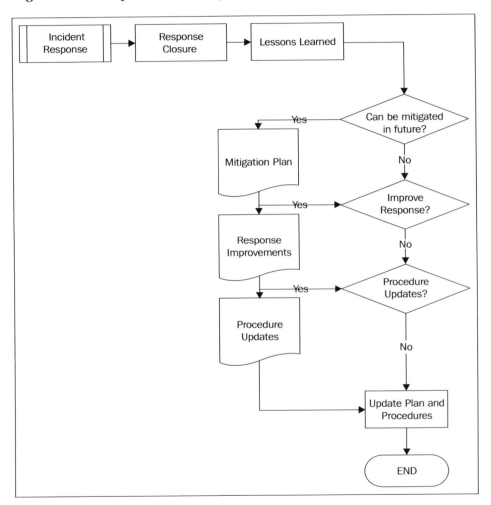

Getting enterprise support

The broad touch that security incidents can have requires complete enterprise support when an incident is raised and an action must be taken. The simplest of external attacks will have a minimum of three teams involved to investigate and take action: security, network, and systems, as the attack would traverse the network, security tools, and eventually reach the target system. In order for the attack in this example to receive the proper attention, there has to be a predefined agreement on the expected response time for the incident type and which team members need to be involved from each team. The fact is that incidents are inconvenient and do not occur based on the ability of the team to respond. The unexpected nature of incidents will require whatever is actively being worked on to be halted and immediate response action to be taken for the incident. The mandate of importance to be given to security incidents will need senior management directive.

Once the directive has been communicated, a series of meetings should be held to communicate the need for the capability and what is required from each team. Valuable perspective can be gained from IT teams and business units that can increase the adoption rate of incident response and establish key individuals for the success of the incident response implementation. The meeting, or series of meetings, can help with the development of the incident response process and establish the precedent of the process development and support, with regards to existing projects and day-to-day work that each team is responsible for supporting and producing, respectively.

Understanding the critical components of each team will drive the decision tree logic for developing a response priority and the overall criticality to the enterprise. Estimated asset allocation can be calculated based on previously observed incidents and will aide management in deciding what resources to commit and when the resources can and should be engaged for incident response. Providing the identified teams an influence in the building of the incident response process ensures the most effective and responsive team possible.

Building the incident response team

Each team identified from previous meetings for building enterprise support for incident response will need to identify resources with areas of expertise that can be committed to incident response in the event the process is triggered. The capacity in which they are engaged is dependent on the severity of the incident and may serve in an advisory role for less severe incidents. Each assigned resource must be made aware of the responsibility of being a member of the incident response team and respond within agreed service-level agreements (SLAs).

The confidentiality of security incidents is as important as a forensic investigation and should be treated as such until the full impact of the incident is understood and communication should be sourced from the communications role in the incident response plan.

Each team member will need to know the correct procedures for already defined incident types, but also be agile enough to take the correct action if an unplanned type of incident occurs. The more the incident response at any level is practiced, the more the process will be refined and the team members will become more proficient, making less mistakes, ultimately reducing the impact of the incident with outcomes that will better secure the enterprise.

The individuals selected on each team will be the decision of the management for each team with management being the first contact for the team and defined in the contacts section of the incident response plan. There may be areas of expertise within each team and those with specializations will be documented to ensure that the right resource is assigned to the incident. Each role will need to know how to interact with the other roles and ensure that the established communications protocol is followed so that all pertinent information is recorded in the incident. In order to build an incident response team it is necessary to define roles, responsibilities, contacts, and supporting procedures.

Roles

Each team involved in incident response has a defined and important role in ensuring that the incident is handled correctly and efficiently. There may be several individuals from a team selected for participation on the incident response team. Each team will be leveraged for the pertinent expertise within the team and responsibilities assigned accordingly. Common IT enterprise and business teams with incident response roles are:

- Desktop support
- Systems support
- Applications support
- Database support
- Network support
- Information security
- HR, legal, and public relations

Desktop support

The desktop support team will have expertise in desktop operating systems and applications at the user level. This team should also have knowledge of the deployed security tools on user desktops and be able to analyze their output as it relates to the incident. Common installed security tools on desktops include antivirus, anti-malware, and firewalls. In addition to security tools, system logs can be a valuable resource for incident investigation.

Systems support

The systems support team is very similar to the desktop team in regards to the operating system and security tools implemented. However, the scope is increased as, typically, servers host critical business applications, databases, and other data that is most commonly the target of malicious incidents. In the case of non-malicious incidents, the aforementioned holds true and introduces potentially greater impact to the business. This team must be aware of data, applications, and processes that each system stores, runs, and manages respectively. This team may have more detailed procedures that need to be developed in order to properly respond to an incident due to the added visibility of server systems including additional notifications and approvals to take action. Another consideration is offloading services running on a compromised or altered system that requires a disaster recovery and continuity plan that can be enacted in an acceptable time frame.

Applications support

The applications teams may have direct or indirect tasks associated with responding to a security incident. Typically, applications will leverage a system in the enterprise but it may be the mechanism used to perpetrate the incident. The team's knowledge of the application including its function, code, and logs will be an invaluable resource when responding to an incident and finding the root cause or method(s) used in the incident. Coordination between the applications and systems team is imperative to further reduce impact on the business in response to an incident. Often the applications team will already have a load balancing or migration process for moving an instance of an application and you should know what the risks and ramifications are when doing so. Understanding the function of the application and the associated processes can also give a perspective of possible scope of the security incident and the data that is at risk. Having this team or teams involved in the development of the security incident response is critical and will ensure complete coverage for business processes.

Database support

The database team is the largest custodian of enterprise data and knows where the most critical data resides in databases. Web applications, critical applications, and other business critical processes most commonly rely on backend database infrastructure to store their data. The end goal of typical security incidents is obtaining enterprise data, whatever that represents for the specific enterprise. This team must be involved to document which databases contain what data and which applications leverage the infrastructure. Additionally, this team must be trained to know what unauthorized or unexpected database accesses look like in logs, in order to aid the incident response team and identify what data was accessed, altered, deleted, and possibly exfiltrated. Without this knowledge and expertise, data that was just accessed and exfiltrated may go unnoticed and the guessing game of what occurred will leave the enterprise in an uncertain state.

Network support

The network team is responsible for getting traffic across the network and therefore has visibility of all the traffic traversing the network. Some network teams are responsible for not only the routers and switches but also the firewalls at the network edge and within the enterprise network. The expertise of how traffic flows on the network and the advanced protocol knowledge will help decipher the network communications of the security incident. Reviewing firewall logs and firewall policies can provide detailed information on how access from the source to destination occurred. This information can be valuable for lessons learned and provides possible areas of improvement, or to drive a new design requirement to further segment and protect valuable assets. Another service the network team may be able to provide are packet captures of traffic that traversed the network related to the security incident. It is common for network teams to have packet capture technology implemented for troubleshooting and monitoring network latency and connectivity. These tools can be an invaluable source of data. Additionally, if the incident is ongoing, the network team can make the necessary network changes to mitigate the threat at the network layer by changing the routing, implementing the firewall rules, and using router ACLs. The network and security teams should already have a good working relationship and know the methods to stop any threat at the network layer. Working with common nomenclature and existing processes for day-to-day operations should create a synergistic approach to security incident response. This team should already have intimate knowledge of all connections to the enterprise network and know the impact of any network-based incident and what effect the changes to the network will have on these connections.

Information security

The information security team has a unique role in security incident response, not only in responding but in leading and in the management of security incident response. After all, security incident response is a primary role of the IT security team. This team must be aware of the environment that they are protecting, the applications, the data, and the processes. They must know what to look for, providing guidance to other teams. The team must be very knowledgeable of protocols and the technologies in use in order to know where to point teams and focus the investigation. A forensic capability may also be a function provided by the security team if the expertise is present in-house. A brief note on the forensic aspect of security incident response is provided in the *Supporting procedures* section of this chapter. Whether this capability exists in-house or not, the information security team must ensure the forensic soundness of the investigation until it is determined that the need for forensic analysis is not required. Beyond providing guidance on what to look for and where, the security team must work with the other teams to stop an on-going threat or help determine how to stop the incident from occurring again. Adjustments to policies, standards, and processes may be the end result of enacted incident response.

HR, legal, and public relations

These non-IT business teams are critical to the incident response process and must be involved in the development of the team and plan. There may be instances where the incident requires the involvement of one or more of these teams. The scenarios include:

- Employee, contractor, consultant, and so on (HR)
- Website defacement (PR)
- Theft (legal)

This should give an idea of why these teams need to be involved in the incident response process. IT security should have a relationship with each team as many functions that IT security may perform will require guidance from each of these teams. A few examples are forensics and legal, policy violation and HR, and publicly visible incidents and PR. It is important that the team members on these teams understand the IT aspect of their practice and are actively involved during incident response.

Responsibilities

There are other responsibilities outside of IT that may need to be defined and leveraged depending on the type of incident and based on agreed incident severity and priority. These responsibilities include but are not limited to public relations, both internal and external, for press releases if necessary, legal, and HR. Generally, responsibilities will be assigned in alignment with expertise and the associated team member. An example is malicious data destruction on a file server. The responsibility assigned to the system's support function would be to facilitate a full assessment and determine through logs and other system data what happened, who took the action, and what data was affected. In this scenario the system's support team would lead with the other teams supporting as necessary. Each team should have a clear understanding about what they are responsible for, providing an expertise and action perspective for the incident response. Example roles and responsibilities are outlined in the following table:

Roles	Responsibilities
Desktop support	• Desktop-related tasks for remediation • Desktop incident analysis • Provide desktop OS and application expertise to the team • Provide data and incident artifacts as needed
Systems support	• System-related tasks for remediation • Server incident analysis • Provide server expertise to team • Provide data and incident artifacts as needed • Knowledge and expertise of data, running applications, and processes
Applications support	• Application expertise • Application migration and recovery • Application log analysis • Other components of application function • Provide data and incident artifacts as needed
Database support	• Database expertise • Incident identification within database • Analysis of database logs • Database migration and recovery • Provide data and incident artifacts as needed

Roles	Responsibilities
Network support	• Network expertise
	• Network incident analysis
	• Provide networking expertise to the team
	• Network disaster recovery and continuity
	• Provide data and incident artifacts as needed
	• Implement the necessary network changes
Information security	• Security expertise
	• Forensic expertise
	• Security knowledge of each area
	• Lead and manage incident response with other teams
Legal	• State, federal, and local law enforcement and adherence
	• Forensic investigation support
HR	• Enterprise policy violation enforcement
	• Employment termination
	• Guidance on employee interaction
Public relations	• Public and private press release
	• Communications lead

Expected response times

When an incident occurs, whether critical, major, or minor, it must be assessed and given a severity and that severity should have an expected response time. This is common practice for general incident management in the enterprise. The response time should take into consideration realistic time frames for an individual to answer the call for action and be in a position to take action. It is important to note that each severity type must be defined and understood by all parties. The times defined must be acceptable to senior management with proper expectations set. A sample SLA table to give an idea of what this may look like for an enterprise incident response plan is as shown here:

Incident severity	Response time
Critical	30 minutes phone, 1 hour action
Major	1 hour phone, 2 hours action
Minor	2 hours phone, 3 hours action

Time-to-resolution (TTR) may be unknown and may only be an estimate depending on the type of incident. There are some cases where the time to remediation is known, for instance, restoring lost data to a server. This is a common practice that an estimate can easily provide. However, a more severe incident, such as a complete compromise of a critical system, may take significantly more time, as forensic analysis will be required, and eventually a complete rebuild of the system, data, and applications. The defined service-level agreements for response and action can and may need to be adjusted based on observed response times as incidents are generated and resolved.

Incident response contacts

Knowing who to call and when is probably the most critical decision when an incident is or has taken place and an action must be taken. For this reason, it is a critical step in the incident response plan to create a complete contact list that is accessible for the first responders to initiate the necessary procedures to resolve the incident.

Typically, management representatives are the first point of contact for critical and major severity incidents, while minor incidents would follow a less urgent communication path and be resolved with little or no cross-team interaction at or below the management level. It must be stated that, in some cases, what is initially deemed a minor incident becomes a more severe incident after initial investigation. At this time, management should be contacted as per the communication plan in the incident response plan.

 Minor incidents should be tracked via a ticketing system to allow reporting, trend analysis, and provide a paper trail of consistent incident response actions. This is important not only for the business but is a requirement for PCI DSS and is a recommended best practice.

Not only will the management of the various teams be listed as contacts, but non-IT roles need to be listed as well. These include HR, legal, public relations, and other senior management members that are business aligned and not directly involved with IT but are dependent on or affected by the incident. The decision to communicate the incident to senior management should be the call of the IT management members and must be in accordance with the incident response plan communication guidelines.

A typical contact list will include the following:

- Senior leadership (CIO, directors, and so on)
- Legal representative
- HR representative
- Corporate communications representative
- Desktop manager
- Desktop responder
- Systems manager
- Systems responder
- Database manager
- Database responder
- Application manager (may be several teams)
- Application responder (may be several teams)
- Network manager
- Network responder
- IT security manager
- IT security responder

For reference you can go to www.cert.org/archive/pdf/csirt-handbook.pdf. There may be contacts outside of the enterprise depending on the response implementation, internal or external. Additionally, third-party contact communication may be a function of a member or team on the list; the third-party contact information may not reside on the contact list to effectively control external communication of an incident. Contacting the CEO and board may be handled in the same manner. This can reduce liability to the enterprise in the event of a critical incident that may have far reaching consequences that should be handled with diplomacy and at the right echelon within the organization.

Supporting procedures

Each team responsible for incident response should have defined procedures for responding appropriately. The procedures should be documented and peer reviewed to ensure that the intended outcome is achieved. Forensic soundness may be of concern depending on the type of incident and the procedures should have this requirement as a basis for the developed procedures. It is important that the procedures are as detailed as possible to ensure consistency and repeatable execution regardless of who from the team actually performs the procedures.

In order to build the responding procedures, each team will need to complete one or more scenario exercises based on predefined incident types and carefully document caveats, challenges, and success criteria. The process of developing procedures may highlight operational areas that need to be developed or refined to better respond to a security incident. There may be some actions that will be cross-functional in nature and will require coordination amongst one or more teams to respond to the incident, and reduce further impact to the enterprise. An example would be an application move and change; this scenario may require the database and network teams to facilitate a successful application move to another system, possibly on another network segment. The database team would have to account for changes in the incoming application connection and the network team would have to account for VLAN changes, routing, and possibly firewall rules to permit the new connectivity while shutting down the previous network access to the application.

Procedures developed by the teams must be peer reviewed to ensure that the actions will produce the intended outcome, impact on the enterprise is reduced, and that the actions follow forensically sound methods. The procedures to be implemented during an incident may require a change management ticket even in the event of a security incident in order to obtain approval and notify all parties that could be impacted by the changes.

A quick note on forensics

Forensics has been mentioned previously in this chapter as this capability is critical for any incident response team. There is significant complexity in a properly set up forensic capability and it may be outsourced if the in-house team does not have the expertise. Forensics may be used for legal gathering of incident artifacts for the prosecution of a perpetrator or to simply investigate the root cause and determine a method to thwart future incidents. Key concepts for forensics include treating the evidence the same as one would for a murder case; having the correct tools and expertise to perform forensic investigations. Training on the forensic tools is highly recommended, as time can be of the essence and completing a forensic investigation in a timely fashion may be warranted. If the aforementioned are not the intent of the enterprise, then outsourcing the forensic capability would be the better option. The enterprise incident response team will have the responsibility to understand basic forensics and how to fulfill the requirements of a first responder team without destroying forensic evidence. Having a contracted service for forensics in the event of an incident will be costly to the enterprise. Furthermore, the incident plan must account for when to enact the costly service. A hybrid approach may be the most cost-effective and functionally correct method for implementing a forensic capability.

In the hybrid model, the enterprise builds a forensic capability, but once it is determined that the incident affects a certain type of system or criticality, then the third party is brought in to perform the forensic investigation. The internal team handles all other investigations and any decision to enact the third party will instruct the internal team to take the agreed forensically sound steps to stop the immediate threat. There are several ways to approach the forensic capability in the enterprise and the decision to use a specific model must be carefully assessed based on current expertise, the budget to invest in the capability and training, and risk reduction leveraging a certified third party.

Developing the incident response plan

The basis and plan must be developed as they are the main resource for the process. The plan will encompass support for incident response and will have been developed formally, specifying the high level details of how to initiate incident response, provide contacts, and if third parties are to be involved, the process to involve them. The plan will also include the team roles and responsibilities along with communication protocols and the response times outlined for the levels of severity. Another item that may be important to have in the plan and process is escalation levels. These can be assigned to various severity incidents to ensure that only the contacts that need to be engaged are engaged and at the right time in the response process. Each team involved in incident response should know what the plan is and what is expected of each member.

A process can be written to illustrate the flow of an incident and should be provided as documentation to the support teams, especially the team managing the incident ticket. The process must have a logical flow and be simple enough to follow, allowing each team to reference their incident procedures, when necessary, for a more detailed understanding of what is to be done and when. The process flow can be further noted with references to other documents providing the incident response team the necessary information to successfully perform incident response in accordance to the agreed process and plan. A process for incident response may look similar to the one provided in *Appendix E, Security Incident Response Resources*, and can be customized to the enterprise.

Taking action

The foundation has been laid for enterprise incident response; only running through mock scenarios and real incidents will find the faults and areas that need to be modified for a more effective and fault-tolerant process. The incident process requires information to be gathered at the identification phase of the incident and throughout the resolution process. There are several pieces of information that should be captured at the time of incident identification and throughout, so that the incident team will know where to focus their efforts, and as the investigation continues and possible scope changes occur, detailed documentation can be developed to be used during and after the incident resolution.

Incident reporting

The sources of incident reporting are many; security tools, analyst observation, and employee awareness. The initial report of an incident may not have all the details, as it may be unknown if there is an incident or not and the scope.

Critical information to capture includes but is not limited to:

- Date and time of report
- Name, title, and contact information of who reported the incident
- Date and time of incident, if known
- Type of incident
    - Intrusion, DoS, virus, system misuse, website defacement, and so on
- Affected systems if known (IP address, hostname, OS, applications, and so on)
- If sensitive data is involved
- Scope of the incident, number of systems, and so on
- Any other details on source

This information can be captured in a form or in an incident management system and is updated as the investigation continues. A sample reporting form is included in *Appendix E, Security Incident Response Resources*.

Incident response

Once an incident has been reported and the process is initiated for incident response as per the plan, the documentation on response must be generated. There may be a significant amount of data and information generated during the response and it must all be logged to the forms or the incident management tool used by the enterprise. Not only is this necessary for active investigations, but it should be retained for future incident response. Additionally, this information can be used for lessons learned to either improve incident response or to tweak other areas of the process to better reflect the real world scenarios observed through continued use of the process.

Information that should be captured will include information from the initial reporting of the incident and also includes all details of the incident learned through the investigation.

Additional information includes but is not limited to:

- Case number assigned
- Case owner and contact information
- Incident summary
- Steps taken during investigation
- Additional parties involved
- Incident handler comments
- Next steps (to be updated by each member working on the incident)
- Incident detail (should be more accurate and detailed versus a report)
- Real date and time of incident
- Detailed description of incident
- Detailed source information
- Impact information
- Evidence collected
- Resolution information

The incident tracking documentation will be more valuable with more detailed information that may also help improve procedures previously defined. The more information that can be gathered, the more effective the mitigation could be for future incidents. The last important aspect of incident resolution is that it should be approved with a sign-off from an IT executive. This will more than likely follow a full briefing of how the incident was detected, all the actions taken, impact analysis, and steps to mitigate the same type of incident in the future. Another outcome of incident response may be the determination to further invest in the in-house forensic capability or contract the entire process to a third party.

In-house incident response

There should be some level of in-house incident response capability, but to what level must be determined by the IT management. For the enterprise that will have a full capability, training and expertise development cannot be stressed enough. Improper handling of an incident can cost the enterprise additional money, increase incident impact, and increase liability to the enterprise. With this understood, it is an investment that can be very beneficial in reducing the day-to-day impact of incidents when the process can be handled properly in-house. Depending on the size of the enterprise, more resources may be required to maintain all facets of securing the enterprise, while gaining the additional responsibility of incident response.

If management decides that due to resource limitations, it will not proceed with building a full capability, the team should still exist and a well documented process must be executed for when the in-house team hands off to a contracted third party.

Contracted incident response

For enterprises that have made the decision to contract incident response to a third party, a small amount of incident response work will still need to occur in-house for maximum effectiveness in reducing further impact on the business. There can be significant benefits to contracting out incident response to a third party. First, leveraging for the most impactful incidents ensures that a dedicated team will be assigned to resolve the incident and second, the liability of improper incident handling is no longer an enterprise concern, as it is owned by the contracted third party. The caution with a completely contracted out incident response is that the incident resolution time frame is extended while waiting on the third party to respond and there is significant cost in this approach. In enterprises with no in-house capability, this may be the only option and all non-critical incidents may be handled by a more generic process. The more generic process may seem effective initially, but repeating the process and not investigating incidents or documenting thoroughly may prove to be more costly in the long run.

The decision to contract incident response is one that must be well thought out with benefits and caveats clearly understood by the enterprise.

Summary

This chapter presented the need for an incident response team and provided a guide to developing this capability in the enterprise. It is important to gain support from the other IT and business teams that will be involved or affected by incidents in the enterprise. Their support will ensure that the incident team is successful and able to remediate the incident in a timely manner and set proper priority to the incident. It is critical that the process be adopted by the entire enterprise to be effective. Deciding whether to develop this capability in-house or to contract to a third party must seriously be evaluated when an incident of significant impact occurs, and the correct route to follow will depend upon which method can return the enterprise to normal business the fastest should be the route to follow. If the enterprise has decided to perform this function in-house, proper training and complete understanding of the legalities involved with incident response must not only be understood by the IT team but also the corporate legal team too. Incident response is a critical business and IT function that can reduce significant loss to the enterprise.

A
Applying Trust Models to Develop a Security Architectuture

Security architectures are not defined designs as much as a blueprint for securing data interactions that influence design. The example in this appendix is not a typical network diagram simply showing security architecture but rather a diagram of the intended network design with a security architecture applied to the distinct data interaction. The security architectures developed by the enterprise are applications of the trust models to the implemented network design. Security architecture should encompass standards in application, examples being required encryption and authentication mechanisms.

Encrypted file transfer (external)

This example is of applying trust models to develop a security architecture that can be applied to an externally accessible file transfer solution.

The numbers in the diagram will be explained as we progress through the scenario.

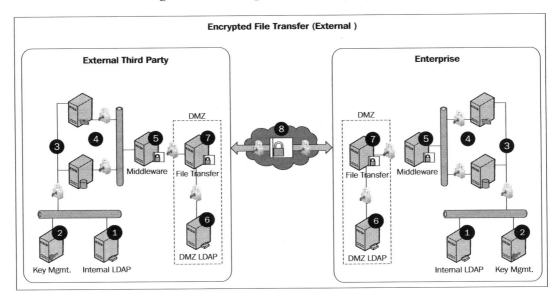

We will start by first referencing our data-centric architecture diagram from *Chapter 2, Security Architectures.*

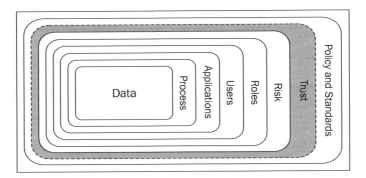

With the designed solution we must consider each layer of the above diagram and determine what security mechanisms must be employed to secure the data interaction. In order to determine this, it must first be understood what data will be interacted with, what process the solution is supporting, applications that may be used, and users who will be using the solution.

Let's start with identifying each component of the trust model by building blocks for this file transfer solution.

Data types	Process(es)	Application(s)	Users	Roles	Policies and standards
PII	Prescription order fulfillment	Prescription order fulfillment system	External Internal	User Administrator Data owner	Data classification Data handling Encryption standard Third party authentication standard

Now that we have defined all the building blocks of our trust model, risk can be assessed and security mechanisms can be chosen.

If there are regulatory requirements for the data in the solution, these will have a significant influence on what security must be implemented. If policies and standards have been developed that need to be applied more direction, then they can be derived from the content of these documents.

It may become apparent that there are missing policies and standards to properly enforce the requirement for security controls. If this is the case and not too significant a risk, then note the present shortcomings, obtain approval from those who can assume risk, and begin the process to correct the identified gaps. It is common for new solutions, projects, and market shifts to drive new security policies and standards.

We now have what is needed to develop our trust models that will drive the security architecture applied to the solution design. Because the trust in this case is based on the user and the data being transferred, we'll focus on these trust models.

External user

User type	External
Trust level	1 – not trusted
Allowed access	Tier 1 DMZ only, least privilege
Required security mechanisms	FW, IPS, data encryption, user authentication, and role enforcement

Internal user

User type	Internal
Trust level	3 – trusted
Allowed access	Internal network systems, least privilege
Required security mechanisms	FW, IPS, data encryption, user authentication, and role enforcement

Data owner

User type	Internal
Trust level	3 –trusted
Allowed access	Internal network systems, least privilege
Required security mechanisms	FW, IPS, data encryption, user authentication, and role enforcement

Automation

User type	Automation
Trust level	2 – median trusted
Allowed access	Least privilege
Required security mechanisms	FW, IPS, file integrity monitoring, and data loss prevention

With the building blocks defined and trust models developed, a data-centric security architecture can be applied to the file transfer design to maximize security and minimize risk. We will now see how the applied security architecture is implemented in the reference architecture for encrypted file transfer accessible to external parties.

Label	Description	Purpose
1	Internal user authentication	Role enforcement and least privilege implementation
2	Encryption key management	Necessary to provide encryption meeting policy and standard requirements
3	Secure network communication	Data protection, data handling per data classification policy, and encryption standards enforcement
4	Automation (file delivery)	Process used to enforce least privilege and provide necessary external and internal separation
5	External user authentication	Role enforcement and least privilege implementation
6	Secure file transfer system	Data protection, data handling per data classification policy, and encryption standards enforcement
7	Encrypted file transmission	Data protection, data handling per data classification policy, and encryption standards enforcement

I have inserted the diagram again for ease of understanding the preceding table.

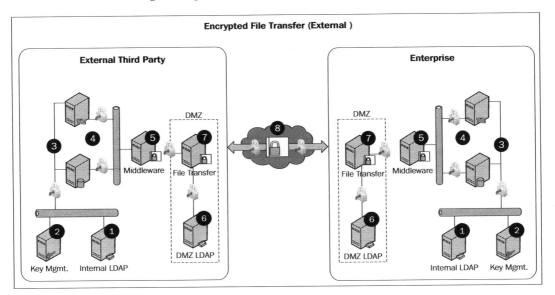

This example is an exercise that should eventually become second nature when developing new solutions or data interactions. Much of what the trust models provide should become standards and a requirements checklist for projects. The key is to provide an agile approach to securing solutions and data interaction that are not confined by the network design. As we have covered in *Chapter 2, Security Architectures*, there is little control over the network design as BYOD and cloud initiatives infiltrate the once trusted internal sanctuary of the enterprise network.

B

Risk Analysis, Policy and Standard, and System Hardening Resources

Risk analysis resources

Risk analysis methods	URL
SANS Quantitative risk analysis step-by-step	http://www.sans.org/reading_room/whitepapers/auditing/quantitative-risk-analysis-step-by-step_849
FAIR	http://www.riskmanagementinsight.com/media/docs/FAIR_brag.pdf
NIST risk management guide	http://csrc.nist.gov/publications/nistpubs/800-30/sp800-30.pdf
CERT OCTAVE	http://www.cert.org/octave/
DREAD threat model	http://msdn.microsoft.com/en-us/library/aa302419.aspx#c03618429_011
STRIDE threat classification	http://msdn.microsoft.com/en-us/library/ee823878(v=cs.20).aspx

Policy and standard resources

Policies and standards	URL
SANS Policy Project	`http://www.sans.org/security-resources/policies/`
CSOonline	`http://m.csoonline.com/article/486324/security-tools-templates-policies`
CSIRT	`http://csirt.org/sample_policies/index.html`

System hardening resources

Operating system hardening	URL
NSA hardening guides	`http://www.nsa.gov/ia/mitigation_guidance/security_configuration_guides/operating_systems.shtml`
Windows 2000	`http://www.microsoft.com/en-us/download/details.aspx?id=15910`
Windows 2003	`http://technet.microsoft.com/en-us/library/cc163140.aspx`
Windows 2008	`http://technet.microsoft.com/en-us/library/gg236605.aspx`
Windows 7	`http://technet.microsoft.com/en-us/library/ee712767.aspx`
Red Hat Enterprise 5	`http://www.nsa.gov/ia/_files/factsheets/rhel5-pamphlet-i731.pdf`
Mac OS X	`http://www.apple.com/support/security/guides/`

C
Security Tools List

The tools listed in this appendix are open source for the purposes of remaining as vendor and product agnostic as possible and to highlight excellent tools provided by the open source community. This list is not comprehensive, but consists of some well-known open source projects for their respective uses. In some cases, the open source project has been acquired by a commercial entity. This is not an endorsement of the commercial entity, but of the open source project only. There are several commercial products available for each of these areas and simple Internet searches will provide the available products and vendors. For enterprise implementation, there may be a mix of commercial and open source tools used to accomplish security goals. Tool selection should always consider the total cost of ownership, support, and effectiveness.

Tools for securing the network

Name	URL
pfSense (firewall)	http://www.pfsense.org/
Snort (IDS)	http://www.snort.org/
PacketFence (NAC)	http://www.packetfence.org/home.html
Suricata (IPS)	http://www.openinfosecfoundation.org/index.php/download-suricata
m0n0wall (firewall)	http://m0n0.ch/wall/
OpenWIPS-ng	http://www.openwips-ng.org/
SpamAssassin (SPAM)	http://spamassassin.apache.org/
The Bro Network Security Monitor	http://www.bro-ids.org/

Tools for securing systems

Name	URL
OSSEC (HIDS)	`http://www.ossec.net/`
ModSecurity (WAF)	`http://www.modsecurity.org/`
ClamAV (AV)	`http://www.clamav.net/lang/en/`
AIDE (FIM)	`http://aide.sourceforge.net/`
Bastille Linux (OS hardening)	`http://www.bastille-unix.org/`
Artillery	`https://www.trustedsec.com/downloads/artillery/`
Open Source Tripwire (FIM)	`http://sourceforge.net/projects/tripwire/`

Tools for securing data

Name	URL
TrueCrypt (encryption)	`http://www.truecrypt.org/`
MyDLP (DLP)	`http://www.mydlp.com/`
OpenDLP (DLP)	`http://code.google.com/p/opendlp/`
GnuPG (encryption)	`http://www.gnupg.org/`
KeePass (password safe)	`http://keepass.info/`

Tools for security monitoring

Name	URL
Logwatch (log monitoring)	`http://sourceforge.net/projects/logwatch/`
OSSIM (SIEM)	`http://communities.alienvault.com/community/`
Honeyd (honeypot)	`http://www.honeyd.org/`
ntop (traffic monitor)	`http://www.ntop.org/`
Nagios Community	`http://www.nagios.org/`
The Bro Network Security Monitor	`http://www.bro-ids.org/`
Security Onion	`http://code.google.com/p/security-onion/`
Aanval	`http://www.aanval.com/`

Tools for testing security

Name	URL
BackTrack (Distro)	`http://www.backtrack-linux.org`
BackBox (Distro)	`http://www.backbox.org`
Metasploit	`http://www.metasploit.com`
Burp Suite	`http://www.portswigger.net/burp`
w3af	`http://w3af.org`
Sqlmap	`http://sqlmap.org`
Samurai Web Testing Framework	`http://samurai.inguardians.com`
Websploit Framework	`http://sourceforge.net/projects/websploit`

Tools for vulnerability scanning

Name	URL
Rapid7 Nexpose	`http://www.rapid7.com/products/nexpose/compare-downloads.jsp`
OpenVAS	`http://www.gnupg.org/`
Nikto	`http://www.cirt.net/nikto2`

D
Security Awareness Resources

General presentation and training

Name	URL
The Exceptional Presenter (Book)	http://www.amazon.com/The-Exceptional-Presenter-Proven-Formula/dp/1929774443
CompTIA CTT+	http://certification.comptia.org/getCertified/certifications/ctt.aspx

Social engineering

Name	URL
Social-Engineer Toolkit	https://www.trustedsec.com/downloads/social-engineer-toolkit/
PhishMe.com	http://phishme.com/
Social-Engineer.com	http://www.social-engineer.com/

Security awareness materials

Name	URL
NIST SP 800-50	http://csrc.nist.gov/publications/ nistpubs/800-50/NIST-SP800-50.pdf
SANS InfoSec Reading Room	http://www.sans.org/reading_room/whitepapers/ awareness/
DISA IA Awareness Posters	http://www.iwar.org.uk/comsec/resources/ia-awareness-posters/index.htm

Safe and secure computing resources

Policies and standards	URL
US-CERT	http://www.us-cert.gov/home-and-business/
CERT	http://www.cert.org/homeusers/ HomeComputerSecurity/
SANS Home/Small Office Security	http://www.sans.org/reading_room/whitepapers/ hsoffice/
NSA Best Practices for Securing Home Network	http://www.nsa.gov/ia/_files/factsheets/Best_ Practices_Datasheets.pdf
Microsoft Security for Home Computer Users Newsletter	http://www.microsoft.com/security/resources/ newsletter.aspx

Security Incident Response Resources

Building a CSIRT team

Name	URL
Carnegie Mellon	`http://www.cert.org/csirts/Creating-A-CSIRT.html`
SANS	`http://www.sans.org/reading_room/whitepapers/incident/creating-managing-incident-response-team-large-company_1821`
SANS	`http://www.sans.org/reading_room/whitepapers/incident/building-incident-response-program-suit-business_627`
Gartner (paid)	`http://www.gartner.com/id=1389613`

Incident response process

Name	URL
NIST SP 800–86	`http://csrc.nist.gov/publications/nistpubs/800-86/SP800-86.pdf`
NIST SP 800–83	`http://csrc.nist.gov/publications/PubsDrafts.html#SP-800-83-Rev.%201`
NIST 800–61	`http://csrc.nist.gov/publications/nistpubs/800-61rev2/SP800-61rev2.pdf`
CIO.com article	`http://www.cio.com.au/article/184145/five_tips_building_an_incident_response_plan/`

An example of incident response process flow

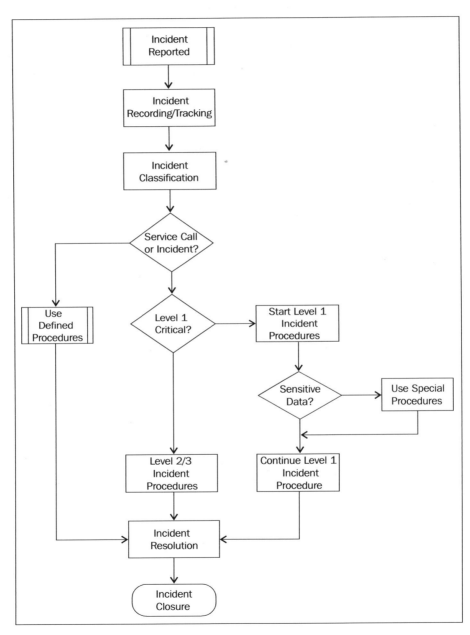

A sample incident response report form

Company CIRT Incident Report Form

Contact Information for this Incident

Date Reported: 10/8/12	Time Reported: 12:11:00 AM
Name:	Title:
Office Phone:	LOB:

Incident Details

Date of Incident:	Time of Incident:

Type of Incident (check all that apply)

☐ Intrusion	☐ Root Compromise
☐ Denial of Service	☐ Web Site Defacement
☐ Virus / Malicious Software	☐ User Account Compromise
☐ System Misuse	☐ Hoax (email, etc.)
☐ Social Engineering (Phishing, Phone, email)	☐ Network Scanning / Probing
☐ Technical Vulnerability	☐ Other (Specify)

If other, please specify:

Optional: Below Fields Are Optional

Affected System(s) Information

IP Address:	Hostname:	OS:	Applications:

Does server store **Sensitive** data (i.e. cardholder, finance)? Unsure

How Many Host(s) Are Affected

☐ 1 to 100   ☐ 101 to 1000   ☐ More than 1000

IP Address of Apparent or Suspected Source:

Source IP Address:	Other Information (DNS, etc.)

A sample incident response form

CIRT Incident Response Form

This form is to be used to document a security incident reported to the CIRT team. Please complete form as detailed as possible.

Current Date: 10/8/12	Current Time: 12:16:49 AM
Case#:	
Case Name:	
Case Opened By: Select Name	Case Assigned To: Select Name
Office Phone:	Office Phone:
Case Status: Select Status	

Contact Information

Name:	Phone:
Email:	Dept:
Location:	

System Notification

Hostname:	Software:
IP Address:	Location:

Incident Summary

Brief Summary of Incident Status:

Steps Taken:

Other Parties Involved:

Name	Role	Phone
1.		
2.		
3.		
4.		

Incident Handler Comments:

Next Steps:

Incident Detail	
Date of Incident Discovery:	Time of Incident Discovery:

Type of Incident (check all that apply):

☐ Intrusion

☐ Denial of Service

☐ Virus / Malicious Software

☐ System Misuse

☐ Social Engineering (Phishing, Phone, email)

☐ Technical Vulnerability

☐ Root Compromise

☐ Web Site Defacement

☐ User Account Compromise

☐ Hoax (email, etc.)

☐ Network Scanning / Probing

☐ Other (Specify)

If other, please specify:

Date Incident Occurred (if known):	Time Incident Occurred (if known):

Current Incident Status: Select Status

Detailed Description of Incident:

Source System(s) information:

Hostname:	IP Address:

Additional Comments:

Affected System(s) Information:

IP Address:	Hostname:	OS:	Applications:

Does server store **Sensitive** data (i.e. cardholder, finance)? Unsure

Additional Comments:

Estimated Technical Impact:

Response Actions Performed:

Other Organizations Contacted:

Name	Type	Comments
	Org Type	

List of Evidence Collected:
1.
2.
3.
4.
5.

Resolution:

Business (IT) Director Approval	
Name:	Title:
Phone:	Email:
Signature:	

IT Security Director Approval	
Name:	Title:
Phone:	Email:
Signature:	

Index

F

feature-rich web applications, network edge
about 24
implementing 24, 25
features, NGFW
advanced malware mitigation 89, 90
application awareness 87
intrusion prevention 88
File integrity monitoring. *See* **FIM**
file share encryption 166
file transfer
about 106
considerations, implementing 107
file transfer protocols, securing 108
user authentication 108
FIM
about 125, 234
considerations, for implementing 126
implementing 127
forensics 260

G

GnuPG (encryption)
URL 276
Gnu Privacy Guard (GPU) 160

H

hardening
about 73
guidelines 74
hashing 125
heuristic anti-virus 132
HIDS
about 235
implementing 236
HIPS
about 129, 130
considerations, for implementing 130
Honeyd (honeypot)
URL 276
host firewall
about 130
considerations, for implementing 131

host-based intrusion detection system. *See*
HIDS
Host-based intrusion prevention system. *See*
HIPS
human element, security
about 187
least privilege, enforcing 209
physical security 213
security awareness training 201
social engineering 188

I

IEEE 175
IEEE 802.1X
limitations 176
using 175, 176
impact
about 49
accessing 49, 50
Imperva
URL 114
incident response contacts
about 258
list 259
incident response plan
developing 261
incident response process flow
example 282
incident response team
building 251, 252
expected response times 257
HR 255
incident response contacts 258
legal 255
public relations 255
responsibilities 256
roles 252
supporting procedures 259
information security policy
about 60
considerations 61
information security team
about 255
responsibilities 257
in-house incident response 264

Thank you for buying
Enterprise Security: A Data-Centric Approach to Securing the Enterprise

About Packt Publishing

Packt, pronounced 'packed', published its first book "Mastering phpMyAdmin for Effective MySQL Management" in April 2004 and subsequently continued to specialize in publishing highly focused books on specific technologies and solutions.

Our books and publications share the experiences of your fellow IT professionals in adapting and customizing today's systems, applications, and frameworks. Our solution based books give you the knowledge and power to customize the software and technologies you're using to get the job done. Packt books are more specific and less general than the IT books you have seen in the past. Our unique business model allows us to bring you more focused information, giving you more of what you need to know, and less of what you don't.

Packt is a modern, yet unique publishing company, which focuses on producing quality, cutting-edge books for communities of developers, administrators, and newbies alike. For more information, please visit our website: www.packtpub.com.

About Packt Enterprise

In 2010, Packt launched two new brands, Packt Enterprise and Packt Open Source, in order to continue its focus on specialization. This book is part of the Packt Enterprise brand, home to books published on enterprise software – software created by major vendors, including (but not limited to) IBM, Microsoft and Oracle, often for use in other corporations. Its titles will offer information relevant to a range of users of this software, including administrators, developers, architects, and end users.

Writing for Packt

We welcome all inquiries from people who are interested in authoring. Book proposals should be sent to author@packtpub.com. If your book idea is still at an early stage and you would like to discuss it first before writing a formal book proposal, contact us; one of our commissioning editors will get in touch with you.

We're not just looking for published authors; if you have strong technical skills but no writing experience, our experienced editors can help you develop a writing career, or simply get some additional reward for your expertise.

MVVM Survival Guide for Enterprise Architectures in Silverlight and WPF

ISBN: 978-1-84968-342-5   Paperback: 490 pages

Eliminate unnecessary code by taking advantage of the MVVM pattern—less code, fewer bugs

1. Build an enterprise application using Silverlight and WPF, taking advantage of the powerful MVVM pattern.

2. Discover the evolution of presentation patterns—by example—and see the benefits of MVVM in the context of the larger picture of presentation patterns.

3. Customize the MVVM pattern for your projects' needs by comparing the various implementation styles.

Troux Enterprise Architecture Solutions

ISBN: 978-1-84968-120-9   Paperback: 248 pages

Driving business value through strategic IT alignment

1. Gain valuable insights about the role of Enterprise Architecture in today's dynamic business environment.

2. Learn about the Troux Transformation Platform and how it supports the disciplines of Enterprise Architecture, transformation planning, and project-goal alignment.

3. Understand the value of integrating metadata from many sources to deliver new management insights about IT effectiveness.

Please check **www.packtpub.com** for information on our titles

Open Text Metastorm ProVision® 6.2 Strategy Implementation

ISBN: 978-1-84968-252-7   Paperback: 260 pages

Create and implement a successful business strategy for improved performance throughout the whole enterprise

1. Fully understand the key benefits of implementing a business strategy.

2. Utilize features like the integrated repository and ProVision® frameworks.

3. Obtain real insights from practitioners in the field on the best strategic approaches.

4. Ultimately design a successful strategy for deploying ProVision®.

Securing WebLogic Server 12c

ISBN: 978-1-84968-778-2   Paperback: 100 pages

Learn to develop, administer, and troubleshoot your WebLogic Server

1. Discover Authentication providers.

2. Configure security for WebLogic applications and develop your own security providers.

3. Step by step guide to administer and configure WebLogic security providers.

4. Quick guide to security configuration in WebLogic realm.

Please check **www.packtpub.com** for information on our titles

Made in the USA
San Bernardino, CA
15 July 2018